Challenges of the Faculty Career for Women

Challenges of the Faculty Career for Women

Success and Sacrifice

Maike Ingrid Philipsen
With Timothy Bostic

Foreword by Mary Deane Sorcinelli

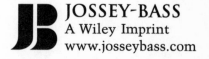
JOSSEY-BASS
A Wiley Imprint
www.josseybass.com

Published by Jossey-Bass
A Wiley Imprint
989 Market Street, San Francisco, CA 94103-1741—www.josseybass.com

Jossey-Bass books and products are available through most bookstores. To contact Jossey-Bass directly call our Customer Care Department within the U.S. at 800-956-7739, outside the U.S. at 317-572-3986, or fax 317-572-4002.

Jossey-Bass also publishes its books in a variety of electronic formats. Some content that appears in print may not be available in electronic books.

Library of Congress Cataloging-in-Publication Data

Philipsen, Maike.
    Challenges of the faculty career for women : success and sacrifice / Maike Ingrid Philipsen, with Timothy Bostic ; foreword by Mary Deane Sorcinelli.—1st ed.
        p. cm.—(The Jossey-Bass higher and adult education series) (A Wiley imprint)
    Includes bibliographical references and index.
    ISBN 978-0-470-25700-5 (cloth)
    1. Women college teachers—United States. 2. College teaching—United States. 3. Feminism and education—United States. I. Bostic, Timothy. II. Title.
    LB2332.32.P45 2008
    378.1'2082—dc22
                                                                                      2008000871

Printed in the United States of America
FIRST EDITION
HB Printing   10 9 8 7 6 5 4 3 2 1

The Jossey-Bass
Higher and Adult Education Series

Contents

To Jasper, Jon Steven, Kendra, Niklas, and Sven,
and the hopes that come with a new generation

Foreword

When Maike Philipsen first asked if I could write the Foreword for her book on how women balance academic careers and personal life, I almost said no. I had recently lost my mother. My siblings and I were now "taking shifts" in an effort to keep my father, alone and failing, at home. Our oldest daughter and her boyfriend had just announced their impending marriage and, a week later, our middle child and her boyfriend followed suit. Our youngest child had graduated from college, scarcely paused at our door, and was headed for the bright lights of New York City. And lest I forget to mention work, I'd been asked by our provost to lead a new campuswide initiative to create mentoring networks for new and underrepresented faculty. We all go through phases when work-life seems out of balance; the mere promise of a book that would shed light on how women faculty might better manage work and life demands enticed me to say yes. I am so very grateful that I did.

Challenges of the Faculty Career for Women: Success and Sacrifice engagingly addresses the broad topic of the nature of women faculty members' lives and, more specifically, focuses on the challenges confronted by—and the strategies used by—women in faculty careers as they manage their professional roles and personal lives. In particular, it brings together contemporary research and personal narratives of work and life outside of work that expand the reader's understanding of the kinds of issues that many women faculty members confront each day as they strive to fulfill multiple responsibilities at work and at home. In addition, it offers a wealth of creative personal strategies and gender-progressive institutional policies that may more fully support the recruitment, retention, and advancement of women faculty members working in universities and colleges.

Virtually all of the research and literature on faculty across the career stages, but especially new and diverse faculty, identifies numerous challenges to professional success and personal well-being. The majority of these potential "roadblocks" fall into five broad categories: understanding the institution, excelling at research and teaching, understanding tenure and evaluation, developing professional networks, and creating work-life balance. Women faculty, in particular, identify critical work-life dilemmas as they seek to balance their teaching, research, and service, develop time management skills, and attend to quality of life issues such as spousal or partner employment needs, parenting, child care, and elder care.

Why is it important to examine and proactively address these work-life concerns? Put simply, if we want to attract, develop, and retain the most talented scholars and teachers to academia, institutions will need to find ways to support a fuller integration of academic and personal lives, especially for women faculty. Women now earn half of all doctorates awarded to U.S. citizens from American institutions and represent nearly two-fifths of full-time faculty. Despite their growing proportions, however, women are still disproportionately relegated to the lowest ranks of the academic profession. At nearly every stage of their careers, married women leave academia at a higher rate than men; women faculty make career sacrifices for parenting and caregiving at a higher rate than their male colleagues; and women at all faculty ranks are significantly less satisfied than white males on measures of work life and career satisfaction (Bracken, Allen, & Dean, 2006).

The forty-six women faculty members interviewed for this book give full voice and rich timbre to the data cited above. What is most striking and quite remarkable about the book is the diversity of these women. They are white, of color, and international faculty. They are employed at a range of institutional types—from community colleges to research-intensive universities. Their disciplinary training is in the humanities and fine arts, social and behavioral sciences, natural sciences, and the professions. Their appointments include tenure-track and non-tenure-track positions and they span the entire career cycle—from entering faculty, to mid-career faculty, to faculty on the cusp of retirement. Even their living arrangements are widely divergent—single, married with children (from infants to twenty-somethings), single with children, adoptive parents, same-sex partners, dual career couples, caretakers for an ill spouse or elderly parents.

Yet despite their remarkable diversity and the unique pressures that each of them face, all of these women are linked by a shared triumph. Every one of them has beat the odds, stayed in the pipeline, and found some measure of success in their academic careers and personal lives, despite obstacles and costs along the way. And perhaps because of the prices paid and repaid, these women are also connected by a common desire. In one way or another, they are asking that the academy find ways to create more flexible career paths—from entry to retirement. Flexibility would allow responsiveness to life events such as pregnancy and childbirth, illness of a parent, a spouse, or a same-sex domestic partner. Flexibility would allow women to advance through the ranks—tenure and promotion—with less chance of stagnating, being marginalized, or leaving academia due to excessive personal or family responsibilities.

In their struggle to balance it all, the place that most academic women in this book start is at the individual level, with a range of inspired, inventive, and resourceful coping strategies. However, personal strategies are not enough. Women in the most fortunate of circumstances (e.g., a house-husband, a house-cleaner) still struggle to navigate the shoals of career and family. Solutions also require changes among the demands, structures, and policies of universities and colleges. Here, the reader will find a multiplicity of examples of real progress in the design of gender-sensitive, family-friendly policies and practices. Even still, the author suggests that institutional initiatives such as mentoring programs or policies such as tenure-clock extensions can't make all the difference. Ultimately, we need to cultivate the kind of campus culture that welcomes, integrates, and supports a diverse faculty throughout their careers.

As I write this foreword, my life has regained equilibrium. My parents are gone, one daughter is married, another wedding is on the horizon, and the son is back home. My university has just been awarded a generous grant from a private foundation to support new and underrepresented faculty through "mutual mentoring," a network-based model of support to encourage non-hierarchal, cross-cultural mentoring partnerships—at work and at home. Maike Philipsen's book suggests many such innovative ways for academic women to combine productive work lives and satisfying personal lives. My hope is that her book will inspire even more initiatives and campus policies that support all faculty members in their multiple professional roles and personal lives. And I hope that institutions of higher education can continue to shape what this book's extraordinary women faculty and all faculty desire and deserve—a humane, productive, and satisfying academic career.

Mary Deane Sorcinelli
University of Massachusetts Amherst

Acknowledgments

First and foremost I would like to acknowledge the contributions of the women who gave their energy to this project. Not only did they take time out of their busy schedules to meet and talk with me, they also read interview transcripts and made changes and suggestions. I am deeply grateful for their openness and trust, and their willingness to share very personal information with me. Without them, of course, this book would never have come about.

I had wonderful support along the way. Jim Anker showed interest in the book when it was little more than an idea, and encouraged me to make it real, take on the project, and finish the writing in a timely manner. Thank you also to Carolyn Dunmore at Anker Publishing, and Erin Null, Cathy Mallon, and Suzanne Copenhagen at Jossey-Bass for their expert counsel and their work to make the manuscript better. I would like to thank my colleague Lisa Abrams at Virginia Commonwealth University, who served as peer debriefer. She spent hours poring over the raw data and then reading the entire manuscript to see whether my interpretations of the data rang true. Her suggestions were invaluable, and her engagement meant I never felt alone with the project. Lisa, thank you also for the subtitle, and the many hours you successfully distracted me from the book so that I could refuel.

Thank you also to Carol Baron and Mary Deane Sorcinelli for your suggestions when I planned the book, and Mary Deane, for your beautiful foreword. Both of you honor me by your investment in this project.

I would like to thank my graduate assistants for their work on the book, including Tim Bostic (by now no longer a graduate student but author of Appendix A in this book), Wayne Slough, Jaimee Woodall, and Shemeka Childress. You did work that may have seemed tedious at times but was essential for the project. Thank you also to my professional home, Virginia Commonwealth University, for the support that enabled me to engage in research as time consuming and intense as that which resulted in this book. I am so glad that some institutions are still willing to invest long-term in their faculty's ideas rather than insist on quick results in the name of scholarly productivity.

I am grateful to my children; they provide perspective, distraction, and hope, and they are simply wonderful people to be with. Finally, my deepest gratitude to my wonderful husband, Jon Wergin, who was there for me every step of the way. He listened to an endless stream of thoughts and ideas about this book, and if his eyes glazed over at times, he made sure I didn't see it. He also lent his expertise in higher education to improve the substance, and he carefully edited the entire thing. Plus, just sharing life with him makes any project so much easier.

About the Authors

Maike Ingrid Philipsen has been employed since 1993 at Virginia Commonwealth University, where she currently holds the position of professor in the social foundations of education. Born and raised in Germany and educated in Germany, the United States, and Canada, Dr. Philipsen came to Richmond after receiving her Ph.D. in social foundations at the University of North Carolina at Chapel Hill. She had previously earned her master's degree in political science at the Free University of Berlin.

Dr. Philipsen's research interests center on issues of social justice and equality in education, specifically the roles of race, gender, and social class in shaping schools and institutions of higher learning. She studies questions relating to equal opportunities at both the K–12 and college/university levels, employing primarily a sociological perspective and qualitative methodologies. One of her primary publications analyzed the cultural consequences of an African American school closing for the sake of desegregation. She teaches students at all levels ranging from undergraduate to doctoral studies and is the lead faculty member at the university's PFF (Preparing Future Faculty) program.

Maike Ingrid Philipsen is married to Jon F. Wergin, has three sons, and two adult stepchildren, and lives in Richmond, Virginia.

Tim Bostic has been employed at Old Dominion University (ODU) since completing his Ph.D. in 2006 at Virginia Commonwealth University. He earned an M.A. in humanities, focusing on feminist theater and English literature at Old Dominion University, received his post-baccalaureate certificate in education from Virginia Wesleyan, and taught high school English in Norfolk for six years. He also has a B.B.A. in finance from George Washington University and a B.A. in speech communication and theater arts.

After spending almost six years in an urban high school classroom, he decided to get his Ph.D. in education in order to work on creating more equitable learning environments for all students. He has conducted quantitative studies on barriers to males entering the teaching profession, teacher empathy's impact on standardized test scores, mobility's effect on elementary school achievement, and evaluation of an ESL curriculum implementation for adult learners. He also researches effective practices for teaching writing. Currently, he is the director of composition for the Department of English at ODU, where he teaches future secondary English teachers how to teach writing.

Challenges of the Faculty Career for Women

Introduction

It's been called "suddenly one of the hottest questions everywhere in higher education" (Marcus, 2007, p. 28): How can female academics have successful careers and have children too? One might add, how might women successfully combine an academic career and a rich life outside the academy? How might they find a balance between the academy and their personal lives, with or without children?

These questions are not only "hot" and curiously understudied, they are also largely unaddressed by policy. Female faculty continue to dominate the lower-paying, less prestigious, non-tenure-track jobs while being underrepresented in the higher-paying, prestigious, tenure-track positions and higher tenure-track ranks (Marcus, 2007, p. 29). They make up the majority of "lecturers and instructors" but are outnumbered at all other ranks. Women represent 46 percent of all assistant professors, 39 percent of all associate professors, and 25 percent of full professors (*Chronicle of Higher Education Almanac*, 2007–2008, p. 24). The American Association of University Professors (AAUP) reports that in 2005–2006, women held only 31 percent of tenured positions whereas men held 69 percent, with the disparity at doctoral universities being particularly striking (only one-fourth of tenured faculty were women). The AAUP concludes that "the gap between men and women has not closed. . . . prospects for women do not appear especially bright in the future without a significant change in hiring and tenure practices" (West & Curtis, 2006, pp. 10, 11). The premise of this study is that the persisting gender gap has much to do with the relationship between women's professional and personal lives. This relationship is what I seek to illuminate in this book.

Although many women in higher education have long struggled to combine the pursuit of an academic career with parenthood, it was not until recently that the topic began to attract national attention. A 2003 article in *The Chronicle of Higher Education* reported results of what is believed to be the first study based on national data showing what women in academic life have known for a long time: having children can have a devastating impact on the careers of academic women without having the same effect on academic men (Wilson, 2003).

Recent research has begun to address related issues such as the bias against caregiving in the academy (Colbeck & Drago, 2005), the (mis)use of work/family policies (Spalter-Roth & Erskine, 2005), and others. I continue this line of research here but broaden the picture in two ways. First, I include women's experiences across their professional life span rather than narrowly focusing on those early formative years when tenure decisions and child-bearing tend to collide. The accounts in this book go beyond the early years and include women's experiences with balancing their professional and personal lives during their mid- and late-career years. I believe that as women mature and age, the problems they face do not go away, they just change in nature. Second, the book is not limited to women with children. Rather, it includes women who are happily single, single and trying to find partners and start families, married without children, child-free, lesbian, divorced, and women whose children are grown.

Gender-based reform in higher education in general is well documented. There has long been a trend to achieve equity by providing women with the same conditions, advancement opportunities, salaries, and so forth, as enjoyed by their male counterparts—equality in the sense of providing the *same* opportunities, that is. Another trend encompasses efforts to initiate change in the very fabric of the academy and mold it to embrace female ways of doing, knowing, and being—in other words, providing equal opportunities for women without the expectation that they become like men. Literature exists accordingly, addressing how to survive in the academic world, "level the playing field," assume leadership positions, and generally be successful in a male-dominated environment (Glazer-Raymo, 1999; Caplan, 1993). Models have been proposed for how to evaluate gender equity in academe (Miller & Miller, 2002), how to help women become transformative leaders in higher education administration (Madden, 2002), or how to address institutional barriers for female scientists and engineers (Rosser, 2002). Papers have been published on cross-cultural comparisons of issues pertaining to women and power, how to overcome discrimination in and outside of the academy, and the role of universities in molding different societies' attitudes toward women in general (Unesco, 2000). The list continues. What these studies do not address, however, is one major stumbling block on the road to success for many women: the incompatibility of their personal lives with the design of an academy that continues to be based on the assumption that the successful academic has a wife at home. Missing, in other words, are the first-hand accounts of female academics on what it is like to be a woman and a faculty member: not only the hurdles and obstacles—professional, institutional, and psychological—but also the enablers and ways to secure success. This book sets out to capture the powerful stories of powerful women who tell of challenges, failure, and regret, of costs and sacrifices; but who also share their coping strategies, their advice and ideas on how the academy needs to change and reform in order not to lose half of its highest potential.

Ultimately, my intent is to capture the challenges and responses of female academics across their professional life span and thus bring to light one of the "dark" sides of academia, one that inhibits true equal opportunities of all its members, regardless of gender. Just as important, however, is to learn from female academics about the coping skills they developed in order to survive, be successful, and, in many cases, flourish. This book, after all, includes only the stories of women who "made it," who got jobs and stayed. It would be very interesting to conduct a study with those who left academia, were not tenured, or were unable to acquire an academic position. Those voices remain unheard.

The People

The participants in this study consist of female faculty members at five institutions of higher education in a mid-Atlantic state. The colleges and universities were deliberately chosen for the diversity they represent in size, charter (public or private), and mission. Included are a large community college (the pseudonym used is simply "Community College"), a large urban research university ("Metropolitan University"), a small historically black university ("HBCU"), the state's "flagship" public research university ("Flagship University"), and a private comprehensive university ("Private Comprehensive University").

Although most faculty are tenure-track, either at the junior or senior level, some are collateral faculty (community colleges, for instances, typically do not grant tenure), and some have administrative duties. The participants are diverse not only in institutional background but also by discipline, working in the sciences, arts, and humanities, as well as professional programs. To protect the women's identities, disciplines are not identified in the text. They are business, criminal justice, dance, education, engineering, instructional technology, law, medicine, nursing, social work, urban planning, theater, communications, astrophysics, Asian studies, biology, chemistry, English, history, mathematics, philosophy, political science, psychology, sociology, and women's/gender studies.

Likewise, the women's lifestyles and personal arrangements vary. Many are married, either without children or with children living with them at home, whereas others' children are grown. Living arrangements also include being single with or without children, lesbian, and "child free."

Twenty-nine of the women interviewed are white-Caucasian, nine are African American, and eight are immigrant scholars from China, Ghana, Italy, Jamaica, Japan, the Netherlands, Pakistan, and Trinidad. The youngest woman interviewed is in her twenties, and the oldest one is in her seventies. The vast majority have doctoral degrees; some have master's degrees.

The Places

The research took place mostly in faculty members' offices. A few women were interviewed in their homes, and a couple preferred to come to my house.

Flagship University is a selective public research institution serving about 20,000 students in a pristine setting, a small university town surrounded by wooded hills. Faculty members typically emphasize research more than teaching and service, and students have the reputation of being strong academically.

Metropolitan University prides itself in being the largest university in the state, serving more than 30,000 students. Its buildings and facilities are scattered throughout a major southern city, space and expansion being a major challenge. MU aspires to improve its research status and rise from "research intensive" to "research extensive" according to the most recent Carnegie categorization scheme. Faculty members tend to have relatively heavy teaching loads and students are diverse in background, frequently first-generation college-going and often part-time. Many need a lot of support to succeed academically.

Private Comprehensive University enrolls about 4,500 students attracted from a wide geographic area. Its beautiful campus, located in an upscale residential district of a large city, and high rankings in magazine surveys have helped make it much more selective in recent years. It offers both undergraduate and graduate professional degrees.

HBCU is a historically black university located in a mid-sized town, serving almost 5,000 students. Due to its relatively open enrollment policy it attracts students with varying degrees of academic preparation, many of whom need a lot of faculty attention. Teaching loads are high and the emphasis on research is relatively low compared to other institutions of higher education.

Community College serves 17,000 students on three campuses in a metropolitan area, preparing students for transfer to four-year college institutions, employment, and more. Although the emphasis on scholarly activity of the faculty has increased somewhat, teaching is by far where faculty spend most of their time.

The Methods

The genesis of this study dates back several years, when I was asked by the director of my university's Center for Teaching Excellence (CTE) to give a workshop for junior faculty. I was asked to contribute to a session that dealt with issues relevant to "women and minorities." My part of the workshop was the "women's part" and was supposed to address how women balance their personal and professional lives.

I remember thinking that it was good the CTE offered such workshops because they could certainly be helpful to beginning faculty. But I also remember thinking that I wished the women's issues would stop being women's issues and workshops of this kind would see men attend just as frequently as women. Not until both women and men begin to seriously think about how to balance their lives around professional and personal obligations, and make these conversations part of institutional arrangements and policies, will the problem ever be effectively addressed, I thought.

Preparing for the workshop led to interesting discoveries. For one, I studied the statistics and realized that although women have made considerable progress in some ways, their status remains stagnant in other ways. One of the reasons, I suspected, had to do with the continuing inequalities associated with childrearing (let alone childbearing) and domestic responsibilities. I wanted more than statistics; I wanted stories. Hence, a qualitative interview study was born.

The study was soon broadened to include women who did not have children, whose children were grown, or who had other personal arrangements. I also designed the study to include various colleges and universities to obtain diversity of faculty backgrounds and to see whether institutional makeup seems to make a difference. Furthermore, I made sure to include many different disciplines, diversity of women's racial/ethnic backgrounds, age, lifestyle, and family status, as well as rank. I interviewed nine (in one case ten) women at each of five institutions, three at each level (early, mid, and late career), for a total of forty-six interviews.

During the data collection process I used a mixture of what qualitative researchers call "purposeful sampling" and "snowball sampling." At times, in other words, I sought out specific participants, and at other times I relied on the faculty members to recommend whom I should interview next. I used a matrix to tell me, for example, when I had interviewed enough early-career women at Metropolitan but still needed mid-career women. In such a situation I asked my participants for specific recommendations of women who "fit the bill." I also strove to obtain diversity of discipline: once I had talked to a certain number of faculty in the humanities and sciences, for instance, I made sure to include people in the professional programs or the arts.

The participants provided me with names and contact information of other potential participants whom I contacted by phone and e-mail. I typically said, "Dr. X gave me your name and contact information," before briefly describing the purpose of the study and asking for participation. The response rate was surprisingly high. Although it seems as if academics nowadays get swamped by requests to fill out this and respond to that, about 80 percent of the women responded positively. I attribute their willingness to make time for me in their busy schedules to a need to talk. In fact, many seemed glad that somebody finally asked.

Although my approach was purely qualitative, my colleague Tim Bostic developed a quantitative survey based on the themes that emerged from my data. He was first involved in the project as a graduate assistant transcribing some of the interviews. Early on, he developed a keen interest in the topic and began to serve as a "peer debriefer." After a transcription we would simply sit down and discuss the data. After his graduation Tim stayed involved in the project and provided a quantitative analysis. We wanted to see whether the issues I found to be true for a limited number of women might hold true for larger numbers. The analysis of his data compliments my qualitative study and can be found at the back of the book.

Back to my study. The shortest conversation—about fifteen minutes—was the only phone interview in the project. All others, conducted in person, lasted about forty-five minutes, some a bit less and some a bit more. The longest interview lasted an hour and a half. After some small talk about the campus, the weather, the office setting, and such, I typically began the interview by formally introducing myself and the project, explaining the purpose of the research, assuring participants of confidentiality and the option not to answer questions, and asking for permission to tape record. The participants provided me with demographic information first, a sketch of their educational and professional histories, as well as the parameters of their personal lives (age, marital status, children, etc.). I then proceeded with a broad question about how they saw the relationship between their professional and personal lives in general. Most women began talking right away, some asked for clarification. My probe was whether they were generally able to establish a healthy balance between their professional and personal lives, and then to elaborate. This type of open-ended question gave participants an ample opportunity to guide the conversation and talk about what seemed most salient to them. They were in the driver's seat, sometimes choosing right away to address questions that I had planned to ask later on. Those included inquiries about the enablers and barriers to balancing their lives. I wanted to know, in other words, what factors helped them balance as well as they did, and what issues stood in their way. These questions were followed by inquiries about coping strategies they had developed. (My favorite responses were "I cry a lot," "I drink a lot," and "I can't tell you on tape!") I also inquired about any differences the women perceived when they compared themselves to previous generations of female faculty, and the mid- and late career participants were asked to make comparisons with newer generations of faculty. I wanted to get at their sense of history and change. The interview concluded with questions about reform and how the academy ought to be changed in order to aid female faculty to better balance their lives. I also asked what advice they had for women just starting out.

At the center of my interviews was to understand the women's experiences through the stories they tell. As qualitative researcher Irving Seidman writes, "stories are a way of knowing" (Seidman, 2006, p. 7), a way for people to reflect on their experiences and give them order. For Seidman, when people tell stories about themselves they are making meaning about their lives by selecting details of their experience from their stream of consciousness. Seidman makes reference to Russian psychologist Lev Vygotsky, who argued that every word people use in storytelling constitutes a microcosm of their consciousness (Vygotski, 1987, pp. 236–237). It is this consciousness that provides access to complex social and educational issues "because social and educational issues are abstractions based on the concrete experience of people" (Seidman, 2006, p. 7). The women in this study leaned back, took a good look at their lives and their experiences, and reflected; they made meaning of what happened to them in the past and sometimes projected these meanings into the future. They thought about the different parts of their lives; older women talked about changes over time and younger women focused on the present and future. They wove together the strands of their experience, building stories that at times had a beginning, middle, and end but at other times were still "under construction," resembling more a puzzle being put together rather than a product. Some women were able to provide narratives that were almost linear in character, with one part neatly flowing from the previous one. Other women spoke of tensions and contradictions, of things that did not necessarily make sense, that did not follow or add up when you first looked at them. Sometimes they were able to put disjointed pieces in place during the course of the conversation, and sometimes they were not.

I loved listening to the women talk, struck by the power of their stories, their honesty, and eloquence. I marveled at the trust afforded me and at their courage to let me glance into intimate facets of their lives. Some interviews were quite matter-of-fact in character, but most were not. What I heard was often deeply moving, sometimes shocking or surprising, and hardly ever mundane. I frequently left their offices impressed, sometimes elated or wiping away tears, never untouched and never indifferent. It took almost ten months to collect the data, and in the process I learned and reflected on what I heard, tweaked my interview protocol a bit, and continued to look forward to yet another female faculty member who would teach me.

People always ask how qualitative researchers know when to stop collecting data. When do you know you have "enough?" Well, perhaps you never really *know*. But you do get to a point of saturation when themes begin to recur and information is repeated. At some point, you also simply run out of time and resources, and that is a consideration. I had set out to conduct forty-five interviews, and once I had slightly surpassed my goal I found not so much that I was "saturated" but that it was permissible to stop because I had good rich data, enough to write a meaningful book. I knew for sure, however, that my journey of learning about female faculty members' lives could easily be continued for a very long time before I would feel I had come even close to "exhausting the topic."

Once data collection ended I had the interviews transcribed verbatim and sent transcripts to all participants for member checking, meaning that I asked them whether they wanted to make changes. A few did, and two participants even decided to withdraw their participation altogether, asking that their transcripts not be used. After the process of member checking, I began the analysis. Using the software program ATLAS I coded the transcripts by marking passages according to what the women talked about in a particular passage (examples: barriers, enablers, coping strategies, parenting, men, policies). A code, in other words, is not so much what a person said but rather what topic she or he talks about. A total of twenty-two codes were assigned. Once the data were coded I analyzed by career stage. For example, I read everything the early career women said about "general balancing" issues or about parenting or about barriers. As themes emerged, the narrative began to almost write itself. The data were so rich, the stories so powerful, the themes so obvious, and the women so articulate that it became clear very soon what the issues were, how they related, how people's experiences resembled each other, and where they differed.

The book was written by career stage, some topics were addressed in each (for example: enablers and coping strategies), whereas others were unique to a certain stage and discussed only once (for example: elder care). The narrative varied between descriptions of general patterns many participants had described and portraits of individual situations. In the last part of the book, finally, I wove together accounts from all career stages in order to make comparisons across generations and to capture the recommendations offered by women across the board.

The Author: "I Had to Get Divorced to Find a Healthy Balance in My Life"

For quite a while I debated with myself how to bring my own experiences into this book. It was clear that more so than my other research endeavors, this one is intimately connected to my own life and my experiences trying to balance my personal with my professional life. I therefore knew I needed to discipline my subjectivity and do all I could to acknowledge my own biases in order to be able to do justice to the stories told by the women in this study. I did not want to have their accounts colored through my personal lenses, or worse, use them to advance a personal agenda.

The question was how, exactly, to make my own story known to the reader so that she or he had a backdrop against which to read this book. I entertained the possibility of interviewing myself but quickly dismissed the idea, given how good I am at self-deception. Then I thought about asking somebody else to conduct an interview with me, using the protocol I had developed. That idea was dismissed as well because I would constantly second-guess the interviewer's skills and approach. Finally I decided to simply write about my journey and make transparent the personal experiences that had a great deal to do with prompting me to write this book in the first place. So, here it is, my own personal journey trying to navigate both the professional and the personal world.

I am forty-four years old, a full professor at a research university in a metropolitan area in the southeastern United States. Born and raised in Germany, I received my education in Germany, Canada, and the United States. I had one child as a graduate student in Germany, got married and had two sons after I came to the United States in 1988. My second child was born while I was in graduate school in the United States, and the third during my forth year on the tenure-track. A few years ago I got divorced and recently re-married.

I care deeply for both my profession and my family but, in a nutshell, I had to get divorced before I was able to find a healthy balance in my life, because then I started having my children only half of the time. My former husband and I share their custody and care. Certainly, my desire for balance was not the reason for the divorce, and yet that's what it took to have a sane life that allowed me to have a successful career, have time for myself and my adult relationships, be a good and caring mother, find joy in domestic activities, and stop feeling so incredibly harassed. After my former husband and I separated in 2002, we began to share the care of our children equally. That means that I had "days off" during which I could work long hours, catch up on sleep, go to the gym, and not only feel that I was able to give enough to my profession but also to take care of myself. Incredibly, other professional women occasionally confessed their envy in the face of the arrangement. Here I was, in the throes of a recent separation, and women thought this was enviable? I remembered having felt that way some years prior when my mother told me about my brother's separation from his partner with whom he shared the care of their child. My mother told me, "Right now he is vacationing without children for a while," and I remember thinking, "wow."

My children are healthy and wonderful people, yet having children and an academic career without a strong support network was incredibly demanding even though my former husband Dirk did 50 percent of the domestic work. In fact, at times it was hell. Sleep became a luxury commodity in our house, something we envied and guarded. It took me years *not* to feel guilty about taking a nap. It always felt as if I were taking something from someone else. It also took years to overcome the paranoia that took hold of me every time I went to bed, afraid to fall asleep because I knew it would only be a short time before the wailing of the baby would wake me up and it was time to either nurse or soothe or do something for the little one. In the morning it was time to go to work. Well, almost. First was getting the kids ready for babysitters, child care facilities, or, later, school.

At work, however, I never talked about my family other than in superficial terms like, "yes, they're doing fine." Most of my colleagues at the time were men in their fifties and above or women who either had no children or whose children were grown. Hardly anybody in my school had small kids when I did. So I felt I needed to make my family a non-issue because I knew how people talked about colleagues who had heart attacks or other impediments. They said, "we can't expect such and such of him, he just had a heart attack." I could not afford to have people say "we can't expect such and such of her because she just had a child." I knew lowered expectations would come back to haunt me at some point, and so I never asked for help, for release time, for maternity leave, or anything else.

My third son was born immediately after I taught my last evening class in Spring 1997; I went home at 10:00 P.M., and my water broke at midnight. Maternity leave never crossed my mind, and I was back in the classroom the next Fall. To my colleagues I talked about my kids as if they were golf or another kind of hobby. I knew playing golf had never gotten in the way of tenure and promotion or perceptions of being hard working and capable. Not being authentic, though, is hard. Not asking for support when you need it can be disastrous. I continued to struggle along and succeeded professionally. I got tenure and was seen as the poster child of a successful academic with children. Other women came to me for advice on how to make it. Meanwhile, my marriage fell apart. And I kept thinking: "why am I the poster child of success? Can't you see that I didn't *really* make it?"

I remember my transformation once I began having the children only half of the time. I started to cherish their presence. When they came "to my house" I was ready for them. I was rested, I had my work under control, the house was clean, and I wanted my time with them. It was then that I really started to enjoy them, to take the time to listen to them, to love their company. Before, when I was responsible 24/7, I more or less managed them as well as everything else in life. I got through the day. My focus was on getting everything done that needed to get done rather than enjoying life. During my pre-divorce days, my then six-year-old once wrote me a memo while I was grading papers (he knew not to interrupt me while I was working). The memo had a title page stapled to it that read: "to Mommy, from Niklas. Plees reed this." The memo itself said: "Plees lissen to me."

What I have always pondered is whether my experience was unique. After talking to many women in the academy, I don't think so. In addition, I wondered what it says about academia, and society at-large, that we make it so difficult for women to have a healthy balance between their professional and personal lives (I believe that is increasingly true for men also: see Philipsen & Bostic, in preparation). One should not have to get divorced and share physical custody to have a sane life if one wants both children and a profession. Is it too much to want both? I have seriously heard the argument being made that women, after all, do have a choice: if they want a profession they can choose *not* to have children. And if they do have children, well, then they ought to just deal with it.

Contrary to such narrow visions, I believe that it is a perfectly reasonable stance to want both a fulfilling profession and a rich personal life that may or may not include children. In my case, it did and it does. I spoke to other women who crafted different family constellations as their lifestyles of choice, and nevertheless found it challenging to balance their professional and their personal lives. My personal experiences prompted me to be curious about other academic women's situations. And I soon realized that it's not just female faculty with children who are struggling to find a healthy balance; this is an issue for women in all sorts of personal living arrangements, single women, with or without partners and children, lesbian women, and women whose kids are grown. This book is about all of us.

Obviously, I am not a neutral observer of female faculty balancing their professional and personal lives. Instead, although I did not use the women profiled in this book as agents to advance a predetermined agenda, now that the data are in I do in fact have an agenda: to shed light on the obstacles faced by academic women, what they look like at different career stages and for women from diverse backgrounds, and what can be learned and ultimately done about them.

Organization of the Book

As mentioned above, the book is organized by career stage, with Chapter One devoted to the experiences of early-career women, Chapter Two to mid-career women, and Chapter Three to women at the end of their careers. Each of the chapters describes how women view the relationship between their personal and professional lives in general, the challenges they face, as well as the conditions that enable them. They share stories and analyses, coping strategies, and suggestions for how to deal with a less than perfect world.

Chapter Four is devoted to comparisons across the lines of gender (women comparing themselves to men) and time (women comparing themselves to different generations). Chapter Five consists of recommendations for change on a systemic level and advice on how to cope on a daily basis. The conclusion, finally, summarizes the main findings, discusses their implications, and points at new directions for institutional renewal and future research.

In all, the book is intended to capture the thoughts, experiences, and stories of female faculty in higher education. It is meant to inspire new generations of scholars and can be used to prepare future faculty. It is also an invitation to older generations of faculty to learn from their colleagues and add to the discourse on what it means to be a female faculty member. Finally, my intention is that the book will add to the chorus of those professors, university administrators, and policy makers who see a need for change, a discourse that I hope will be engaged by both women and men. Specific recommendations for the long run, and practical advice for now, are all included in the hopes of contributing to the efforts of those who wish to make academe more humane, for everyone.

1

Early Career

"It Is Tenure or It Is Nothing"

The earliest years in a faculty member's career life-cycle are likely to be the most difficult ones (Olsen & Sorcinelli, 1992). Many factors contribute to these difficulties, and life balancing issues are among them. Indeed, with few exceptions, early-career faculty in this study find it challenging to establish what they would consider a healthy balance between their professional and personal lives. The reasons are manifold, and some cut across lifestyles and family constellations. These general issues are addressed first in this section before the analysis moves on to topics that vary depending upon the faculty members' specific life circumstances.

The Curse of Ill-Defined Expectations: "It's a Moving Target"

"Am I able to balance. . . ? I would say 'no.' Not at all" are the words of Flagship University's assistant professor Dr. Miller. She is convinced that what she sees as her rather limited success at establishing a healthy balance between the personal and professional spheres of her life is symptomatic of the academic profession. It is not just she, in other words, who is struggling at finding balance. It simply comes with being a faculty member in a high-pressure environment. Not being able to find a satisfying balance is, furthermore, not exclusively a trait of faculty with families but typical for most faculty members. It is also not limited to women but faces men as well. In Dr. Miller's words:

> In terms of personal life, family is just one aspect of personal life. I would be hard-pressed to name more than a handful of people in my field total who have thriving personal lives outside of the field, because there's just so much pressure in general on performing academically that there isn't much room left for personal life. . . . I was told early on when I was a grad student by one of the senior faculty in my department that I could have at best two of the following three things. I could have a career, a life, or a family but you can't have all three. I found even having two was hard, but I can't do all three successfully. Even for the men, you can barely do two successfully.

She elaborates that one of her biggest struggles derives from feeling that nothing ever gets done to the extent or with the quality she would like. Academics, she explains, tend never to know how much work is enough and, subsequently, carry a constant sense of guilt because they are never doing as much as they could. The academy is remiss at providing clear expectations, and as long as faculty don't know what, exactly, the expectations are and what it takes to succeed, they are doomed to try to do as much as they possibly can. She recounts attending a meeting on the tenure and promotion process called by the deans of her institution, hoping to learn specifics about work expectations. She left empty-handed.

> I wanted to know, and I didn't expect they could give this, and they didn't. I wanted to know on average how many papers I need a year. On average, what do my teaching evaluations need to be? I know it's a very

complicated formula, and it's a moving target, and they can't give those numbers, but if I could have those numbers in front of me, I could say: "OK, this is my goal, and if I can meet that goal, I'm OK and I don't have to worry about it." But they don't exist.

Dr. Miller explains how unclear expectations in the academy are reflected by a lack of boundaries within the self. She describes finding it difficult to say "no" when an opportunity presents itself, although she may not have the time to devote to the task. She may also say "yes" to activities not essential for her pursuit of tenure. Puzzled with herself she asks:

Why would you choose that? Why would you choose to live your life out of balance? I don't know. It's not that I choose it consciously . . . Maybe that's the obstacle. Maybe the obstacle is I don't know how to say 'no' effectively. Or that I don't want to.

Perhaps what plagues not only Dr. Miller but many other academics, namely the inability to say "no," has its roots in how she generally feels about her job. It, according to her, "isn't just a job. It's sort of my life, for better or worse. What allows me to have a life is that my job is my life, and I'm passionate about it." She cannot conceive of leaving her job because of her family, for instance, knowing that she would "feel totally ungrounded" given that her field "is so deeply part of who I am; without it, I would be totally out of balance. It is not something I can give up."

The curse of ill-defined expectations echoes throughout interviews with early-career professionals. These are the words chosen by different people to describe the same phenomenon:

Not always being sure that you are doing everything right. Not always being sure you are meeting the invisible line that has been drawn, so you don't know when you are just taking on too much.

It feels like I'll get a big pass/fail grade in six years, and I kind of know what I need to do to get a pass, but not very directly. . . . The lack of clarity, . . . if you don't get the information through the grapevine, then you might not know.

Even faculty who seem fairly happy with their own balancing act are plagued by the great unknown. Flagship University's assistant professor McLeod, mother of a two-year old and pregnant, talks about her balance working "pretty well." She is happy that her daughter has the same day care schedule as her work schedule, and reports that she does not work much in the evening or on weekends. What she does not know is whether her lifestyle is going to "produce the appropriate level of productivity" and, accordingly, writing papers is "probably the major thing on my mind."

Coupled with the problem of ill-defined expectations is the paradox of flexibility. Academics have the reputation of benefiting from relative freedom to define the boundaries between their personal and professional lives. Dr. Calhoun, assistant professor at Private Comprehensive, however, is not able to enjoy this flexibility. This is what she has to say:

Part of the problem for me at least is that when you don't have a clearly defined 9 to 5 job it is not like you can leave at the end of the say and say "I'm done." Your project is always with you in a certain sense. On the one hand, I feel like I have a lot of free time because my time is not scheduled. On the other hand, I feel like I don't have any free time because since my time isn't scheduled, or as scheduled, at any moment I could be working or arguably should be working. Sometime I think if I could set banker's hours in some way and sort of tell myself that I'm working from 8 to 6 and then I'm done, but thus far I haven't had a lot of success holding myself to those commitments.

Quite a bit has been written about unclear expectations and ill-defined boundaries. Colbeck observes that faculty may have much discretion over how they allocate their time and integrate roles, but they work under intense pressure to meet high expectations that are often unclearly specified. She quotes a colleague saying that faculty "enjoy the freedom to work themselves to death" (Colbeck, 2006, p. 47).

The consequences of unclear expectations can be exacerbated when faculty work in isolation. Assistant professor Dr. Adams at Metropolitan University describes that, in her case, isolation does not necessarily stem from colleagues' lack of interest in her research area. Nor is it due to their unwillingness to help. Rather, she finds, they are simply unable to find the time to help her, and she feels as if she would bother them given their workload. The end result is a sense of isolation and a lack of what Dr. McMillan, assistant professor at Metropolitan University, calls "structures" necessary to ensure that people succeed in whom the academy has made tremendous investments. Success, for her, means tenure. She finds it "a shame" that assistant professors often need to learn on their own how to design a research plan. If you learn to plan ahead, she explains, lay out your work, make sure you know when you have to submit proposals, you can "make decisions pretty far out in terms of your scholarship," and then "it takes off some of that pressure because you're tenure-track." She explains what many tenure-track faculty members know only too well:

You know there's an expectation, and you're teaching; it takes a tremendous amount of time because if you don't really have a plan for your scholarship, it gets lost.

It is time for change. According to research by Cathy Trower on "Generation X" (born between 1965 and 1980), young scholars have a "new view" of academic employment policy that is markedly different from the "traditional view." Among other things, Gen X scholars want clarity of the tenure process, criteria and standards, and the evidence required. They want clarity of expectations for scholarship, teaching, advising, colleagueship, and campus citizenship. In addition, they are asking for reasonable and consistent performance expectations, as well as consistency of messages from senior faculty and administrators (Trower, 2005, p. 17). They are, in other words, asking for all the things Dr. Miller at Flagship was hoping for when she attended her deans' meeting.

Although this discourse about academic reform is well under way and suggestions are ample, in short, it does not appear that much progress has been made. What is just beginning to be explored and needs to be added to the conversation, furthermore, is how the stress resulting from muddied expectations affects faculty members' attempts to balance their professional and personal lives. As Dr. Miller at Flagship so vividly captured, undefined expectations, both within the academy and the individual scholar, result in the extremely stressful situation of faculty striving to do ever more, without knowing whether what they do is going to be enough. Work spills over into the personal sphere, which, too, is affected by stress.

Research indicates that beginning scholars of either gender are increasingly seeking work environments that permit them to effectively address both their personal and professional responsibilities (Rice, Sorcinelli, & Austin, 2000). Doctoral students note the constant pressure and stress in their teachers' and advisors' work, leaving some to wonder whether a balanced life is possible or even to rethink their career goals (Austin, 2002). As Austin argues, it is therefore imperative to take action and improve the quality of the academic work life given that it is not merely a personal but an institutional issue (Austin, 2006, p. xiii).

Parents on the Tenure-Track: "I Always Feel Like My Attention Is Divided"

Whereas the issues discussed previously apply to tenure-track faculty members regardless of family status, others stem from the individual makeup of their personal lives. Being a mother while on the tenure-track, for example, poses unique challenges. Both the academy and the family are, after all, "greedy institutions" (Letherby, Marchbank, Ramsay & Shiels, 2005, p. 211). This phenomenon, however, has only recently begun to attract national attention.

The public seems well aware that women have made progress in academe. It is often emphasized that they constitute the majority of bachelor's and master's degree recipients and about half of all Ph.D.'s (National Center for Education Statistics, 2005). It is less often articulated that women continue to lag behind in the upper echelons of the professoriate and are underrepresented at both the associate and assistant professor ranks (Chronicle of Higher Education Almanac, 2007–2008, p. 24). This problem in the pipeline has much to do with female faculty having babies and continuing to carry the lion's share of family responsibilities. Not until recently has research begun to document and address these issues.

The "Do Babies Matter?" project, for example, examined the effects of family formation on career progression, the effects of having a faculty career on family patterns, and the nature of work–family conflict for academic parents. According to the research, marriage and young children have a strong negative effect on women entering tenure-track positions, and tenure-track women are less likely to gain tenure than their male counterparts (regardless of family formation). Once on the tenure-track, women and men possess different family formation patterns. For example, tenure-track women are less likely than tenure-track men to have children. When attempting to answer why women opt out of the academy or are pushed out, and why men and women have different family formation patterns, the researchers find one explanation in the tension between work and family responsibilities. This tension, they underscore, is more strongly felt by women than men (Mason, Goulden, & Wolfinger, 2006, pp. 11–17).

The following testimony gives life to the numbers. Women faculty reflect on what it is like to be or become a parent on the tenure-track, how having babies has changed their lives, and what, exactly, the causes are for the tensions between work and family responsibilities. The stories of women who are in later career stages are woven into this section when relevant.

Division of Labor: "I Wish It Were a Little More Equal"

Dr. Carver is a thirty-five-year-old assistant professor at a small, private, liberal arts comprehensive college. She is married and has an eight-week old infant. She talks about having lost control over a situation she called "well balanced," something she had been able to establish before the birth of her child. Before its arrival, she was able to carve out time for herself and for activities she enjoyed away from work. She chose, in other words, a fairly rigid boundary between her professional and her personal lives and was happy with the arrangement until the birth of her daughter changed everything. Now she feels that her personal and professional lives are more in competition with each other.

> Up until I had this baby, I think it was really quite well balanced. I wasn't constantly bringing work home all the time. I certainly worried, and still worry about going up for tenure, and there's a fair amount of anxiety around that. So I don't mean to suggest that I have this great separation, I really don't. But I've always managed time outside of work for other things. I played music with some friends, and would spend time on weekends with my husband and friends, and my dog. So I felt like up until very recently it was well balanced.

Dr. Carver struggles with a tension within her, wanting simultaneously to take care of the infant and needing a break. She emphasizes that her husband does a lot of the domestic chores, a situation that leads to a more even division of labor than most couples experience, something that is "incredibly enabling" to her career. Yet he is not as involved in child care as she would want him to be, although he has, according to her, "this great flexible schedule" as post-doc fellow at Flagship University. She describes how they are still trying to negotiate the division of labor and "every woman I know says in the early period they do much more work with the baby. It's just a standard." Part of the problem, she explains, has to do with breastfeeding, but even if that is not an issue (her baby is mostly bottle-fed), she nevertheless does most of the feeding. She describes being torn in these ways:

> I am mostly pumping [breast milk] and he could give her a bottle. . . .That means he could just take over a lot of these feedings and he does, some, but I do much more of it. So we're trying to negotiate because sometimes that's just fine with me because . . . I want to have this time in my life, . . . but there are other times when I just kind of feel overwhelmed with taking care of this baby, and I want a break, and I wish it were a little more equal.

She elaborates that there is a "cognitive difference" in that she monitors the baby much more than her husband. Even when they are both at home, she feels in charge "even though we're both sitting there in the same room with the baby. It's easier for him to get absorbed in concentrating on something else. I always feel like my attention is divided." She describes how as long as she is physically near the baby she is monitoring the baby, feeling that "it's just my nature." The only way she can imagine to get a good stretch of concentration is if she leaves her daughter with her husband and leaves the house herself because otherwise "I feel I just have to be attuned to her." Her husband, however, doesn't seem to feel that way, and in her mind that's a "real asymmetry" that doesn't play out so much in the couple's behavior but in the way they think.

Dr. Young-Powell, first-year instructor at Community College and married mother of a three-year-old and an eight-month-old, talks about her difficulty letting her husband take over domestic duties. She describes herself as being "very hands on, and I like to control. I like things the way I want them done." She elaborates further:

> For me it is harder to let go of the kid responsibilities. I feel like I should be the one giving them a bath at night, giving the last bottle of the night, reading bedtime stories. Sometimes I need to be doing other things and he'll say, let me read the story. And I think, no, that's mommy's job. There's certain things I'm not willing to say, daddy do. I feel like that's mommy time. . . . And financial things like paying the bills, where he'll say "I'll do it." That's a control thing for I need to know where everything is going.

Dr. Young-Powell's need to control manifests itself in the words she chooses when she describes the division of labor between herself and her husband. She talks about "giving him grocery shopping and bath time" or just generally "giving him more responsibilities around the house." She clearly is the one in charge, in other words, of domestic affairs, either by being "hands on" and doing it herself or delegating, managing, and telling her husband "I need you to do x, y, and z today." She seems to be looking forward to the summer when she will teach only one Internet class and "other than that I'm home. I think I do pick up a lot more responsibility during the summer."

Sacrifices: "It's Tiring"

Life with small children certainly makes it difficult for most female faculty to craft what they would consider a healthy balance between their personal and professional lives. In their efforts to "do it all," care of self is sacrificed first. Dr. Miller is an assistant professor at Flagship University, married with a three-year-old daughter and pregnant with her second child. In response to my question about balancing, she replies:

> I guess for me the way I balance, if you can call it that, is I put out the biggest most immediate fires as they come and juggle as necessary. There is always something falling through the crack.

Dr. Miller has learned to "prioritize ruthlessly" but "what goes in that prioritization is nothing for myself." Anything that has to do with taking care of herself, she explains, comes last. She recounts how "exercise has gone pretty much out the window," and so have quiet meditation and journaling. Dr. Young-Powell at Private Comprehensive University describes a similar reality. She lacks sleep and gave up hobbies and things she enjoys doing in her free time such as the gym or working on scrapbooks.

There were other stories of sacrifice. Dr. Nelson at HBCU told the story of a female colleague who had to sacrifice success in her career because she got pregnant and had a child.

> She went up for [tenure] last year in August. She got pregnant, she had a baby . . . while she was pregnant, she went up for tenure. One of the guys put her down and said she hasn't published enough, she hasn't done enough. But she goes, I was pregnant, and I was getting ready to give birth. The whole committee decided not to grant it to her. She tried again this August and she still didn't get it, so she is up for it one more time.

She elaborates how pregnancy is a nine month process, and not all women are fortunate enough to be able to fully function during that time. Some develop physical problems, and accommodations need to be made (such as extending the tenure clock) that allow all women to have a chance at success.

Sacrifices occur even when women with families are professionally successful and able to have babies without being pushed out of the academy. Dr. Nelson, instructor at HBCU, has ample support from her husband and extended family to free her up for professional duties. Yet she mourns the fact that she cannot spend significant amounts of time with her three small children. There simply is not much time left when she comes home in the evening. She does not think she has been able to establish a balance but concludes "right now I have to establish myself in my career, so it takes front row."

While grateful for her family support, Dr. Nelson is torn between her career and her desire to be a parent. These are her words:

> There were many instances I wanted to quit but then I didn't quit because of my support system. . . ." I can't bear this, there's too much work". . . . and people keep going "it's just a couple of years. You have the job." "I'm never with my kids." They go "think about it, you have them on the weekend and in the evening." I'm like "that's nothing. I would like to be home with them all the time." They go "remember who chose this path. Nobody chose it for you. It's what you wanted to do."

She recounts wanting to quit her Ph.D. program but continuing because of her family's encouragement. They told her once she was finished, she would be able to spend time with her kids. "I'm done," she says, "and still don't get that time." She has come to the conclusion that "I have to learn that since you make the optional choice to work, you have to give up something. With a family, you can't do both equally. One will have to give." She perceives a clear gender component in her ruminations and says, "I think if it's a girl pursuing a career, they will have to learn that that is going to become the focus. Although the family is number one, the family kind of takes a back seat when you go to work."

Dr. Nelson is looking forward to a time when the tension eases up, either because she can use grant money to buy back time that she can devote to her family, or because her small children will go to school, in which case "it doesn't become such a big problem anymore because they're gone and you're gone." As for now, however, the pain in her face is obvious when she says that even though things may not be bad long term, they are short term between the kids' ages of zero and five. "That's when the emotional attachment problems become more predominant. At least for me." She sums it up by saying, "to a young girl trying to get where I am, they have to be focused."

Dr. Nelson's analysis of her dilemma is based upon the notion that women need to choose whether they want to pursue a career *or* have a family. This notion may well be shared by many women themselves, Dr. Nelson being one example. However, choice is an insidious notion here, despite its seemingly benevolent character. Being an immensely popular societal construct, it seems inconceivable to oppose "choice" on rational grounds. How can anybody be against "choice"? And yet, in certain situations asking people to make a choice is simply wrong. In cases of women such as Dr. Nelson, the idea of choice is just as perverted as a choice between shelter and food would be. People need both, food *and* shelter, not a choice between the two. Likewise women, and men one might add, need to be able to pursue *both* a career and a family life if they wish, and they need to be able to do so without major emotional or physical costs.

Ms. Young-Powell's life is illustrative here. Echoing many of Dr. Nelson's dilemmas, the instructor and administrator at Community College is the married mother of two children under four years of age. She, too, craves "mommy time" with her children, and rather than doing without, she goes home, plays with them, and then waits until they go to bed before she "reverts back into the academic mode." This modus operandi is not without costs. Explains Ms. Young-Powell:

> For me it's tiring. I do find myself a lot of times at eleven, twelve, one o'clock in the morning doing more planning and other administrative duties. I don't want to stay [at work] until six every night because I want to go home to be mommy. . . . Sometimes when [I have] time off, when they're napping, instead of doing things that I need to be doing at home, I'm spending time doing things for [work] at home. . . . I spend a lot of time [working] when I'd really rather be sleeping when they're in bed.

In addition to fatigue, Ms. Young-Powell also battles feeling guilty because she is not a stay-at-home mother. Feeling insufficiently available, however, is a sentiment shared by other mothers on the tenure-track, including those of older children.

Dr. McMillan, for example, a fourth-year tenure-track faculty member at Metropolitan whose children are fifteen and twenty-three, talks about the difficult adjustments she had to make after leaving a K–12 teaching environment to begin her work in higher education. She used to think of her job as an extension of her life; she socialized with her colleagues, and her family was involved in her school. All that changed when she entered higher education. Now she is no longer as available to her children. One of her sons experienced difficulties in middle school, and she talks about his challenges given that his mother was "whacked up in her new position that demanded a tremendous amount of time." She recalls coming into the office on Saturdays at least twice a month, working at home on Sundays. In short, she "wasn't that available." She struggles with that, she says, and explains:

I think women, more than anything else, struggle with that. Men for the most part, I don't see that as a big struggle for most men. Work as hard as necessary to attain that goal for my job, and struggle over how much time I give my family, or how much quality time. . . . I see that is something that women, because we are nurturers and because culturally, we see our role as being available, that we struggle with it. But you know I am surprised, some Saturday mornings I would be waking up to run out to do some errands. . . . and my kids would say 'are you going to work now?' They expect me to work all the time. It bothers me a little.

Female faculty on the tenure-track, it seems, rarely have options both workable and healthy. They are asked to make choices, furthermore, that their male counterparts hardly ever have to make, namely the choice between family and work. In fact, recent research shows that women who enter the tenure-track without children have less than one in three odds of ever having children. Furthermore, a majority of men (60 percent) are married with children twelve years after receipt of their Ph.D. whereas only a minority (41 percent) of women on the tenure-track are married with children (Mason, Goulden, & Wolfinger, 2006, p. 16). As this study indicates, if women refuse either–or propositions and pursue both, a career and a family, they suffer the consequences of doing something that is simply "too much to ask."

And yet to pursue both is not too much to ask in a society in which work is plentiful and families are needed, if for nothing else than reproduction. A civil society simply cannot afford to force people into false dichotomies and ask that they make *choices* that require them to abjure one if they want the other, or suffer dire consequences if they pursue both. Instead, the focus ought to be on how to design support mechanisms and realistic expectations to enable people to have a fulfilling career *as well as* a family life without paying the price in degrees of sanity or physical health. Of course, the women in this study had many suggestions in this regard, summarized in Chapter Five.

Single Parenting: "I Was Paying for Having Some Relaxation"

There are single mothers on the tenure-track, and if being a parent is challenging for women with partners, it can certainly be daunting for women without. Dr. Adams became a single parent because she took a tenure-track position at Metropolitan. Her husband was unable to find work in the new city and stayed behind. It was up to Dr. Adams to take care of their teenage daughter. She describes the transition:

> My husband and I are geographically separated. He's not here. So when I started this position not only was I separated from someone I'd been with for thirty years, but I suddenly became a single parent and moved to a city that I was not even familiar with, and left a city where I'd lived for over twenty years.

Living in limbo for two years was difficult. Dr. Adams began to realize that she, too, had to "make a choice between my career and my family, and I chose my family." She decided to resign from her position at Metropolitan, move back to her old town, and apply for a job at a less research-intense institution. Again, the paradox of choice. According to Dr. Adams, this is a choice she would not have made twenty years ago. In her life stage, however, she prefers to make a difference professionally without the strains that come with the competitive nature of a tenure-track position, which, in her field, heavily relies on federal grant funding. Says she: "The research opportunities have been here, but my decision [to leave] was based on what was most important to me, which was my family."

Dr. Adams worked hard all her life, juggling her professional obligations and her family. She is fifty-one years old and has two grown children in addition to the teenager. She received three degrees while building her family: "It seems like I got another degree with each child. I got my bachelor's degree when I only had one child. My master's when I had two children. And I got my doctorate when I had three children." Despite the fact that she is certainly experienced at working hard and multitasking, always doing more than one thing at a time, it is her most recent tenure-track experience that was simply too much. As she recalls:

> Being in a tenure-track position has been more difficult than anything I've done in the past. I've worked full-time and gone to school full-time and taken care of a family. Yes, it was very stressful, but it also provided time for me . . . to spend with my family and do the things I enjoy doing. That probably could have been done here, but there was always something that needed to be done as far as work was concerned. . . . I was paying for having some relaxation. . . . I was always playing catch-up.

She found it difficult to find the creative spaces necessary for research and writing. And if she got a break from work, she did not get one from her family.

Being separated from her husband, and the daughter from her father, was not only emotionally difficult for Dr. Adams and her daughter, at times it was also a logistical nightmare. Her field demands faculty teach in clinical settings, and she explains what it means to be given an evening clinical course:

> Not only was I in a new town and being a single mother with a teenager, but I had to go to a setting from three to nine in the evening weekly. . . . . Which drove me

crazy mentally because I'm thinking 'I'm in this town where I know no one, and I'm away from my child in the evening.' So that was difficult.

Her contract, she points out, is not a traditional nine-month contract running Mondays through Fridays. Instead, some work needs to get done on evenings and weekends because her clientele consists of licensed professionals who are coming back to obtain degrees. They are busy during the week, and faculty are expected to accommodate the students' schedules. This kind of flexibility, however, is exceedingly difficult to offer for a faculty member who, as a single mother, is solely responsible for a child.

The observation that faculty appointments involving clinical work are exceedingly demanding is echoed by her late-career colleague at HBCU, Dr. Noah. She points out how challenging it is to have a family and teach in her field because of the clinical hours. She explains: "You're spending an enormous amount of time in a clinical setting, and then having to evaluate your students on their performance with their patients in their clinical settings. . . ." Being a single mother, of course, exacerbates the challenge.

Dr. Adams surmises how much more of a logistical challenge being a single mother to her teenage daughter would have been if the girl had been more involved in school activities than she was. "If she was involved in a whole lot of things, and I had to take her this place and that, . . . I don't know what I would've done."

Being a single mother is not always easy for Dr. Yong either, a young immigrant scholar at Metropolitan. Dr. Yong's fourteen-year-old son was raised by her parents in China before joining her just over a year ago in the United States. Since then, she has been a single parent.

Dr. Yong is well aware that some of the challenges she faces have much to do with the fact that she is not only a single mother but also a relatively new mother to a teenager who, in addition, grew up in a different culture. She feels stressed simply because parental scripts taken for granted by many of her American counterparts are not always known to her. In her words, "nothing is routine."

> For single moms there are so many little things that you cannot skip. Because a child there depends on you. I had very limited experience because my parents took care [of the child] until last year, and that's why I feel so stressed because many times I don't know whether I am doing the right job as a parent. . . . Little things like making a choice about extra-curricular activities. I don't know which is the right choice for him, who I can ask for support. This is already routine for many parents; they do this all the time. For me it's kind of a learning; it creates a lot of stress, and you cannot always just ask people because people do it as a routine, but for me nothing is routine. Everything is new. Even . . . parent meetings.

To deal with the challenges of single parenting, administrator Dr. Lilian at Community College decided to stay close to her extended family. Dr. Lilian is thirty-four years old, divorced, and the mother of a thirteen-year old daughter. She describes making the decision "to stay local" in relatively close proximity to her parents and sister. Says she:

> As a single parent I didn't want to go far from my support, meaning that if I had to fly somewhere for a conference, then I could be at my parents' house in an hour where they could take care of [the daughter]. Whereas if I lived on the West coast, I wouldn't have that support line.

"Staying local," Dr. Lilian admits, came at a cost. She simply could not take advantage of professional opportunities that presented themselves. "There are so many career opportunities, you know, in different states and so forth. As a single parent, I really needed to stay close to my support line."

Maternity Leave Policies: "It's Something the Deans Kind of Do"

For mothers on the tenure-track, academe is a mixed blessing. It allows an uncanny degree of flexibility, and is one of the few professional environments that does not strictly regiment employees' time and place. The benefits are huge. Parents are able to attend children's special events, take time off without fearing for their jobs when children are sick, bring children to work, and bring work home.

Academe is also uniquely detrimental to parenthood with its "up or out" promotional system that renders it difficult to take time out for childbearing and rearing without repercussions. A faculty member who leaves the tenure-track to take care of family responsibilities will not find her job waiting for her when she comes back. Tenure-lines are valuable commodities snatched up at once upon a person's departure. Faculty careers are certainly possible outside the tenure system, but they tend to be second class and unprotected.

Official university policies designed to lighten the load of female faculty members with children at the institutions represented in this study are currently in various stages of infancy. All do, of course, offer the provisions of the Family and Medical Leave Act (FMLA) of 1993 (U.S. Department of Labor, 2007, pp.1–18). FMLA allows eligible full-time employees to take up to twelve workweeks of unpaid leave per calendar year for the birth, adoption, or foster care placement of a child or to care for a child. It also allows for paid leave which at the universities in this study is typically granted if the employee requests to use annual, compensatory, overtime, or sick leave during a Family and Medical Leave period. Additional provisions are possible, but the policies are neither uniformly applied nor well known. Universities do not appear to put forth much effort to publicize them and, therefore, implementation is largely capricious.

At Metropolitan University, for example, a special program sponsored by the Alfred P. Sloan Foundation allows faculty one-semester paid leaves of absence for birth and adoption of children. It also provides faculty with the option of extending the promotion and tenure review by up to one year. However, only pre-tenure faculty in the College of Humanities and Sciences are eligible. The program is not widely advertised. Says Associate Professor Dr. Schumacher at Metropolitan: "It isn't publicized very well. Every time I bring a new faculty member in, I tell them, you go take advantage of this."

The lack of awareness of existing maternity policies is a problem well beyond the colleges studied here. Even at the University of California-Berkeley, with its extensive maternity leave package, researchers found that faculty were ill aware of its availability (Mason, Goulden, & Wolfinger, 2006, p. 20). Compounding the problem might be uninformed human resources personnel. This is how Dr. Schumacher sees the situation at Metropolitan:

> The other barrier is that the university human resources system has no idea what to do with maternity leave. They give out wrong and bad information, and it is a very poor system. . . . It is terrible. It is an awful system. I actually got cheated out of a semester of leave . . . after the birth of my first child because I was told by a person in human resources, unequivocally, that I was not eligible for it because she was born in May. And because I was a nine-month faculty, any time-off had to be continuous to the birth when indeed I was entitled to twelve weeks of combined paid/unpaid leave. I specifically asked this person in human resources this; they said "no, you are not entitled to it." So, I came right back bleary-eyed with a three-month old.

Flagship University appears similarly unpredictable. Faculty do mention that a paid semester's leave is granted, and the tenure clock can be temporarily stopped. However, the policy is not "official," meaning sanctioned, put in writing, advertised as part of employee benefits packages, and equally available to all. Dr. Miller at Flagship, pregnant with her second child, describes the situation as follows:

> It's not well publicized though. I couldn't find it on the web, my chair didn't know. It's something I think the deans kind of do, but it's not publicized . . . . There certainly is not [a policy] university wide. I think each school within the university might have its own policy somewhere that's not readily available. It many not be in writing.

Dr. McLeod at the same institution, also mother of a three-year-old and pregnant, corroborates:

> [Flagship] has a fairly good maternity policy but it's not like a real official policy. It's sort of an "ad-hoc" policy. . . . Most people get a research leave. They usually give us a semester off from teaching. . . . I'm not sure about [people's] knowledge because it's not on the web anywhere. . . . So I feel like if you didn't talk to anybody who'd gotten it you might not know that you can get it.

She explains that the official policy at Flagship is based on the Family and Medical Leave Act and, therefore, whether or not a woman is granted maternity leave (disguised as research leave) depends on the department. With this practice, she elaborates, the university obtains an element of flexibility and can grant faculty leave that staff members do not get. "And I'm guessing that's part of the reason there's not an official policy."

Serious equity considerations would arise should pregnant women have to take their "research leave" to have children while others use it for its intended purpose. Yet Dr. McLeod insists that she is certain to be granted research leave again, in addition to the leave she will enjoy after her baby's birth. She also disagrees with colleagues who think that maternity leave ought not carry with it any expectations that you are scholarly active. Says she: "it's freaking nine months. It doesn't seem that extreme what we're expected to do. Come on. Let's face reality here. Because if you time your birth correctly, it's a summer-plus-sort-of-thing."

Dr. McLeod timed the impending birth of her child "correctly": the due date is in June. She will be able to take the summer and the fall semester off. Not everyone is so lucky. Her colleague, she recounts, is expecting a baby in October, in the middle of the fall semester, and "she had lots of pressure from her department to take [leave] in the fall." Concludes Dr. McLeod: "It's just, if you get lucky at the time. . . ."

Luck is a relative term here because faculty are typically on nine-month contracts. Taking the summer off entails not being able to supplement one's income through summer teaching and, although it might "buy time," it nevertheless means financial loss. Even if something as fickle as a pregnancy could be reliably planned, the "correct timing issue" is complex, as explained by Dr. Miller at Flagship:

> I think if you were to have the child in May and wanted to take time off, the university would probably not pay you, but I don't know. I think you would just not take your summer salary [supplemental income from teaching or grants] and then have the fall semester off when you would be paid. So that would be financially a hit if you were to have a child in May. . . .

Timing is an issue brought up by Dr. Schumacher at Metropolitan as well. She explains that since the Family and Medical Leave per se is unpaid, faculty have to use such things as accrued sick leave to convert it into paid leave. They can, however, only use 33 percent of accrued sick leave for maternity leave. In her case, she was able to use more than 300 hours of her 1,000 hours accrued, a number that translated into eight weeks of paid leave and four weeks of unpaid leave. Her second child was born in July. She faced a dilemma:

> So I said, "what would I do if I took eight weeks paid leave?" We work on semesters. "What does it mean if I take eight weeks of a semester off, and we have seven weeks of a semester left? What does that mean?" No one had ever thought of it, or had an answer. They said "well, you come back and we'll put you in the administration office and you do administration work for seven weeks." I thought, I'm not going to do this. The last thing I want to do is shuffle paper. I mean, I'm an academic, right?

Dr. Schumacher approached the problem by negotiating based on "some obscure rules in the University system about half-time Medical/Family Leave use." After having her baby, she took half-time leave for sixteen weeks rather than full-time leave for eight. The arrangement was awkward at best.

> Once we got that agreement set for half-time leave, I said OK, what are my responsibilities? What is half-time for an academic who teaches a three/three load and [serves on] twenty-five committees? So we futzed around, and I taught one class with a brand new baby and a C-section, and did some administrative work, and wrote and published.

She reiterates a familiar theme: "There were no policies. There were no guidelines." What happens when there are no guidelines, she emphasizes, is that faculty have to "sort of tentatively feel out what is possible. It is sort of like pushing until people say 'no.' Yet you never know where 'no' is." The process, in short, is completely arbitrary.

Tenured professor Whitehead recounts policy perversions similar in nature dating back to times prior to the Family and Medical Leave Act. After the C-section birth of a child with health complications, she asked for a tenure delay and was put on half-time work. Her paycheck was also cut in half, and she lost her health insurance altogether: "So there is a time when I really need it, and they cut my health insurance."

Back at Flagship, Dr. Miller did not run into quite the same obstacles and finds her institution's one-semester paid leave "quite generous by U.S. standards." Those standards, however, are low, and discussions about maternity policies in academe do, after all, occur in the national context of a country that is unique among industrialized nations in its absence of viable maternity or paternity policies, as even the popular press noted recently.[1]

USA Today reported that, with the exception of some American states, the United States and Australia are the only industrialized nations that do not provide paid maternity leave. Australia does, however, offer a one-year job-protected leave whereas the U.S. Family and Medical Leave Act only provides twelve weeks of job-protected leave, and only to those who work in larger companies. Canada, in comparison, offers fourteen months of paid maternity leave and Sweden provides sixteen months of parental leave for mothers or fathers. To illustrate the point differently, out of 168 nations studied recently by Harvard University, 163 provided paid maternity leave, "leaving the United States in the company of Lesotho, Papua New Guinea, and Swaziland." In response to the question why the United States fares so poorly in comparison, the article cites experts who explain that whereas some countries such as France needed expanded maternity leave policies after World War II to combat falling fertility, the United States could rely on immigration to ensure population growth. Likewise, the feminist movement in the United States, unlike its European counterpart, did not advocate for mothers, specifically. Be that as it may, at this point American women and men seem to consider a three-month maternity leave to be the norm (*USA Today*, 2005, p. 1).

Besides leave, stopping the tenure clock is often discussed as an option for new mothers in academe. Dr. Carver at Private Comprehensive is currently on leave after the birth of her baby six weeks ago and had her tenure-clock stopped. She is grateful for both, convinced she has gotten good support professionally and hopeful that she will not be expected to produce more scholarship just because she has more time. Yet she concedes: "Of course I don't really know how that plays out in people's judgment of you." Despite her support, Dr. Carver cannot deny that simply being on the tenure-track adds a component of pressure to an already stressful time following a major life event:

> I think the nature of the job, and being on the tenure clock, it adds a certain sort of stress to this period of our lives. As I said, they extended the clock for me which is great. If they hadn't, I think this would have been a very stressful period. As it is, I don't think I'm a shoo-in for tenure, and it's something in the back of my mind I have to manage, but I don't think I could reasonably ask for anything better than the extension that I got. I wish I had tenure; that would be better. . . . I feel like if I had a rough year, it wouldn't throw my entire career off-track. But I do feel that to some extent it's not really anybody's fault. It's just the period of my career where I am at. The nature of being on tenure-track.

Although maternity policies are neither "official," uniformly implemented, nor well advertised, colleges may well provide more to women than originally meets the eye. Yet even if female faculty know about and are theoretically able to take advantage of policies, they may not necessarily be inclined to do so. University policies suffer, in other words, from a "bane of unintended consequences," to use the words of educational historian David Tyack (Tyack, 1974). Though intended to help, they may actually hurt or, at the least, be perceived as potentially hurtful and thus underutilized.

Dr. McLeod at Flagship illustrates the point. She wonders: "I don't know how you really change the institution because once you start dropping requirements or creating a perception the bars are different for people based on their family, I think [you create] really big problems." She alludes to debates about whether stopping the tenure clock helps or hurts. Her tenured colleague Dr. Sutherland puts it more decisively:

> At [Flagship] if you have a child before tenure, for each child you're allowed a one-year extension of the tenure clock, but . . . oftentimes there's increased expectations that go along with that. It's hard to balance whether you should take it because it's viewed that you had an extra year, and maybe they expect more of you.

In response to the question whether she knew of people who decided not to take leave for that reason, she responded, "Yes. Lots of people decide not to take it for that reason." At Private Comprehensive, associate professor Pryzinski, echoes the sentiment. She tells the story of a colleague who took sabbatical, maternity leave, and stopped the tenure clock, and who talks about "all of that as this beautiful life resource. And yet, she fears backlash that is now more subtle and more hidden than anything that would have happened prior to these institutional resources." The insecurity is fueled by the fact that maternity leave entails an expectation for continued research, and the question is how this expectation will affect tenure standards in comparison to those for men or women without maternity leave. Dr. Pryzinski recounts having talked to other junior faculty women at her institution who share the worries and wonder "how it is all going to pan out. So there is this new anxiety of the unknown. . . ."

This finding is consistent with quantitative research that found that faculty do not make use of available policies for fear that doing so might hurt their careers. This phenomenon, the authors conclude, "points to deeply rooted problems of institutional culture and climate" (Mason, Goulden, & Wolfinger, 2006, p. 20). How those problems might possibly be addressed will be discussed in Chapter Five.

Single Women

The Ability to Focus: "My Job Is Much Easier Because Women with Children Have Two Jobs, and I Have One"

Being single seems to make it easier for some women to perceive their balancing act as successful. Assistant professor at Private Comprehensive University Dr. Rossi talks about having a "really sweet job, very flexible job, no family," and being able to see her friends whenever she wants. She is convinced that single persons have a lot of control and, comparing herself with women who have children, simply states: "My job is much easier because women with children have two jobs, and I have one."

Ms. Ohler at Community College feels similarly. She is twenty-eight years old, a relatively new instructor who watches her friends get married and have children. That, however, is not for her. Says Ms. Ohler:

> Looking at that situation and looking at them trying to manage family life, and all of them have ended up either working just part-time or staying at home full-time while the children are small. Certainly to balance that sort of personal situation would be difficult to me because I just

enjoy working on my own academic interests too much. I think I'd have a hard time giving up that stimulation that would go along with that.

When asked whether she thought that having a family necessitates going part-time or staying at home altogether, she replies that people can combine work and family successfully; examples do exist. For her, however, "it seems like a daunting prospect . . . I see what they struggle with. . . . I think 'wow, how do they do it?'"

For now, she simply wants to be able to focus on her academic pursuits rather than being torn between family and work demands. According to another single faculty member, thirty-six-year-old Dr. Calhoun at Private Comprehensive, women get a pretty bad deal, furthermore, when compared with men. These are her observations.

It does seem awfully easier for men. I have this one colleague who has three children under the age of nine. His wife is a lawyer; it's not like she doesn't have a career, but I was once chatting with him and a female colleague who also has young children and sort of inadvertently comparing how much they were talking about how much they had to do around the house because the issue was having kids at this age. What she was describing was all about picking people up and taking them places and dropping them off and making lunches. What he was describing was all about interacting with them when he got home at 7:30 in the hour before they went to bed. I was sort of thinking at the time, 'he has got a good deal.' It is kind of a nice little set up. He comes home at 7:30 and plays with the kids for an hour and half, and then they go to bed. My poor colleague Annie was talking about all of this stuff, and it just seemed very poignant, and it was enough to make me think I wasn't

so sure I wanted to have kids even if I were so lucky to
find someone to have them with.

Despite her doubts and the gender inequities she observes,
Dr. Calhoun joins the ranks of those women who are very
much interested in giving up the single life. Yet they face difficulties of their own. Research indicates that single women on
the tenure-track, who are within three years of receiving their
Ph.D.'s, are significantly less likely than single tenure-track men
or single non-tenure-track women to get married. They have a
37 percent lower probability than single tenure-track men and a
34 percent lower probability rate than non-tenure-track female faculty (Mason, Goulden, & Wolfinger, 2006, p. 15). The following
section sheds light on the dynamics behind the statistics.

Racing the Biological Clock: "I Have to Sort of Roll the Dice on Whether or Not I Will Ever Be Able to Carry Children"

Not all single faculty members in this study describe their balancing
acts in glowing terms. Having trouble establishing a social life,
making friends, and dating were identified as impeding their sense
of a good balance. Dr. Calhoun, for instance, assistant professor
in her fifth year at Private Comprehensive University, describes
the relationship between her personal and professional lives as
"vexed." She finds that the pressure to get publications out and
make herself indispensable in her department has made it difficult
to prioritize relationship building. Her problems are exacerbated
by the nature of where she lives, a town she describes as a "pretty
married place." She elaborates:

Most of the friends I have are married. All of my
colleagues are married, so there is no single culture, or I
haven't found much of a single culture at this point.

In order to "find a slightly more conducive social life with a few more single people in it," Dr. Calhoun is planning to spend the next summer with friends in Manhattan, just to get away. Back home, however, given the difficulty of finding a "singles culture," Dr. Calhoun chooses to immerse herself in her work and get her research done rather than "trying some online dating, or really nudging my friends to introduce me to people, or join groups that would introduce me to people." Dr. Calhoun emphasizes that for her, questions about balancing are about finding a partner with whom to start a family rather than dealing with a family that already exists. This aspect of the single life tends to get lost in discussions about balancing one's life. Dr. Calhoun talks about friends who have infant children and who resent the fact that she does not.

> They say things like how nice it is that I have all this free time to myself, and how great it must be to be able to get your research done whenever you want and not to have to worry about changing someone's diaper and getting food on the table.

She points out, however, that her lifestyle comes with certain costs, such as the worry about whether she will ever be able to find a partner or have a family. She is irritated by the fact that she cannot make finding a partner more of a priority because "my career has such a rigid understanding of what it means to be successful in the first stage of your career. It is tenure or it is nothing." Her college is trying to increase its research profile, she explains, by growing from a medium-sized, regionally recognized liberal arts university into one with a national reputation. To this end, enormous pressure is put on junior faculty to publish quickly and profusely. Simultaneously, however, the college does not want to lose its reputation as a teaching-oriented college, leaving faculty in the double bind of having to meet both high research and teaching expectations. Not much time is left to craft one's personal life. She explains that if one is not lucky enough to find a partner as a graduate student, one is "out of luck" until after tenure. Most of her friends who are married, she elaborates, got married in graduate school. The ones who didn't get married then, got married after tenure, not before.

Trying to find a partner and start a family once you have tenure is not always easy, however. The biological clock ticks ruthlessly. Dr. Calhoun puts it clearly:

> The thing I worry about the most in terms of this question about balance is the . . . whole biological clock problem which is that my pre-tenure years are also, for whatever reason, in sync with the years in which I should probably, if I want to have a child, I should be doing it. I will get tenure provided everything goes all right when I'm 38. According to a lot of doctors that is getting late to start a family. I haven't found a way to start a family yet while on the tenure-track. The one thing that would make a difference to me is if there was a way to make tenure sort of not coincide with one's child producing time. It isn't that I don't want to get tenure. Obviously I do. It would be nice if tenure didn't have to be such a rigid thing. As it stands, I don't feel like I can really prioritize finding a partner and getting pregnant right now. So, I have to sort of roll the dice on whether or not I will ever be able to carry children. Which scares me. To get a more flexible schedule for tenure would make a big difference, I think.

Dr. Calhoun recounts the example of her forty-four-year-old friend who was thirty-nine when she was granted tenure. After that she made her social and romantic life a priority but was not able to build a lasting relationship. Menopause hit early, and she had to give up on having children. Dr. Calhoun admits that her friend's example colors her attitude and contributes to her sense that she needs to meet and commit to somebody during her pretenure years if she wants to have a family. Although she is not opposed to the idea of tenure per se, she finds the system rigid. It simply "doesn't take into consideration how complicated people's lives can be, and how maybe your life doesn't fit into this very clearly defined five-year clock." Consequently, she sees herself facing a dilemma: "It feels like a risk to wait [having children], but it is also a risk not to do everything I can to establish myself in my job."

Dr. Sutherland at Flagship echoes Dr. Calhoun's sentiments and says the timing of the tenure clock is just "really crappy for a woman's biological clock." She was lucky she did not meet her husband and get married until after tenure, she says, and so she was spared the difficult question as to whether or not she wanted to risk having children before tenure.

Lives are often complex and not amenable to the five-year tenure-system. What makes things more complicated, furthermore, is the nature of the academic job and the typical requirement that people move, often long distances, in order to take a tenure-track position. They are forced to uproot and possibly jeopardize social networks they may have established in graduate school. In Dr. Calhoun's words "you have to kind of rebuild your networks."

The notion that female faculty may be forced to choose between having a career and having children was confirmed by Dr. McLeod, assistant professor at Flagship University, married, one child and expecting a second one. She stated that there are "obviously a lot of people who put off childbirth ... until after tenure," something that just did not make sense to her. She did not want to sacrifice her personal life and build her life around her job. Consequently, she chose a field that she thought would be less intense than others and made use of a "couple of windows" to have children, such as graduate school when "nobody's counting the time."

Dr. McLeod is also very clear that she would never have become an academic if she hadn't been married. She defines academe as a "crappy place to meet people. . . , a sheltered sort of life" that compares unfavorably with businesses who may sponsor trips and events. She recalls her pre-academe life in a consulting firm:

> We were always going out for happy hours. They would sponsor parties; they would rent out restaurants, bars. It's such an entire social structure built around work. And some of that, they were deriving from a very homogenous set of people, like all Ivy league grads, all kind of following a similar career path. So there's more social interaction than you would have at a later stage in your life.

The Two-Body Problem: "People Have to Think of This More as a Package Deal"

Dr. Ingersen-Noll at Flagship calls it the "Two-Body Problem," more commonly referred to as the "dual career" or "spousal hiring" issue. No matter what the name, it is one of the most vexing dilemmas in higher education.

An obvious place for academics to meet potential life partners is academe itself, and if one or both partners are not yet institutionally established (if they meet as graduate students, for example), the couple has to deal with the "dual-body problem." It faces a competitive job market with institutions interested in specialized expertise. Finding a suitable job may not be easy for one person; multiplied by two, the barriers can be insurmountable. If both partners are housed in the same discipline and do similar work, they must find an institution that needs "two of them." More likely, they will end up competing for the job. If they are of different backgrounds, they are searching to find homes in different departments at the same institution, or at geographically close ones. In most fields, and for most people, the problem is close to intractable and may well mean that one spouse truncates career aspirations at least temporarily to do adjunct work, accept visiting professorships, work part-time, out of field, at a less desirable institution, or abandons academic work altogether.

By the time of this writing, Flagship University had already lost Dr. Ingersen-Noll due to the two-body problem. Her husband and she joined a university in another country because Flagship could not satisfactorily accommodate two promising scholars in similar fields. Here is Dr. Ingersen-Noll's story.

She came to Flagship after completing a post doc at a major research university in the United States. Before that, she received her Ph.D. in the Netherlands. Dr. Ingersen-Noll is thirty-one years old and married to a scholar who shares her field of research. He followed her to Flagship but did not receive a tenure-track position. Instead, he was offered what Dr. Ingersen-Noll calls "a dead end job" as system administrator. "There is no career path," she says, "no progress. . . . There is nothing like that, and it has been made clear to us that that's the case." She relates that there are no future prospects for her husband in the department and perceives "unwillingness to solve this." The couple finds the situation "not very satisfying."

Dr. Ingersen-Noll is determined to move forward in her career but seeing her husband confined to his job is not "very motivating for either of us." This is her analysis of the university environment:

> . . . this university in particular is a very male dominated environment. . . . A lot of people here, especially if you look at the generations before us. Men who came to work here at the university have had their housewives come along with them, and they stayed at home to take care

of their kids or something. Women were only admitted
here—both professors and students—in the 1970s. It
was quite late; so it is still a bit of a male-dominated
community.

While acknowledging that Flagship is doing its best to make women
part of the institution, she diagnoses a real problem in the absence
of consideration given to the partner situation.

What they do they just apply the same strategies. They
assume you can move people around whether they're
men or women without thinking about what their partner is going to do. That's something that they're not
thinking about here at this university. And it's a big
problem.

According to her, the university is now willing to adjust its
modus operandi and make women the breadwinner but is not at
all concerned about the partner. Her conclusion: "We are actually
looking around for other jobs because we've been told that there
is no solution for him here. This is the consequence the university
has to deal with."

Dr. Ingersen-Noll knows many people with partners who leave
their institutions because of the two-body problem. "And they're
good scientists," she emphasizes. The university, she explains, often
is interested only in one person, in "one half of the deal." People
have to get over this perspective "because you may not get either
of them if you're being so restricted to only one of them and not
both."

Universities may argue that one of the partners is simply better
than the other, but, in Dr. Ingersen-Noll's experience "this is not
very often true." Once people have obtained their Ph.D.'s and even
gone beyond and are engaged in research, they have to be pretty
good scientists. Universities have to start thinking "of this more as

a package deal." If you want to hire one, you have to come up with a solution for the other. Otherwise, you will lose them both.

Dr. Ingerson-Noll relates the story of a couple that includes a scholar hired by Flagship in a department different from hers and a spouse who receives a post-doc in her department. Her department chair resists giving the spouse any kind of permanent position because he feels the person has "been sort of dumped on us." In Dr. Ingerson-Noll's opinion, the university should at least make an effort and offer the spouse a teaching appointment. "He's a good scientist," she says. His research may not be completely what the department wants to do but "it is more important to keep people happy than to try to be very precise about what kind of science you want to have." Besides, she argues, if a person is hired for twenty or thirty years in a permanent position, they might change their research trajectory anyhow. She elaborates:

> Maybe today they're hiring me because I'm doing [topic A], but they give me tenure. The year after tenure I'm just "oh, I'm really so interested [topic B]." And I'm going to change my topic. There's nothing they can do about that, right?

Today's realities, according to her, require a different way of thinking. And if there is a partner, there should be a backup plan. The couple ought to be appointed in whatever way appropriate. Universities may just have to be creative and "think of a couple as more than the sum of the halves." Her own situation serves as an example:

> My husband and I, I'm doing [topic A], he's doing [topic B], but we're both interested in [topic C]. . . . If you want to start a group in this field and you hire us both, then you have a good start because we're both doing this thing, but we're not doing exactly the same

thing. That's a way to think of it, but there are also of course couples that are completely different. You might get two good people, and if you can appoint them both and make them both happy, then that's worth something.

Being an international scholar, Dr. Ingersen-Noll knows that universities in other places are struggling with similar issues. She tells the story of how her husband and she both applied for jobs at a university in Ireland. Her husband got his job, but she came in second for hers, and "number one" accepted the offer. The couple was left empty-handed. Irish universities, according to her, go strictly by the book and make decisions solely based on "a check list." Whereas the United States may be concerned about not denying equal opportunities on the basis of race, Ireland is concerned about religion. Here is how it played out:

> When we applied it was clear to the department that we were married. If they were smart about it they would sort of think about it but . . . they have all these issues about Catholics and Protestants. They have a very strict rule about how, if you appoint someone, how to make it as fair as possible because they don't want anyone to say he's appointed because he's Protestant, or he's appointed because he's Catholic. . . . They basically had a checklist. . . . They gave points for everything that we did, and then added up the points. The person who had the most points was going to be offered the job. There were no other considerations. You couldn't say "well, here we have a couple. If we give them both a job they are very likely to come and they are very likely to stay."

Dr. Ingersen-Noll was the runner-up for the job in Ireland. It was accepted by a woman with a partner who, given that the two-body problem cannot be considered in Ireland, was not offered a job by the university.

This is what Dr. Ingersen-Noll has to say about this hiring decision:

> By doing it this way, strictly following the protocol, they're basically not taking the opportunity to solve a problem and keep people happy. They're actually creating problems. . . . It would have been really easy if they had the power after they made the list and they have the points that they could circumvent that with a good reason to make the offer to number two rather than number one. They're not allowed because of the whole discrimination issue. It has to be as fair as possible. The woman might be number one, come work for a year and leave again because she finds a job closer to her partner. And they should have the possibility one way or another to solve this.

Dr. Ingersen-Noll makes an excellent case. The old mode, according to which dutiful wives follow their husbands around, is long obsolete. Institutions of higher education must pay attention to the "two-body problem." Dr. Miller at Flagship faces the same problem, having a highly qualified husband who finds it difficult to find a permanent position. Yet she views the problem as complex and concedes that "the department can't just hire spouses and throw their strategic planning out the window for the next decade, and not hire the best people in the field."

Simply disregarding hiring criteria and turning "number two" into "number one" because there is an eligible spouse might also create new forms of discrimination. Minority faculty are sparse in higher education, and perhaps the two-body problem is primarily a "white" problem because more non-whites have non-academics as partners. If search committees were to give preference to dual-academics, they would very possibly engage in a form of discrimination that has received little attention in higher education, namely discrimination against academics whose life partners are non-academics.

Another issue seldom discussed is that of divorce and what happens to "spousal hires" afterward. Oberlin College's Assistant Professor Anne Trubek writes about the problem. Years ago, she accepted her part-time position as part of a "package deal" with her husband. Now they are getting divorced and share custody of a four-year-old. She has seen other women choosing to share a job or work part-time in order to balance work and family obligations but "[r]arely does the question arise of what might happen should women divorce. The prospect of becoming a single mom is simply not mentioned" (Trubek, 2004, p. 1). Trubek attempts in vain to turn her part-time position into a full-time one but is not mobile due to the shared custody of her child. In hindsight, she questions the wisdom of spousal hires and making employees' personal lives a consideration during the hiring process (Trubek, 2002, pp. 1–6).

The two-body problem is not easy to solve. It is clear, however, that it needs to be addressed. Institutions of higher education, however, are just beginning do so.

The Immigrant Scholar: "I Feel Many Times I Live Between Cracks"

An increasing number of scholars in the United States are immigrants.[2] Many of their challenges are similar to those of their American-born counterparts, but some are unique. The latter may be caused by immigration laws and policies, both in the scholars' home countries and the United States, that produce unpredictable life situations and therefore stress. Other problems derive from sacrifices, cultural norms, and cultural barriers little understood by American colleagues.

Dr. Yong from China, assistant professor at Metropolitan University, for instance, went back to China while in graduate school and was denied a visa to come back to the United States, according to her a rather common occurrence: "it happens all the time." She was eventually able to return, finish graduate school, and stay but then encountered other challenges. For one, she continues to suffer from what she calls "identity paradoxes." Explains Dr. Yong:

> I feel many times I live between cracks. Two cultures. My original culture and this new culture. Every time I go back to China to visit I don't feel I fit anymore. I have lived in this country for ten years; I feel many times I am never completely accepted.

Dr. Yong finds it difficult to establish a strong social life in the United States, a recurring theme for her because she suffered from isolation back in China as well. A gifted student, she went to college young, beginning at age fifteen, which made it difficult for her to fit in socially. She recounts how, given her talent and academic accomplishments, everybody thought she was going to have a very successful life, but she says, "I define success differently. . . . I did not have a normal life."

She explains that life decisions were always made for her rather than by her: she did what her parents or the Chinese government wanted her to do. Her parents sent her to college early, and the Chinese government sent her to the United States (she initially came as a Chinese representative to work for a U.S. corporation). Says she: "I never had the choice to think 'what is the best choice for myself?'. . . . Most of my life decisions were not made by myself."

Not only did others decide the course of her life, Dr. Yong herself made sacrifices for others. She stayed in the United States after completing graduate school, for example, because she wanted to provide her now fourteen year-old-son with opportunities she did not think he would have in China. Dr. Yong could have enjoyed a fine career back home and easily moved into the professoriate in China after her U.S. graduation. She tells stories of other Chinese immigrants in similar situations; they gave up professional accomplishments and status they had achieved in China in order to raise their children in the United States in hopes that they will enjoy more opportunities and freedom here. Elaborates Dr. Yong:

> There were very few professionals in previous generations [from China] who came who ended up teaching in higher education. . . . [T]he previous generations came first of all to survive. Many of them, as I witnessed, sacrificed their own profession for the next generation, their children. Many of them just picked up whatever work. I had doctor friends . . . and when they were in China, they were already medical doctors and very successful, and now they have research fellowships at Harvard University Medical School. They are in their fifties or older but none of them are now doctors.

When probed as to why successful professionals come to the United States to raise their children, Dr. Yong repeats that they do it for the next generation. In response to the question of what, exactly, makes life better or gives people more opportunities in the United States, she explains that China is currently changing and opening up but until recently one did not have many choices. She gives the example of people not being free to move from city to city without official permits that were at times difficult to obtain if you were needed in your place of employment. She, for instance, was not able to live with her husband because they did not get the permits that would have allowed them to reside in the same city. She lived with her parents as a married woman.

I applied. I went to the president of the medical school where I worked, showed him the marriage certificate, "see I got married; he [the husband] works in another city." He [the president of the medical school] said "well, maybe he should move here." So then I said "can I just leave?" and he said "no," because at that time in most higher education they needed teachers, and I was one of the top students and was selected to teach at the medical school. They typically would not let you go.

Moving to the United States to gain an education and establish a life for her son, however, involved more hardships for Dr. Yong than merely leaving her native land. She had to leave it without the child. He grew up with her parents in China while Dr. Yong went to graduate school in the United States, a difficult choice that once again her parents had made for her. Dr. Yong recounts that it was not only painful to live without her son but she was also confronted with people asking her, "How could you leave your child behind?"

I said "I did not leave him behind, I had something to do"; I had wanted to make a better life for him. Also I was doing that because my parents wanted me to, it was part of my family's priorities. They wanted me to achieve. It was not like I wanted to leave my child behind. But that was very hard.

Dr. Yong was divorced from her husband years ago and has found a new significant other. Her son joined her recently in the United States, once her parents felt comfortable to have him transition to her because she now has a stable job as an assistant professor. Unfortunately, even today the thirty-eight-year-old is of the opinion that she does not have a "typical happy personal life" because it is "missing a lot of parts." Though successful professionally, she feels that she "missed a lot, as a person, as an individual." She shares that she does not have many friends in this country, nor a strong social life. She often feels lonely and uncertain about where, exactly, she belongs. One particular challenge is to connect to people on a level that goes beyond superficiality. Dr. Yong illustrates the point:

> There is an obstacle of communication between me and my colleagues. One particular example I remember so clearly. . . . My mentor, she was a very nice lady, she wanted to help me succeed professionally. At this point I really needed to talk about my personal dilemma. I'm lonely, I want a friend. . . . I tried maybe three times when we had a mentor-mentee lunch. I felt very, very lonely. My child at the beginning was not there with me, and I wanted to share some of my struggles. It started when she asked me "how are you doing?" And I started to share my problems but I was interrupted. And then I began to realize, OK, when people, some people, nice people, when they ask you how you are doing, the response they want from you are not really the problems. It's a courtesy. It's a social courtesy. You're supposed to answer "I'm doing great," and if you cry, close your door but you're not supposed to tell them.

Dr. Yong finds it culturally difficult not to be able to share personal dilemmas or problems, a situation that leaves her feeling isolated. After her disappointing experiences trying to connect to colleagues in a former position, she followed their example and kept her office door closed. Her isolation mounted.

> If I did not go out and ask a question or say "hi" to people, I realized some days if I didn't teach I did not say a word. I was in the office the whole day, got some

lunch and came back, didn't see anybody. I said "that's really very weird." I feel very abnormal to live that way.

Dr. Yong is not alone in her isolation, and though non-immigrants certainly experience their share of isolation too, that of immigrant scholars may be compounded by cultural barriers and the lack of family. Dr. Marx at HBCU, a full professor originally from Jamaica, talks about rarely getting integrated into the community, a fact she finds particularly odd because she is a black woman feeling rejected by African Americans. In her words:

> I'm a foreigner. We very rarely get integrated in. . . . I'm Black in African American society. . . . I have been invited to dinners by non-African Americans, not by African Americans. . . . It's African Americans in relation to other blacks from other countries.

She describes how she gets together with other immigrant scholars, and this group is inclusive of "whites, Indian, all kinds," but African American colleagues in her immediate work environment tend to be exclusionary. Dr. Marx has previous work experience in another historically black university, and recounts that there, too, she found her colleagues unwilling to share information. She attributes this attitude to past hardships African Americans endured that led them to think that "OK, if I had to go through it you go through it too. I'm going to keep my information, whereas the culture I come from, we share." She concludes that if she had to live her life over again, she would not choose a career but stay home. She says, "I cheat my personality going into the workplace," which she finds very harsh. She elaborates:

> I must say if I had been in Jamaica or in the islands I would definitely prefer to work but I find the American workplace very harsh. So, for me, if I had to do it over, I

would stay home with my kids. . . . I do very well, don't worry. But all I can think of is I'm going to walk out one day and not work again because I found it traumatizing, as it were. . . . I've been very successful at it. . . . So I have achieved but it's not the life I would've chosen had I thought it through before.

Dr. Koshino from Japan, full professor at Flagship University, believes that although she may have been exploited because of her minority status, being an immigrant scholar has its advantages, too. She feels that her cultural background helped her a great deal in that it prepared her to be organized, a perfectionist who likes to do "things almost 110% right." She compares her basic education in Japan with basic education in the United States, and is simply relieved she got what she did. Says Dr. Koshino:

I can't believe the problem of literacy in this country. That American natives can't spell, cannot write grammatically correct English, that's very, very disturbing for me. So then I say to myself, wow, I got something right from being Japanese.

Interviews with other immigrants confirmed that isolation seemed to be the resounding theme. Some relayed, however, how they had found ways to prevent or break through isolation by relying on their families. An assistant professor at Metropolitan University, Dr. McMillan came to the United States from Trinidad at the age of nine, and she recalls the importance of her family throughout her life. Her family had immigrated to New York, and she found it painful to be far away from them while at college, so she transferred and moved back. She got married, had two children, and moved South; her extended family followed. She concedes:

I'll be honest with you, I forced a lot of that. I said I needed to have my mom close by so we really worked with her on selling her house in New York City. We talked seriously to my in-laws about not retiring very far away because we wanted them to have a close relationship with the children. My mother came, and subsequently my sisters came, and when my sister got divorced, I said you need to be with your family because you need the support. Do not leave. You need to have the family to hold you up. We've generally been that support for each other. Even growing up, because we moved from another country, your family was always the nucleus of everything you were doing.

Currently her sister lives next door and her mother resides in her house. It is this family that has kept her grounded, as she would say, and has also supported her and made it possible for her to go to graduate school. Her mother and mother-in-law took turns cooking and taking care of her children while she went away to obtain her Ph.D. Whatever friends she makes, they become integrated into her family, and so "you stay within that hub, it's fine."

There are few Caribbean scholars at Metropolitan University but her extended family life, or "the hub," helps Dr. McMillan deal with the fact that as Caribbean people "we have really different cultural lives." When I asked her to elaborate on these "different cultural lives," she explained:

Coming to this country as immigrants, my parents let us know very early, especially my father, that Americans were very different from us, and we didn't live like they did. . . . It was pretty clear, they have their lives, we live here, we will get the best of what's here but we will always be who we are. . . . So we always had that thing of we have our family and our family will be our friends. We would have interactions with people on the outside but it wasn't as important. One of the really strange things is that we would always look at my sister who always had lots of American friends. It was like "why does she do that?" It was like she always has these people around her, and we would always kind of turn up our nose and see that as something not being very right about that. We'd see them as a little bit unsavory.

To be sure, Dr. McMillan and her family opened up and befriended other people on the outside given that "I realize that you do need people outside of your family that you are friends with, that you are close to." The extended family does remain her most immediate support network, however, and a major factor in preventing the feeling of isolation other immigrant scholars confront.

Dr. Sikka from India, full professor at Community College, emphasizes that though "as a family we tend to be more Americanized than anything else," her husband and she were greatly aided by her parents who moved to town after her father's retirement. Their move coincided with the birth of Dr. Sikka's daughter "and that did enable me to continue working at a pretty intense rate. . . . They watched her and juggled her preschool and all that schedule, so that helped."

Extended family is equally important for Dr. Nelson at HBCU, who immigrated from Ghana at age thirteen. Her family was instrumental in helping the twenty-eight-year-old Ph.D. pursue her career while having three children who are now six, five, and two years old. Dr. Nelson stresses that she has family support and never took any time off to have or care for her children. Says she: "I went to school while giving birth and taking care of them, but I had family support. They would come watch them while I went to class and come back." She attributes her professional success to the help of her husband, parents, and parents-in-law.

Reflecting on the immigrant experience more generally, Dr. Nelson echoes sentiments expressed by other immigrant scholars. Dr. Kochino from Japan explained that being an immigrant was a positive influence on her work because her education prepared her well. Dr. Yong from China shared the investment immigrant parents make to provide better opportunities for their children. Dr. Nelson recalls that being an immigrant made her "work harder" and "strive to be better. That's why I was brought here. Otherwise I would have failed my parents because the only reason why they came here was to give us a better education. It was my job to take that opportunity and make something out of it."

Immigrating to the United States without family not only means forfeiting the daily support one might otherwise gain from family members but it also can produce hardships because of prolonged periods of separation. Flagship University assistant professor and recent immigrant Dr. Ingersen-Koll describes how the teaching schedule makes it difficult for her to go home and visit her family back in the Netherlands. She describes the teaching schedule as "very fixed," limiting her to travel over the holidays and not being able to go home during the summer because tickets are prohibitively expensive:

> So we're not going home. If I weren't in a teaching schedule, we could go in October but we can't do that right now. It [being an Assistant Professor] is not as flexible as it used to be when I was just a researcher.

Since the job market for academics is a national one, many American scholars face long-distance separations from their families, to be sure. And yet they may have the opportunity to look for academic jobs closer to home, if they so desire, or move their families closer to them. Unless immigrant scholars came to the United States with their families in the first place, they do not have these options. Parents and other family members live in different countries, often on a different continent, speak different languages, and are restricted by immigration policies. In short, they tend to face insurmountable hurdles if they consider joining their daughters in the United States. Being an immigrant scholar, consequently, might well mean enduring a permanent separation from those to whom they feel closest.

Immigrant scholars face some of the same barriers to professional success as their American born counterparts. They need to find ways to balance busy lives and overcome isolation. And yet in some ways their balancing acts are unique. They negotiate webs of relationships based on conventions markedly different from those in their native lands, as Dr. Yong's battle with prolonged loneliness illustrates.

Another example is Dr. Ingersen-Noll's negotiation of attitudinal difference between people in two countries. She grew up in the Netherlands, and the Dutch simultaneously strike her as more and as less traditional than people in the United States. Back home, they are much more closed-minded about working mothers, she says: "In the Netherlands, if you have children and you keep working five days a week, you are pretty much considered a bad mother." And yet the Dutch are more open-minded toward different living arrangements:

> This is a very strong difference between Western European countries and being here. Back home you can just live with someone, and that is considered the same as being married. Here you actually have to have the paper that says you're married.

Her husband and she realized the difference in perception and got married, whereas "if we were in the Netherlands, we probably wouldn't have been married by now."

In addition to navigating of conflicting cultural norms, immigrant scholars may carry burdens that are invisible to others and little understood because they are culturally scripted in ways unimaginable to most Americans. Dr. Yong's forced existence as a burgeoning scholar without her child serves as an example.

But perhaps some immigrant scholars are uniquely positioned to deal with the challenges of academe. They may, for instance, have close-knit families who support them and serve as enablers for their careers, particularly by providing child care. They stay together, move close to each other, and live the notion that it takes a village to raise a child.

Immigrant communities can also serve important emotional functions, as in the case of Dr. Marx, who experienced black-on-black racism. Rejected by the African American community at her college, she found solace not only in her immediate family but also in a community of immigrants who were more embracing and open minded.

Being an immigrant scholar, finally, might positively affect the scholars' work in that it enhances their work ethic and increases their motivation to succeed. Dr. Nelson, for example, personifies what educational anthropologist John Ogbu describes as "voluntary minorities" in contrast to "involuntary minorities." Ogbu defines involuntary minorities as having become a minority against their will, through conquest or enslavement. Examples are African Americans or Native Americans, who look back at a long history of oppression and exploitation and tend to see little experiential evidence that hard work will lead to success or will remove discrimination. Consequently, Ogbu observes, members of involuntary minorities, especially adolescents, are likely to develop oppositional cultures. They may be inclined to view hard work in school, for instance, as "selling out" and instead engage in actions intended to subvert the system. The behavior backfires, and they often undermine their own educational success. But voluntary minorities, such as those found in this study, came to the United States by choice in search of economic, political, or religious opportunities or to flee oppression. Voluntary minorities are much more likely than involuntary minorities to accept a temporary second-rate status in order to prove themselves worthy and to work their way up through society. They tend to have a strong work ethic and seek success within the existing educational system (Ogbu, 1987).

Making It Work and Dealing with It: Enablers and Coping Strategies: "Keep Moving and Getting It Done"

Despite the fact that early-career faculty members face a host of challenges, they also enjoy a variety of enabling factors in their lives. Most of these are personal in nature, some institutional. Institutional enabling factors include advisors at alma maters who continue to be mentors, graduate assistantships that made Ph.D. work possible, colleagues who are friends or who share information freely in a collegial atmosphere, flexibility, and the ability to set one's own schedule. Some institutions grant one-semester maternity leave and one-year extensions of the tenure clock. Also mentioned were positive attitudes of colleagues and administrators who understand that faculty may have a role to play at home in addition to their work, or mentors and advisors who served as role models because they were able to combine families and successful careers. Flagship University's Dr. McLeod tells a poignant story:

> My main male advisor was . . . an incredible, not sort of your standard run-of-the-mill advisor. I'm not sure he's emblematic of the standard male. . . . He was talking about meeting with junior faculty members at Berkeley who would tell him outright that they weren't going to get married because that would affect their tenure-track. He was just like, "if you're miserable, how is that going to help you get tenure?"

Dr. Miller at Flagship describes a "critical mass of people with children" in her department, a fact that fosters an "understanding of what it means to have children and what you can and can't do when you have children." Decent day care is close to the university, which is important because the university's child care center has a waiting list of two years.[3]

Dr. Miller also benefits from what she calls "serendipitous things" such as her husband's office being close to hers. Therefore, they are able to bring their child to work on days that day care is closed.

Not many faculty enjoy the set-up of Dr. Miller, and yet others do find their institution supportive of them as parents. Dr. Carver at Private Comprehensive and mother of a very young child, for example, credits her encouraging colleagues who extended her tenure-clock without question, rearranged classes to accommodate her leave, and even gave her a baby-shower, an important symbolic gesture of their support. She is happy to be able to take her baby to work:

> The work environment is also very enabling because I bring the baby to work with me. I go in a few hours a week here and there to meet with students who are doing research with me. . . . I'm not working anywhere near full-time but I'm trying to keep my foot in the door and be a presence in my office. So I just bring the baby with me. I strap her in a carrier, and nobody bats an eye about the fact that I'm working with the baby strapped to my body.

Dr. Carver made a conscious choice not to go to an Ivy League or Research One university that would have higher publishing and grant writing standards. She did that "for the sake of work-life balance" and is happy about her choice. She is of the opinion that her work environment ought to be standard in academia, and if she had a nonacademic job, things would be more difficult to manage. She marvels at the flexibility of both her work and her husband's schedule and wonders "how women with nonacademic jobs manage and do motherhood."

While institutional enablers play a role in some women's lives, other women rely on family members, including husbands, parents, siblings, and in-laws who look after children and households while women work.

Greatly relieved that her sister is a stay-at-home mother, Dr. Young-Powell at Community College takes her small children to her every day.

> They're not stuck at a day-care center somewhere. They're loved and they're rocked, and it does help me because with my oldest one I had to take her to day care when she was eight weeks, and it almost killed me.

Dr. Carver at Private Comprehensive considers herself lucky to have a husband who not only has a flexible work schedule but also is willing to do more than half of the housework, thus helping her making the adjustment to being the parent of a newborn. She calls their division of labor incredibly enabling to her career and is convinced that "a lot of women don't have that." Without it, she would expect a "real strain on the marriage because I would feel resentful, and a strain on the career. It's valuable. I appreciate it a lot."

HBCU's Dr. Nelson credits both extended family and her husband with being her main supporters. Her husband makes sure, she explains, that she is being left alone so she can get her work done, and he is the one she can turn to for advice. Her parents and in-laws, furthermore, used to take time off and drive long distances to baby-sit until her children were old enough to attend day care.

The same holds true for Dr. McMillan at Metropolitan, who recounts that obtaining her Ph.D. would not have been possible without her family, who "was very supportive. My husband and my in-laws and my mom took turns cooking meals for the family." Her mother moved in with Dr. McMillan's family and continues to cook, and the cleaning is hired out so that "most things are taken care of from the home front, the day to day, the cleaning the house, fixing the food, the basic necessities." Dr. McMillan's husband supported her desire to obtain her advanced degrees; "he almost does it without question. . . . I would meet people who would say 'oh, your husband talks bout you all the time.' I know he's really proud of me, and I couldn't do this if it wasn't for him."

The McMillans are of Caribbean background, and Dr. Mc-Millan relates that her husband tells stories about his Caucasian co-workers, mechanics and electricians, who warn him that "your wife is not going to want to be married to you after [she got her Ph.D.]. That was his way of saying . . . that that could be a concern for him." Counters she: "I've always made it very clear to him, I'm not going anywhere. We've been married twenty-seven years this year. There's nobody I want to start over with. He's a great guy." She relates that being an academic, while her husband is not, has caused some friction at times in their relationship. She also knows "it's an issue for some men, machismo and all that stuff." Yet she points out, the bottom line is that she will never earn as much money as her husband, and both realize they have different strengths. She respects her husband highly for his willingness to come into her circle of friends: "I know it is not easy for him when we sit around and talk about our stuff at work and all that. He's willing to be there because he loves me enough that he's going to be a part of it." She concludes: "It speaks to a strength, I think."

Whether enabling conditions are plentiful or sparse, early-career faculty employ a wide variety of coping strategies. Some strategies focus primarily on replenishing their bodies and souls whereas others are practical in nature, intending to "make it all work." Women mention exercise, enjoying the outdoors to "get grounded," and being nurtured by friends and support groups. There is talk about spirituality and prayer as a way to refocus the mind on the purpose of the profession and the people who might benefit from one's work. One woman describes self-talk and finding inspiration in "little sayings in my office, words people have sent to me." Self-talk comes in particularly handy, she explains, in dealing with the "imposter syndrome," common among academics who often assume they know much less than people expect them to know.

Instead, this faculty member works on "being positive," seeing opportunities, and downplaying negative parts of life.

For some, "refueling" through hobbies and personal pleasures may not come easily. Ms. Ohler at Community College sometimes wonders whether she is missing out on social things, given that she is one of those academics she describes as "consumed by academic interests" so that it becomes "sometimes difficult to extricate yourself from that world." Her questions resonate with Dr. Calhoun at Private Comprehensive, a single faculty member. She talks about "forcing myself out of the house," "trying to make sure that I take time to do things like actually go see a movie rather than just write about them," and "scheduling that kind of activity . . . instead of assuming at the end of the day that I'll find something to do." She describes being "rigid" with herself about going to the gym on a regular basis and using the workout as a boundary between work and home. This, she emphasizes, makes it easier for her to release whatever it is she is working on, a way of "sort of becoming free of the work environment." She is then ready to relax, fix dinner, get in touch with friends, and talk on the phone.

Talking to people who find themselves in similar situations appears to be an effective coping strategy, as in the case of Flagship's Dr. McLeod, who shares both motherhood and a passion for her work with a female colleague at a different institution. She also enjoyed Flagship's first-year-teacher program, which gave her an outlet to talk to people, get acclimated to the institution, and build bridges outside of her department. "Decompressing" at the end of the day with her husband, a scholar in her field, is seen as helpful by Dr. Miller at Flagship. This is how she captures their relationship:

> I find it's been very helpful to have a spouse who knows exactly what I need when I describe a situation, or a problem, or an issue. They don't just smile and nod and say "yes" or "that sounds awful," they really know,

he really knows what it is I'm talking about. And he can offer concrete responses and concrete suggestions. That has been immensely useful to have someone to talk to. . . . So I do have an outlet to decompress, and that helps me stay sane.

Her sanity is further aided, she describes, by her daughter, who "laughs and you laugh, and for a couple of hours at least before bedtime I can most days put work aside and not think about it. I thing that's good for me."

An effective coping strategy shared by some women derives from self-determination and simply making sure to meet deadlines and achieve goals. Women find various ways to remain inspired and on track. Dr. McLeod at Flagship finds it helpful to remind herself that, because she has a family, she cannot afford to go off on tangents, and this is her chance to be more effective in the time she has available to work. She states: "You're a little more focused because you realize you have constraints." She also embraces the idea of dedicating certain times to doing things that easily become distracting if allowed to penetrate the entire day. The example she used was reading e-mail only during a child's swim practice, and otherwise "not touching it." Such measures can be used to free up the limited time that faculty members have to be productive.

Ms. Ohler at Community College makes lists. Carrying around her calendar and her "little notebook," she finds it essential to keep lists and, therefore, keeps herself organized. Her colleague Dr. Young-Powell sits down every night and plans the next day so as to not "lose sight of my responsibilities." She separates the "has to be's" from the "kind of needs to be's" and "would like to be's." After prioritizing her day, she makes peace with the fact that she cannot get everything done, and then she tells her husband what she needs him to do. She had to work on that last step after her second child was born and she realized she needed to give up the assumption "that I could do it all."

Getting her husband involved in the care of her newborn is an important coping strategy for Dr. Carver as well, who is trying to carve out periods of time each week when she can "just leave and not think about [the baby's] care." She is planning to hire students to baby-sit on campus while she is doing work in the office and arrange full-time day care once the child is older.

At Metropolitan, Dr. Yong pursues very sophisticated motivational strategies. She likes to travel with her son and life partner, and on those trips read and write novels instead of professional literature. She sets deadlines for her projects and searches for external motivators (she used the last day of the month of November—national novel writing month—as a deadline, and indeed wrote 50,000 words). Says she: "I set deadlines by looking at something that I really like and make it work." Dr. Yong explains how she uses a powerful dialectic between personal and professional writing to increase both her pleasure and her productivity:

> . . . getting it [the novel] published is not my priority. I try to balance, and reading only academic research articles would drive me crazy. And I feel I'm not productive by only focusing on one thing. Actually, it makes me more productive, like this month, November, while I was writing my novel, I also wrote an academic peer reviewed article, and it was already accepted. So I'm trying to do both. That part makes me really happy as a person. . . . That's one of the strategies. Find something really interesting that you're good at. And do it.

Another example of a refined coping system is personified by Dr. Lilian, who masterfully integrates various aspects of her life. She invites her family along on business trips, for example, and while she attends meetings they go sight-seeing. Everybody has dinner together, however, and "just knowing that they were there,

and knowing that they were in the hotel. . . ., that was fun."
Dr. Lilian combines her work and personal life in other ways
as well; she takes pleasure, for example, in volunteering in the
community fully conscious of the fact that she represents her
college. She also combines care of self and family activities by
sharing personal pleasures with her daughter:

> I just need to go and do some things that take care
> of myself. For example, I want to get a pedicure or a
> manicure, or something simple, you know, and so I find
> that I have to involve my daughter into those things and
> make it a fun day. Let's go get our nails done together.
> So that way, we're spending time together, we're doing
> things we need to do, and we're doing things we like
> because we like to reward ourselves with certain little
> things.

Dr. Lilian is a master at "multitasking," another coping strategy
that helps her manage her busy life as a successful professional and
single mother.

> Having an only child, I found that after 9 o'clock I am
> very productive because at 9 o'clock she is in bed, and
> I'm not tired and ready to crash myself. . . . I can be
> doing a load of laundry, watching television and reading
> e-mail all at the same time. . . . And I'm content. I don't
> feel like I'm burdened to be sitting there reading these
> e-mails. I'm watching my favorite TV show, I have on
> my favorite slippers, in about an hour you hear the drier
> 'ding,' which is fine. I'm doing things that I need to do.
> What's stressful is if I couldn't do these things, and they'd
> pile up on me. That's when the stress comes in but as
> long as I can keep moving and get things done, I'm fine.

When comparing her generation to previous ones, Dr. Lilian finds significant differences that enable her to cope with a busy schedule. For one, she describes herself as not knowing "anything other than fast pace." Technology is a part of life, a phenomenon accentuated in her daughter's generation, who, at age thirteen, "can already do all those technology programs, PowerPoint, access databases, Excel . . . because she started with the computer from kindergarten."

Technology, she explains, means change, and she finds it easier to adapt to change than members of previous generations. This ability to adapt, however, helps her cope:

> If you are accustomed like my mother to dinner every night, and just couldn't imagine walking through the house with dinner in your hand, so I guess for her that would be a big issue to adapt to because you should be sitting at your dinner table at six o'clock. But you can't because the child is still at basketball practice, and basketball practice ends at eight thirty. So then we're going to get home, and we're not going to set the place setting here at the table. We're probably more than likely, if we haven't grabbed something from the gym, we're going to go home and grab something quick. So you're really trading off the personal dinner table time. That can be a big issue.

Making adaptations in routine is not stressful for Dr. Lilian, given her generation's adaptation to fast paced life. Again, her lifestyle clashes with that of previous generations:

> And that's what I hear from my grandparents too. My mother just said last week: "your grandmother's getting kind of upset with you because she hasn't talked to you in two weeks now." So I have to take time . . .

and be sure that I call her as much as she thinks I should call her that week or that I am even answering the phone when she thinks I should be answering the phone because in her mind we're not getting enough sleep because we're always gone. In our mind we're not always gone, we're home a lot. So it's really a generational thing.

Integration is also used as a coping strategy by Dr. McMillan, who employs it primarily to prevent isolation and stress in her professional life. Specifically, she collaborates with people in other departments, reaching out and making connections with scholars who do similar work. She remembers realizing that "I have to be the one to make those connections to allow this thing that I do to work." She describes doing a small study with a colleague at a neighboring college as a "tremendous lift."

So now I remove myself from my workplace almost every Friday . . . and we work all day. . . . we can off-load our stuff on each other, then we jump into our work. That is just like the most "wow" thing for me."

Despite many enabling factors in women's lives and the coping strategies they themselves develop and nurture, early-career faculty agree that much reform is needed in the academy. Their ideas are summarized in Chapter Five.

Notes

1. For a detailed comparison, both historical and contemporary, of U.S. social policies toward children and their families with those in other industrialized (mostly Western European) countries, see: Kamerman, S. B. (2005). Europe advanced while the United States lagged. In J. Heyman & C. Beem (eds.), *Unfinished work: Building equality and democracy in an era of working families.* New York/London: The New Press, 309–347.

2. The exact number of immigrant scholars, defined here as first-generation immigrants who hold faculty positions in academe, are difficult to obtain. The group includes immigrants who are nonresident aliens (people with visas that allow them to work), resident aliens (green card holders), and citizens. According to the National Center for Education Statistics, 21,200 full-time instructional faculty in degree-granting institutions were nonresident aliens in 2003 (NCES, 2005). To obtain an accurate picture of the size of what is here defined as "immigrant scholars," one would have to add green card holders as well as first-generation citizens to this number.

3. In fact, a visit to the institution's website reveals that faculty are encouraged to "research your desired childcare provider and then to place your name on the appropriate waiting list(s) as close to the *time of conception* as possible."

2

Mid-Career

"I'm Not Sleepwalking; I'm Making Decisions"

Mid-career faculty members in this study continue to be busy people, of course, yet over time change occurs. They tend to struggle just as much with how to find a healthy balance between their professional and personal lives as early-career faculty do, but the issues have shifted. It appears, furthermore, that mid-career women have more developed coping strategies and somewhat more definite "lines in the sand" that demarcate what they are willing to do, and what they decide to give up.

In most cases, pregnancy and childbirth no longer occur. Children are older now but continue to play an important part in many women's daily lives. Some women have "come out," be it in a sexual sense or in terms of defining who they are as professionals and as people. For those on the tenure-track, tenure is no longer something they worry about, but workload as a senior professor certainly is.

In fact, one of the ailments voiced by early-career women, namely the inability to say "no," to some extent continues to plague mid-career faculty as well. "A big obstacle is knowing when and how to say 'no.' It used to be an honor to be asked [to do more]," associate professor Whitehead at Metropolitan says, "[but] now it's just a drag."

Workload comparisons are thwarted by subjectivity, but senior faculty may well be experiencing rising expectations as they advance. Many of them mentor junior faculty, and some take on disproportional shares of duties to protect their relatively vulnerable colleagues. Annual reporting and accountability continue to structure most academics' work lives, and so does the passion for their disciplines. "It's not like you can kick back and play golf every afternoon with tenure," is how Dr. Whitehead summarizes the situation.

Lumbering Under the Load: "It's Only Work, Work, Work"

Dr. Foster is fifty-one years old and unmarried. Neither her two grown children nor her grandchildren are living with her. She has been at HBCU for seven years where she serves as a tenured associate professor. When asked about the balance between her professional and personal lives, she replies: "There is no balance. It is only work, work, work." She misses her previous non-faculty job because "it would be nine to five, and I knew I would be home at six doing what I wanted to do." A separation between work and home is no longer possible, she finds, because she goes home and prepares for her classes or gets things organized for work. She finds the setup "frustrating as all heck" because she feels that "you're not calling the shots about your time" and describes her life in these terms:

> I don't have a life outside of here; I work here all day. I go home at night and work all night. I work on weekends. The only time I really have a break is when school is done. . . . I don't have a personal life. I really don't. I'd love to go home and be with my grandchildren on the weekends, you know. To be with my family, just to be with my family. I would love to have been home over the break and spend time with my sons, and my grandchildren, but I couldn't do it.

Her isolation is partly the result of her workload and the lack of time to make friends. It also stems from a cultural disconnect. Dr. Foster had to move away from her hometown in the North, her family, and her comfort zone. Now she is struggling to fit into southern culture, which she finds very different.

> I couldn't befriend people quickly. . . . I used to wear dreadlocks, and I'm slowly changing my looks. I went from dreadlocks to straight hair and contacts and make-up to fit into the mold here, to be more acceptable to people around here. When I go home, I close the door, and there is absolutely nobody there; and it is just very lonely, very lonely.

People need to be forewarned before entering academe, she says. Since it is not likely that they get jobs in their hometowns they may well find themselves struggling with the same sense of isolation she confronts. "In the process of getting that degree," she says, "they need to be told . . . how lonely it can be for them. . . . They may find themselves in the middle of nowhere, isolated in the middle of flippity-ga-blip somewhere."

Struggling to balance work with the rest of her life is not easy for Private Comprehensive's Professor Pelletier either. Dr. Pelletier is forty-six years old and lives with her female partner. Although her partner is able to leave her work at the office, Dr. Pelletier feels that she never is and, instead, is robbing one part of her life in order to maintain the other. If she does not want to do this, her only option, she says, is to "do just the reverse, and rob this set instead of that." She believes that women in the United States, regardless of socioeconomic status, simply do not have enough time. This is a puzzling phenomenon to her and, being the successful intellectual she is, Dr. Pelletier expects to be able to figure out a solution, given that she thinks about the problem so much. "And I can't. So you have to write this book," she concludes.

Dr. Pelletier works twelve hours a day most days, and on Sundays while her partner is at church. Her current schedule is the *scaled-down* version of what it used to be before she got together with her partner. It is a concession to her, so to speak; before she entered Dr. Pelletier's life, the professor worked "seventy-five hours a week on a regular basis with no stress as far as the home life is concerned." She finds it frustrating sometimes to see her work life "severely curtailed" although, she concedes, now at last she is able to cut down on work she does not much like, such as committee work.

"Time" is a major issue for fifty-four-year-old Dr. Littlefield, untenured associate professor of HBCU. She lives with her male partner, and wishes she had more time to relax and take a vacation. She describes that between her own and her partner's professional commitments, work takes up 18 to 19 hours a day, "and the rest is sleeping. There's not a whole lot of sleeping going on. There's just not enough time."

Community College's Dr. Sikka says that she has "just sacrificed my own life for the sake of everything else." Her two children get as much attention as she can give, and so does her work. Collateral faculty member at Flagship University Dr. Seidman experiences similar pressures. She is fifty-seven years old and the married mother of three grown children, one of whom just moved back in with her baby twins. Dr. Seidman cannot isolate her personal from her professional life, and even though she feels that she is able to find a healthy balance personally and emotionally, she experiences "lots of stressors at work and very high expectations, so I think it's a challenge for me to balance that." She basically works two full-time jobs, as faculty and administrator, causing her to spend personal time on professional duties.

At Community College, forty-three-year-old Ms. Ehrenreich is married and child-free, a distinction, she explains, denoting people who *choose* not to have children versus people who *cannot* have children due to fertility issues. Currently able to establish a healthy balance between her personal and professional life, she remembers difficult periods during which she had to piece together several part-time jobs. "That," she remembers, "was extremely stressful to me because I was just pulled so thin so much of the time preparing for so many different classes." She describes the miseries commonly associated with patching together an existence through part-time or adjunct work, traveling even among campuses.

> Whenever you teach full-time you're limited to just a few preps. You're not going to have that many classes. But teaching part-time you take what you can get. Oftentimes that means very early morning classes that nobody else wants, or night classes. It was very common for me to have 8:00 A.M. classes and classes that ran from 7:00 to 9:30 P.M., sometimes 45 minutes away from where I live. The very long days and oftentimes four different class preps. Different textbooks used on one campus versus another. . . . That was just extremely stressful, and I found myself just exhausted and stressed a lot of the time.

Time issues, in other words, and the pressures deriving from multiple sources, determine to a large extent how mid-career faculty describe their lives. The demands on faculty members' time do not end with tenure, and neither does the stress generated by those demands. The next section focuses on the situation of mid-career female faculty with the added burden of children at home.

Mothering in Mid-Career: "We Are the Ones Who Never Have the Cookies Baked"

"'Mothering' and academia still don't belong together," writes professor emerita at San Diego State University Kathleen B. Jones. "Mothering," she points out, "encompasses caretaking not only of children, but of the elderly, the incapacitated, and for partners, both gay and straight" (Jones, 2005, p. 181).

Faculty members who are mothers are, of course, not a mono-lithic group in and of themselves. They differ in income, marital status, sexual orientation, domestic involvement of partners, points in their career when they had their children, and more. Some remain the exception in their department or school, working with faculty who either do not have children or whose children are grown or are cared for by wives. Some feel well supported; others do not. The following sections capture some of this diversity.

Partners as Enablers: "It Is Really What Makes Possible the Mosaic That We Live"

A strong theme through the conversations with mid-career female faculty members who have children and partners is the supportive role played by the latter—in this study typically male spouses. The same holds true for early-career women also, but their testimony is not included here to avoid redundancy.

When asked about enablers or factors that helped her in her attempts to balance her personal and professional lives, Dr. Newton, Flagship associate professor and married mother of three, replies, "First and foremost, without a doubt, is having a supportive husband. There's just no question about it." Before she began her career at Flagship, she explains, she was more the children's caretaker, but when she took her new position, her husband made a career move that allowed him to work from home. He became what she calls "the houseparent, basically."

> And he is the one who met them after school and provided milk and cookies, and did a lot of that kind of thing, and was home with them if they were sick. And he covered for me when I went away to conferences for four to six days. His presence in the home meant that I could be here late teaching. I typically teach in the

evenings, so I'm here four to seven, teaching. Not a very conducive schedule for a mother of three, but he made it work by covering for the kids. And being in the home. He really anchored our household.

Dr. Nelson characterizes her parenting relationship with her husband as more of a 50/50 relationship than many men establish in women's lives. She "anchored" the household when she was home, but her husband covered when she was not.

Other women tell similar stories. Community College's Dr. Ephron says of her husband that "he jumped into this whole parenthood thing much more than I did" and "his active role is a little more than mine." What helps her, she says, is "definitely my husband. You have to have a partner who is supportive, and he has been throughout my whole career. Almost to the point of pushing me sometimes."

Dr. Sikka at the same institution, mother of two children, describes her husband as a primary enabler, and her relationship with him as "a real balance in our marriage and in our lives." An academic himself, he does just as much work around the house as she does, and sometimes more of "the traditional domestic stuff." Never has there been a real gender difference in doing anything, she says, except outdoor work, which her husband does alone. "There's no real distinction in gender concerns inside the house," she explains. "I think our daughters have a real sense that dad is just as much involved in the family as mom is. That's been consistent ever since they were born." The couple's lives revolve around work and the children, and they both support each other as a result of that. "There's no struggle in that."

Metropolitan's Dr. Kaminski, forty-nine-year-old associate professor with two children ages thirteen and eleven, describes herself as very lucky. Her husband not only moved geographically so that she was able to build her career in what is now their hometown, he also gave up his high-powered position as an attorney to take one that allowed him to scale back, have more flexibility, support his wife's career, and spend time with their children. Says she: "That was a real compliment, and his real investment and respect for my career that I think has made a lot of this happen. . . ."

Similarly, her colleague, Associate Professor Whitehead, shares the care of her three children with her husband, whose job allows him "to just take over" when she travels, which is "really critical." She does "the morning stuff with the kids," and "he does the afternoon stuff," an approach that has been called "split-shift parenting" (Gornick & Meyers, 2005, p. 371). Echoing her colleague at Metropolitan, Associate Professor Schumacher describes her husband and father of her two small children as being as much a full-time parent as she is. "I work a lot and well with my partner in the sense of child issues," she says. Despite the fact that he is an academic, he is not on a tenure-line, which he never pursued because "he was afraid he would never get tenure because he is such an engaged parent, and he doesn't have time to write." Her husband "settles" for an administrative job outside of his area of interest, which allows him to have flexibility in his schedule and spend more time with his children than "most men afford themselves." "Our entire conversations," she tells, "are about who is picking up whom, who is dropping off whom, what did they have for lunch, whose diaper got done. In that sense, it is really what makes possible the mosaic that we live."

Women with children and partners in this study were greatly supported, in sum, by men who seemed to respect their careers and were willing to do more than merely "help out" at home. They had become truly equal contributors to child rearing and domestic work. Yet a note of caution is in order: these women represent, in significant ways, success stories. They did not drop out of academe or significantly alter their professional dreams. Some may have scaled back to some extent (see "Scaling Down Professional Aspirations" in Chapter Three), but none gave up. Stories about partners and spouses are likely to sound quite different coming from women with children who had to abandon or at least curtail their careers.

Some women's partners go beyond equally sharing domestic duties and childrearing. They adopt a traditional model in the sense that one person is the primary breadwinner while the other one takes care of the home—except they reverse the roles, and they become "stay-at-home dads."

Stay-at-Home Dads: "A Necessary Requirement to Succeed Here?"

Flagship's full professor Dr. Sutherland characterizes her life as a "see-saw, one or the other side is always winning." Forty-one years old, she is married to the stay-at-home father of her four- and two-year-old children. She knows it is impossible to attain perfect balance in the sense that both her personal and professional lives get equal amounts of attention. If one can be happy, she thinks, with the fact "that occasionally one is favored over the other like a seesaw, then perhaps you can be more comfortable with it."

> There's time when I won't get home in time to see the kids for the day, and you feel like a failure if you were trying to balance that day. But there are other days when I take off early so I can go see my daughter do ballet in the afternoon. That day the family is winning a bit more.

Dr. Sutherland concedes that she would feel "like a totally in-adequate mother" were it not for her husband's ability to dedicate so much time to the children. Her job is extremely demanding and involves a lot of travel, and so she is grateful for her husband's ability to be there for the kids. "I am very comfortable I think with the relationship I have with my kids and my family," she says, and "without a doubt the most important enabler is my husband."

Having a stay-at-home husband is not unusual in Dr. Suther-land's school. This is her story:

> When I came [to Flagship University] I was not married.
> . . . I remember being absolutely terrified when I first got
> here because within my first semester I went to a lunch
> that was there for all the women within the school. . . .
> The dean's office used to sponsor these, and when I got to
> meet all the women, it became blatantly apparent very
> quickly that all of them had stay-at-home husbands.
> There was only one . . . who had a working spouse.
> Everyone else had stay-at-home husbands. I wasn't even
> dating anyone at the time, so suddenly the prospects
> of finding a husband in this tiny town . . . who was
> willing to stay home. I was like "oh boy, I'm doomed."
> I remember that really hit me like a ton of bricks.

Dr. Sutherland wonders whether a stay-at-home husband is a "necessary requirement to succeed here. . . . What's the deal?" She recalls that she, herself, came up for tenure early, was promoted to full professor early, and got married the year she was tenured. Married, she says, "to a stay-at-home dad. I had to go to [Washington,] D.C. to find him."

Dr. Sutherland tells of "trailing spouses" of faculty in her school who often have advanced degrees yet are unable to find a position in the small university town. Her husband, for example, holds an MBA but got tired of the rat race in Washington, D.C., and is now content working out of his home. In addition, of course, he takes care of the children.

Despite having a partner mainly responsible for child-rearing and domestic work ("He does all of the laundry and the house-cleaning and the cooking and the shopping plus the yard work. It's a role reversal."), Dr. Sutherland experiences both pressure and guilt. She works sixty to seventy hours a week, often starting to work again once the kids are in bed. Exercise and relaxation fall by the wayside. She experiences intense feelings of guilt about not being available more to her children, especially when they are ill. Says she: "If I had to do it over, would I do it mostly the same way? Yeah, but I do have a lot of guilt about it."

Having a stay-at-home partner may seem a luxury to some but unless it is seen truly as a calling by whoever decides to stay home, simply reversing the model does not seem to efficiently address the many issues that come with the marginalization of caregivers, regardless of gender. More beneficial long-term would be a societal reorganization, and the implementation of effective work-family policies that recognize the central importance of caring for dependents. Europe has many lessons to teach in that regard; it "advanced while the United States lagged" (Kamerman, 2005, p. 309).

The Hostile Institution: "A Very Old and Very Patriarchal Model"

Many women do not have stay-at-home husbands. Instead, they have a lot of "balls in the air" and feel stretched "way thin," according to forty-six-year-old associate professor Dr. Whitehead at Metropolitan. She is married with three children (two of whom were born before she received tenure) ages fourteen, ten, and five. Not only does she juggle the needs and schedules of her children, she also carries a heavy workload. As senior professor she does not want to unduly burden her junior colleagues who are still facing tenure, and therefore she takes on increased responsibilities that have arisen lately due to budget cuts and staff shortages. One enabler in her balancing act is her partnership with a cooperative spouse, but academe, as an institution, has been of little help to her.

Mother of three grown children, Dr. Nelson at Flagship remembers how for years before tenure she woke up at two o'clock in the morning, unable to go back to sleep. She had panic attacks trying to figure out how to get everything done. How could she finish teaching her class, get to the high school for parent-teacher conferences, and get that paper submitted tomorrow? Where would the time come from to do all this, she wondered, and should she get up right then and do it? Some nights she did, and just worked until the rest of the household got up too. Sometimes, she says, it was the only thing she could do. Her husband was greatly supportive of her as a parent, but the university was not.

She sums it up by saying: "I don't think institutionally the university did anything necessarily to enable me. There was no day care here available if I needed it for my kids. There's no tuition waivers for my children. There really aren't any support systems in place. . . ."

Dr. Seidman concurs. This mother of three grown children does "absolutely not" think Flagship instituted anything that helped her balance her life. "No structures and no formal assistance that I am aware of."

Dr. Schumacher feels similarly about Metropolitan. Shortly before the interview, the forty-seven-year-old associate professor at Metropolitan had just left the hospital where she stayed with her sick child. She is married to an academic, and together they juggle the care of a toddler and a four-year-old. At the time of our conversation she is visibly upset, and this is why:

> My youngest daughter caught a pretty bad stomach virus and ended up in the hospital. . . . She is very sick, and she is little. I stay with her in the hospital around the clock because the only thing she wants is mom, and she is still nursing. . . . Tuesday morning my partner came in which gave me time to take a shower. I run down here so I can get my classes for Tuesday and Thursday set up and the video tape that I was going to show later in the semester, I had my teaching assistant show. . . .
>
> I have a Wednesday seminar . . . , and I couldn't. I literally knew I couldn't meet them. . . . In all honesty,

I didn't know if I was going to come down with the same stuff. It was highly contagious; she was in an isolation unit. Everybody who came in had to be gowned and masked, except me who was with her 24/7 pressed against my chest. . . . They said it was a 48 hour incubation period. She got sick on Saturday; I'm counting . . . if I get it, it will be Wednesday, and I'm in a seminar room that is the size of a bathroom with 18 students, right? I cancelled it. I sent out an e-mail, and I sent out all of this information ahead of time, and I apologized, and said we'll make it up in the semester. I'm taking a day of family sick leave.

I came in to my office Wednesday. I had a couple of urgent e-mails that I had to answer, and I was sitting at my desk at 4 o'clock when my class was supposed to start, and two of my students had shown up for class. . . . My chair came in and yelled at me, I mean yelled at me, and said, "You should be having class." And I said, "My daughter is still in the hospital, and I haven't slept in days. I'm not fit to have class. And I explained it to them in an e-mail. . . ."

She calls the experience "uncivil," "deeply hurtful," and "cruel." The only concern, according to Dr. Schumacher, was that the job was somehow not getting done when, in fact, she does her job very well. She was concerned about her students and did everything she could to take care of the problem and be responsible. "That kind of stuff," she concludes, "is unconscionable."

Children, of course, do not just shape faculty members' lives in special situations. Rather, they affect simply everything, including time allocations, routines, and work habits. Dr. Schumacher at Metropolitan remembers the flexibility she used to enjoy before she had children when she was able to "get up and write at 3:00

in the morning, or I could stay home and sleep the next day if I wanted if I didn't have classes. . . ." Now, she says, she does not have that time.

> I mean, if I'm up at 3:00 in the morning, it is because a kid is throwing up. I don't have that flex to, you know, sort of stay home and lollygag the next morning or to make my schedule more flexible.

She has changed how she does her job because of her children, and now "negotiates out" rather than "negotiating in." When asked what she means by that, she explains that she used to suffer from "Ado Annie syndrome," being a "girl who can't say 'no.'" Now, however, she has "this little picture in my head of two little faces," and she wonders, "hmmm. Do we need that, or do I do something with them, giving them time. I'm much more likely to say 'Sorry, I can't.'"

As illustrated by the story about the yelling chair, reactions of her colleagues, students, and administrators are not always positive; in fact, they can be downright hostile. Dr. Schumacher tells of another recent incident in which she had to bring her then 16-month-old daughter to an exam in her 300 student course. The day-care center had closed that day due to inclement weather, and the baby-sitter was already committed. The child was, in her opinion, not overly distracting, and the classroom was "cavernous." Yet at least one student complained, and though Dr. Schumacher offered students the opportunity to retake the exam if they felt they did not do well because of the child's presence in the classroom, she was reprimanded by the administration.

> I'm still catching grief about this. I have had administrators call me and tell me that it was inappropriate to have my child on campus, and that it was a huge distraction

for the students, and they had gotten all these complaints. So I said to one of the administrators . . . who called me on the carpet for this, I'm a working mother. The reality of my life is, I'm a working parent. The other working parent was in a meeting full of deans and could not take this child. The child caregiver was otherwise committed. I had the choice of canceling the exam for 300 students, bringing her into the classroom, or I could have brought her to your office, and you could have taken care of her. I was a little pissed off at that point.

Students have "come out in droves" to support Dr. Schumacher, but she has yet to face an administrative panel.

Although she did not suffer negative repercussions for her actions, Associate Professor Whitehead at Metropolitan faced the same dilemma. She had to bring her sick five-year-old to an exam because there simply was no place else to take her. She placed the child on pillows behind the podium and administered the final. A care center that admits mildly sick children in some special section would have been helpful, she says. "It would have been nice if there had been a place I could have brought her to just for an hour or two, where I could feel comfortable in knowing that she was entertained and comfortable, and I could go do what I have to do." Many faculty, she points out, do not have family in the area, and are left without support in case of emergencies. "But," she concludes, "they are really not that family-friendly here."

Dr. Schumacher certainly concurs. She calls the university "family-unfriendly" or downright hostile to families. She points out that there are no facilities on campus that are family-oriented, no family housing units for students, no playgrounds for kids, no designated nursing spots for faculty, staff, or student mothers, and no adequate child-care facilities.

I think that from the top down the university is hostile
and works on a very old and very patriarchal model of
what an employee is because they all had wives . . . or
they don't have children themselves. . . .

Dr. Schumacher faults a patriarchal model according to which
"home is where the children are, work is not where the children
are." Children are labeled a "private problem" and if "you wanted
to be a working mom, it is your problem. Resolve it."

Child-care centers are certainly available in town, but they, in
and of themselves, are not the solution. Leaving a child in day care
too long goes against Dr. Schumacher's idea of parenting, which
she defines as a "real important, hands-on responsibility . . . , a joy."
She refuses to "put my child someplace from six in the morning
to six at night." When asked what she is trying to accomplish and
what her idea is of balancing, she replies that she had hoped to
be the same kind of academic that she was and an active, fully
engaged, and present parent. Yet she is failing miserably, she says,
and elaborates:

We are at the point that all the other parents are
making jokes at the day-care centers. We are the ones
who never have the cookies baked; and it's time to turn
in the project for X, and we have no idea the deadline
was even there. My oldest daughter had a project. . . .
Neither one of us ever got to it. . . . We are the parents
who are always, you know, who can't do this stuff. On the
other hand, most of those parents have a stay-at-home
parent in some capacity or are part-time workers.

Looking generally at her life, Dr. Schumacher concludes that,
overall, her job has not suffered but she, her partner, and her kids
are bearing the costs of trying to have both, a family and a career.

I don't think my job has suffered in the slightest. The suffering that goes on is the emotional suffering. . . . I see it sometimes in my oldest daughter when we have to get out the door, and we have a domino effect because she has to be at school at 9:00, and her little sister has to be at school at 9:30, and I have a 10 o'clock meeting. If any of those things gets out of order, I get stressed. When I get stressed, they get stressed. She is four, ands she wants to dawdle. On the way to the car she wants to pick a flower and play with a rock. We gotta go. It ramps her stress up which I had vowed I would never do, but I do. I think that the costs are borne by parents and children. I don't see any evidence that the university suffers whatsoever.

Mid-career mothers talk of not being able to "do everything" and, just like their early-career counterparts, sacrifice care of self first. Exercise, book clubs, friendships with other women, to name a few examples, fall by the wayside. Having children is certainly not everybody's goal or aspiration, and many people live happily child-free. As discussed in Chapter One, however, many women would like to become parents yet feel they need to choose between a career and a family. Some women do have both. Although they may be considered success stories because, at first glance, they "have it all," a family and a successful career, they suffer the hidden costs of stress, pressure, and guilt. As journalist Judith Warner so aptly captures in *Perfect Madness: Motherhood in the Age of Anxiety*, working mothers tend to be stressed near the breaking point. Describing the women she knew, Warner says their standards for high-quality parenting were no lower than those of mothers who did not work outside of the house. In addition, they often carried the "burden of Guilt, a media-fed drone that played in their ears every time they sat in traffic at dinnertime: had they made the right choices? Were their children well taken care of? . . . Were they really good mothers?" (Warner, 2005, p. 13).

Tarshia Stanley at Spelman College also claims that mothering and guilt go hand in hand (Stanley, 2005). She finds the phenomenon particularly difficult to accept as an African-descended American. African women, she writes, have always worked in the fields with babes strapped to their backs and not adhered to the Western dichotomy between work and motherhood. While she perceives "motherguilt" as a widespread occurrence in society, she is convinced that academia takes guilt to new levels. Flexibility serves as an enabler but "the tenure clock waits for no man and seems in a particular hurry to leave women with children behind" (p. 86). As a single mother she feels particularly isolated and misunderstood by those who are not sharing her lot, people without children or people who have forgotten what young children are like. She realizes over time that what she had diagnosed as guilt was really fear, the fear that being a mother was somehow undermining her status in her colleagues' eyes. Academe as an institution, in other words, was just as unsupportive of her as a mother as it was for many of the women in this study, and, to quote Joan Williams: "If we as a society take seriously children's needs for parental care, it is time to stop marginalizing the adults who provide it" (Williams, 2000, p. 63).

Having Kids in Grad School: "It Was Just Part of Life"

Being a mother in academe is not always portrayed as a harrowing experience. Female faculty also talk about how their children keep them balanced. They help them put professional challenges in perspective, force them to leave their offices and enjoy life beyond work. Dr. Newton at Flagship recalls how her children kept her sane through the tenure process and under the pressures many faculty members face. According to her, children make it very clear what is important in life:

There's nothing like the immediate very human needs of a child to have your attention and to snuggle, read a book, and to help them when their homework has totally swamped their world. You just need to set aside things and think about what's going to be important five years from now. Is it going to be the article you're writing, or is it going to be reading with your child? It is usually not either/or but it's how you prioritize your time, and maybe how many articles you write. And really thinking through how to keep a proper perspective on the mania we create in higher education around publishing and presenting at conferences.

Having children has been very healthy for her and makes her feel "like I've had a very rich and wonderful life . . . I've had the best of both worlds."

Thirty-six-year-old associate professor at Private Comprehensive Dr. Jacobs, single mother of two teenagers, would agree with Dr. Newton. This is what she has to say about the influence of her children on her life:

There is the sort of work ethic . . . , like these young earnest assistant professors staying in their office all day long until way into the night, and never go out, never do anything, never have a social life. I couldn't live that way. And I couldn't live that way because I have kids. I think having kids in a way doesn't allow you to live that way, right? You can't be in your office 14 hours a day; you have to be home, you know, you have to. It forces you to sort of leave it behind 'cause you've got to get home for the kids, and that opens up the possibility to recognize that there is more to your life than just your office.

Not only does Dr. Jacobs fully appreciate what her children add to her life, she is also glad she had them at a young age. She doubts the wisdom of waiting to have children until after graduate school and the establishment of a career. Her decision to have children was less disruptive and dramatic as it could have been at an older age when people tend to be more established. "I know a lot of people," she says, "who have waited until they are established in their careers, and they seem to be such self-conscious parents, like it becomes such an event, having this baby now. . . . I've waited, you know, twenty-five years, and now I'm having this baby, it just seems it skews things in some way." For her, it was just part of life. "It was just like, OK, kids and grad school."

Dr. Jacobs echoes the sentiment described by early-career Dr. McLeod that having children provides a healthy structure to one's life. Whereas her friends in graduate school "had all the time in the world, and so they just didn't do anything because it was like, well, I can drink beer," Dr. Jacobs made wise use of her time and finished her degree quickly. With her children being older now, those healthy constraints are gone, and she even feels her colleagues give her more credit than she deserves. Everyone in her department is very understanding, which, at times, makes her feel uneasy given that in her estimation she no longer needs all the support she gets. This is how she describes the situation:

> One thing that is kind of odd is that I get a lot of credit. . . . It's almost like an excuse that is given to me all the time like "well, she's a single mother." . . . This is just my own little paranoia or whatever but there's like sometimes a subtext of "oh, look how well [Dr. Jacobs] has done for a single mother." I get cut some slack . . . because most people who know me [in this town] only know me as a single mother.

Even somebody as optimistic as Dr. Jacobs, however, talks about hidden costs and sacrifices derived from being a single mother, and in a low-paying academic field. Younger colleagues, especially, tend to ask her admiringly "how have you done all this? I can barely take care of myself and get my work done, how did you . . . ?" People don't always see what you *don't* get done, she emphasizes, mentioning "my incapacity to have a proper home" and "being financially destitute."

Dr. Jacobs concedes her financial troubles are partly caused by her choice to live in a part of the city with inflated real estate prices rather than the suburbs. She simply needed what she calls a "pseudo-urban" experience and could not see herself buying a house in the suburbs. Be that as it may, low salaries for beginning academics in many fields are clearly a hardship, especially for single parents who are unable to share the expenses for their dependents with a partner.

Irrespective of their parent(s') specific life circumstances, children have a tendency to grow up, and most eventually leave the house. For faculty mothers, their children's departure may mean the possibility of a more deliberately chosen balance. They certainly continue to be busy, but now many find themselves increasingly in the driver's seat of their lives, better able to determine how to allocate their time and spend their energies. HBCU's forty-nine-year-old "happily divorced" tenured associate professor Dr. Pritchard, who is the mother of a twenty-year-old, talks about juggling her life. As an African American woman, she says, she was born juggling, and the juggling was purposeful, something she always wanted to do. Yet the juggling seemed different when her daughter was at home. She made her daughter a priority and had to forgo scholarly opportunities such as studying abroad; after all, she did not want to interrupt her child's schooling. Now, with her daughter in college, she is still juggling, and things have not slowed down for her. However, she says, "I juggle now different things." Work is not her life, she says, but she does spend time on scholarship, writing, and meeting the needs of her students. She also devotes time to her faith community and her friends. She has come to a point, she explains, where she stopped comparing herself and her scholarship record to others "because I can just do what I can do." She finds wisdom in pacing and taking care of herself. It is that kind of opening up of possibilities that is most characteristic of late-career faculty, as discussed in Chapter Three, *Late Career: "This Is Who I Am, and I'm Going to Be Who I Want to Be."*

Defining Your Identity: "I Didn't Want to Play This Game Anymore"

In some situations, admitting that you are an accomplished intellectual makes you burst out laughing. It happened to Dr. Pelletier, sitting in a booth at Claire's, a lesbian bar, wearing her cowboy boots. The place caters to working class patrons primarily, and is home to line dancers and pool players. It was crowded that day, and when some people sat down in Dr. Pelletier's booth, and they started talking and asking her what she was doing for a living, she replied she was a full professor at the local college. And "then I just burst out laughing as if it were the funniest thing I could have said." "It was so funny to say that," she repeats, "in that place dressed in my cowboy boots."

When asked about the relationship between her personal and professional lives, Dr. Pelletier quickly relates how difficult it is for a lesbian professional in her town to find a social network of people similar to her, namely middle-class academics or professional homosexual women. She has not been successful connecting with such a community, and while she believes it exists, "it is very closed. You have to know somebody who knows somebody to get invited to the right party to find people." Instead, she was able to gain access to a much more open and diverse, primarily working-class community. "So I socialize with people who drive bulldozers, and I line dance, and I learned to two-step, and I play pool."

It is different for homosexual men, she thinks, who have established an extensive gay male professional network in town. "Doctors, lawyers, dentists, businessmen, there are a bunch of them." Dr. Pelletier concedes that, "of course, there are more professional men than there are professional women," but is nevertheless convinced that lesbian professionals can be found somewhere. "I think you have to play golf," she says. "I'm just not willing to do that."

Dr. Pelletier enjoys her friends but does feel that she is often "the odd person out."

> I almost never talk seriously to anybody about what I'm reading, much less what I'm writing. That is hard. [My partner] reads all my papers and things like that, and she does, actually, she has become pretty well educated on [a scholar in my field]. But it is not something that she finds entertaining to discuss over dinner. That's just not the substance of most of our conversations, even with her. So, certainly not when we go to a party. Most of the time people talk about current events maybe, television, their dogs, the sorts of things that people talk about when they don't know each other very well, I guess. It is something that I try not to think too much about, but it is definitely an issue for me. Something that I wish I had but I don't imagine that I'll ever have.

Although she misses not being able to share her work in depth, Dr. Pelletier does appreciate how her partner complements her and "gives me something else to think about when I need something else to think about besides work. That is important." She recalls having been consumed by her work during the years prior to meeting her partner. Now she sees it as "a really positive thing" that her partner "and the lesbian world that I live in part time are radically different from academics." She describes her community as "very non-intellectual, lots of people didn't even go to college, much less graduate school. People are laborers, of course lots of lesbians who kind of followed the 1970s separatist or dropout model, or dog walkers or landscapers, and things like that." There are things about that kind of life that make a lot more sense to her than what she does, she says. She grew up blue-collar, and this is what she would have been "if I hadn't just been weird"; therefore, she feels comfortable in a working-class world in ways she does not feel in academe. "It keeps alive a part of me that is real but doesn't have a place in the academy," she says.

Especially for gays and lesbians, emphasizes Dr. Pelletier, your friends are your network because often you do not have an extended family to rely on. That, she says, tends to be true for women in general, regardless of their sexual orientation. "Most women are going to end up without a partner. Many with children far away if they have any children at all." Despite the premium she puts on friendships, she is not always able to devote as much attention to her friends as necessary, a fact that scares her for the long term.

> It's wonderful that I have some friends who haven't disowned me yet because of the little bit of time I put into seeing them. Friendships take energy and time. Same as any relationship. Americans in general these days—and maybe this is true for the industrialized world—but friendships have become suspect or something you only do when you are a child or an adolescent. They are not things we put any worth on at all.

Friends and a network seem a core part of Dr. Pelletier's identity, and so is her need to be open about her sexual orientation. She used to be married years ago but at some point was "ready for it to be over" and to come out. She recalls having been frightened for a long time to be openly gay, seeing it as a dead end and thinking "I would never have a life." So she tried to conform to

a heteronormative society, but when she got her first job, change
was imminent.

> I got my first job, and I really realized I was good at it,
> and I met the first out lesbian couple I had ever seen in
> my life, and people were not killing them. So my con-
> fidence level went way up. That job was a tremendous
> boost to me, compared to a graduate student when you
> are just dirt. Then I had this example of a fairly happy
> couple that people just accepted; I thought "that is what
> I want." I really didn't want to play this game anymore,
> and it really was a game.

She decided to come out after she had been hired at her
institution, having made up her mind that "if I can't be out and
work at a university, I just won't work at a university anymore; I
don't care if they fire me." It took a few years to get to that point,
but now things have worked out very well at her university, where
she considers herself to be "the resident lesbian." Together with a
colleague in another department who is "the resident gay man,"
she formed a vocal political organization. She benefits, she says,
from her reputation of being very honest, not just about her sexual
orientation. People know she does not like secrets and, whenever
possible, she insists that things not be done behind people's backs,
something that happens so frequently in academe. "I think it has
turned out to be a source of respect among my colleagues," she
concludes.

Being true to herself is important to thirty-eight-year-old
Dr. Pryzinski at Private Comprehensive as well. There is not
much of a boundary between her professional life and her life
outside the academy as long as the former is primarily defined as
being a teacher who brings her research to her class. In that case it
"is just one big life" without distinction between different spheres.
In fact, "if there were a distinction that would be bad because

maybe I would be teaching out of a textbook instead of teaching my research. That would be ludicrous to me."

Things are changing, however. Ever since Dr. Pryzinski got tenured and promoted, she finds herself being asked to act in the "academy part," meaning the politics of the academy, a space she insists she never really owned. Having to play a role in it makes it necessary for her to erect boundaries between her personal and professional lives. "I'm starting to see," she says, "that work is work, and life is life, and there has to be this gap between the two." This is what she has to say about the gap:

> The introduction of that gap comes from me because I've been asked to participate in university, academy service, like the directing of the curriculum, or the admission of students, or selection of the president, or development of a more inclusively diverse culture. I think that the more I get involved in all of that, the more I see that professional space of the academy is very different from my scholarship and writing. So when I think about the academy as my scholarship and writing and teaching, there is no difference between the academy and my life at home. If I think about it in terms of the administration of a university or the politics of a university, I'm starting to see that not only is there a division, but I will be harmed if I don't construct that division actively. Do you know what I mean?

Dr. Pryzinski is convinced harm would result if the identity in her personal life were to become the same as the identity she needs to adopt to perform political or administrative roles in the academy. For example, she will become department chair soon, and as an actor in the (political) space of the academy, her identity will be constructed around questions of resource allocation. As liaison between her faculty, students, and staff and "those people who are doling out the resources," she knows the way she will have to act to get those resources "is not [a way] I would want to adopt as a generalized way of being in my personal life." She will become a competitor, she says, a notion she has "actively giggled at because it is something that is not part of who I am as a scholar." She expects to have to manage the economy of her speech very differently than she does now, be strategic, utilitarian, pragmatic, and politically astute. After all, she has learned in this more politically charged space as a tenured associate professor that

> . . . people can be a little shitty. That is something that I never had to deal with when I was just the identity of a [scholar]. I never thought about people being shitty, and the kind of back stabbing and undermining that can take place in the politicized space when you participate in that space.

Part of the political sphere Dr. Pryzinski finds alienating is the challenge to deal with power relationships with colleagues. She prepares for participating in junior colleagues' personnel reviews and wonders how to navigate power differentials in healthy ways, how to be a good mentor without being paternalistic, how to use power to help people thrive rather than wield it in such ways as to make them panicky, insecure, or floundering. How can she avoid being seen as the "bad guy" because she is casting judgment on them, and how can they possibly trust her? Merely thinking about these issues creates anxiety for her, she says, and is an "energy suck."

To be sure, being "just a scholar" had had its costs for Dr. Pryzinski as well. After years of working "all the time like a machine" and "being wildly and massively productive, and wildly rewarded in terms of resources," she finally learned to "secure freedom from work," realizing how exhausted she was and "how destroyed physically, emotionally, relationally." She was given a sabbatical and used it to work on balancing her life, at a time that her marriage was coming undone, in part a result of excessive work habits. The trauma of her divorce, however, helped her put professional stressors in perspective, and postsabbatical she reentered the academy more focused on things that gave her joy as a scholar. She remembers her state prior to the sabbatical as one under a panic that she was not good enough, or somehow might make a mistake and be found out, that she would not get tenure, or a job, or a Ph.D., all fears that undermined her self-respect. "So I was always fighting this external threat that my life would be taken away." After the sabbatical and the divorce she felt that "I already had my life taken away. . . . The thing that I feared most had already happened, so I didn't need to carry that fear anymore." She came back still productive but better able to take care of herself and her relationships.

The stories of Drs. Pelletier and Pryzinski are illustrations of mid-career female faculty defining their identity, their place, and how they want to be in the world of academe. They come out, not necessarily in the sexual sense of the term. They decide to stop playing games and to sort out what is important for them in order to be who they are and protect themselves and their identities. For that to happen, tighter boundaries between personal and professional spaces may have to be drawn, as in Dr. Pryzinski's case. Workload may have to be renegotiated and priorities redefined, as in both scholars' cases. In any case, these women are powerful agents in negotiating the academy in ways that are conducive to their scholarship and productivity but also their humanity. It is not enough for them to be cranking out articles or negotiating the universities' resources in their favor. They put emphasis on how they are as persons while "doing academe." Dr. Pelletier is known for her honesty, and Dr. Pryzinski will most likely make an excellent chair *because* she is so concerned about not misusing her colleagues' trust. They both serve as exemplars of female leaders at mid-career stage who are "wildly successful" in more than one sense despite considerable obstacles they had to overcome.

Making It Work and Dealing with It: "Psyching Out What Does Really Count and Reconciling That with My Own Values and Priorities"

Mid-career faculty, much like their early-career colleagues, have enablers in their lives that help them be successful, and they employ a wide array of coping strategies to deal with barriers to what they would consider a successful balance of their personal and professional lives. Considerable overlap exists between their testimonies and those of their early-career colleagues; for example, the presence of supportive partners and extended family, as well as the flexibility of the work schedule. Yet there are also differences. For instance, with the few exceptions of women who became mothers later in life, maternity policies and other issues related to pregnancy and child birth are no longer important enablers for them. Some do, however, list flexible schedules, tenure extensions, maternity leave, temporary part-time options (for non-tenure-track faculty), the ability to bring children to the office, and child care on campus as enablers they used to enjoy years ago when their children were young.

Women whose children are older but still living at home enumerate enablers that are relevant in their current life stages. Dr. Kaminski at Metropolitan, for example, tells about when she took educational leave one summer and went to Costa Rica for ten weeks with her children. They learned Spanish, benefited from immersion in a different culture, spent time in a biological reserve learning about the rainforest, participated in a volunteer force to save turtles, and more. Dr. Kaminski and her children greatly enjoyed the experience, and the university benefited from

Dr. Kaminski's increased knowledge about Hispanic culture and heightened level of preparedness for Hispanic outreach programs. One of the outcomes of her stay, she says, is the initiation of a conversational Spanish class for faculty and staff. "I just felt very fortunate to have [the leave]," she says, "and I felt like I really needed it."

In addition, and as described in detail previously, major enablers for the mid-career women in this study are supportive life-partners who go well beyond "helping out" around the house. And children, too, can become enablers of their mothers' careers. Dr. Ephron at Community College lists her children as enablers who are "stepping up" if she needs support. Dr. Jacobs at Private Comprehensive finds it enabling that her kids are "good kids" who do not have significant problems, and Flagship professor Newton relates how her three children (twenty, eighteen, and fifteen years old) from a very young age were taught to respect and not interrupt their mother when she was writing at home. They entertained and took care of themselves, she says, and now are "pretty independent kids."

> Quietly we'd set them up with activities, and then I'd go up in my room and do some of the writing I had to do; so from when they were very little, they got used to the idea of me needing space. And got used to giving it to me and taking care of themselves. They weren't ignored, but they learned how to be more self-sufficient.

In addition to giving her space, Dr. Newton's children were also involved in household duties. "I wasn't going to be the person cleaning the whole house or cooking all the meals, or taking on all those housewife duties," Dr. Newton insists. "So we divided it up." The kids cleaned their bathrooms, did their own laundry, helped with dinner and dishes, and so did her husband. Everyone pitched in, she says, and the family created a "much more egalitarian home situation." Her children also realized that she would not be able to drive them "all the time anytime," and learned to set up car pools.

> We did lots of negotiation like that, but it was something that they became accustomed to right from when they were very young kids. They got used to a give-and-take that's made them, I think, probably, better people.

Dr. Newton assumes her children will be good partners later in life because they know how to take care of themselves and work a household. Never did they think twice about doing their chores, she explains, because they were part of the household routine. "It was just survival. It was how we were going to make it all work."

Mid-career faculty with children may enjoy relatively little institutional support to balance their lives, and yet they do talk of enabling individuals or sometimes departments at work. Overall, the findings mirror what University of Nebraska professor Christina Brantner published in her account of managing two adoptions as a single mother: "Although the official university structures proved largely incompatible with developing a modern family life, I was relieved and grateful that the individuals in my department and program turned out to be extremely supportive" (Brantner, 2005, p. 199).

Dr. Jacobs of Private Comprehensive has a similar opinion. She sums it up by saying that "I don't see the institution supporting families. I don't really see it. Departments are good, but the institution, I don't really see it." Dr. Sutherland at Flagship describes her colleagues as appreciating that she has a family and young children. She does not hesitate to bring her kids to work, for example, but despite these enablers she characterizes her university as essentially unsupportive: "I don't think there are any particular enablers for succeeding well at work that the university or my department provides. It's up to me to find them."

Flagship's Dr. Newton agrees. Despite the fact that her institution offered nothing to enable her balancing, she has good things to say about her former advisor, who distinguished himself not only through encouraging her and involving her in projects, but also through his flexibility as to when she would work on these projects. "He understood about kids," she says. "If I had to bring a sick child to work with me for some reason, that wasn't a problem. We'd work around it." Her advisor helped her establish good work habits in terms of publishing and presenting at national conferences, and their close working relationship continues to date. He was an enabler both professionally and personally, she emphasizes, because of his "respect for families. . . ."

Dr. Ephron at Community College formed close friendships with colleagues at work. They "made a very close pact" which helps her "get through a lot of the stuff that goes on here in terms of politics and personalities." Getting involved in the local chapter of a national professional organization has also been a major enabler for her, providing numerous opportunities she may not have otherwise had.

Along similar lines, Ms. Ehrenreich at the same institution recounts how people accommodated a pregnant faculty member's schedule and covered classes and committee assignments. She remembers also the supportive power of colleagues and students who helped her get through difficult times when her husband had a stroke. Being at work was also a welcomed diversion from sitting at her husband's bedside, and it helped her "to have something else to focus on."

Dr. Pryzinski at Private Comprehensive also mentions having colleagues with whom she coauthors and collaborates, as well as "fantastic mentors" in her life, as major enablers. She remembers one particular person who once told her that "the best way to be an academic is to be so good that everybody just leaves you alone." She followed his advice, and now she is "so good at what I do, that no one picks on me, you know what I mean. Everyone just leaves me alone. I think that's an enabler because I'm not being picked at, I'm not a subject of judgment all the time." When people leave you alone because of your excellence, she explains, you have the "potential for balance and to open your life up to other dimensions that can work to sustain you and make you more healthy in a holistic way."

Being single after her divorce and without children, Dr. Pryzinski may not have needed the *same* type of institutional support some of the women with children described earlier. Yet she did need support of a different type that enabled her to make corrections to what she perceived as a highly imbalanced life. It was her institution's junior sabbatical that helped her do so. "It was just like the university went 'boop, okay, you're over there now. You don't have to be in this space for one semester.'" It felt to her as if the college was sending her the message that, as a junior untenured professor, they wanted her to figure out how to bring more of her research to publication and how to create a sustainable future for herself at the institution. The junior sabbatical, she explains, is "their way of saying we want you to get tenure, and here is some extra time you can take for that very purpose."

While mid-career faculty talk about the many enablers in their lives, they are also asked about coping strategies they may employ. In response, Dr. Schumacher at Metropolitan insists she does not know how one copes. She is reading some of the early feminist writings on the complexity of motherhood and work, and thinks, "oh my God, it hasn't changed in the slightest." Many of the women who identified as working feminists or working mothers in the 1960s and 1970s, she says, went crazy and "emotionally burst at the seams. They all kind of disassembled in some ways." Lessons have not been learned, she concludes, and no institutional, cultural, or structural changes have been made that make working mothers' lives easier nowadays. "I'm sorry there aren't any more coping mechanisms," she says, "literally you just suck it up and run. That is a terrible coping mechanism."

Given the dire situation, Dr. Schumacher cries a lot. Perhaps it's hormonal, she thinks, but she cries more than she used to. Other than that, she works faster than she ever worked before; "some days I feel like I'm on fast forward." She has learned to economize but is uncertain whether her strategies help students.

> I used to write really good, involved, helpful letters of recommendations for students. Well now, I spit out a paragraph and send it, and I'm not sure it is helping them anymore, but I've got to get it done.

Dr. Ephron at Community College feels similarly. In response to my question about recommendations she may have for other women that might help them balance their lives, she responds: "I don't think I have an answer for that. What I do is just work harder." She characterizes herself as a person who does not need a lot of sleep and as someone who wakes up at 6:00 A.M. "with things buzzing in my head." This buzzing in her head, she explains, is her self-evaluating, something you have to do. She asks herself:

> What is important to me? What is not important to me? Is the conflict I'm feeling at work important enough to try to fix, or just let it go? Sometimes you just have to let it go because if you try to fix every conflict you're going to drive yourself crazy. There are some times you just have to say "it's not that important to me. I want to focus on *this* instead." . . . I would say that I self-evaluate a lot in my life. Constantly saying: "Am I doing the right thing? Can I do something better?"

Other women did tell of coping strategies they employed such as exercising, running, gardening, talking to girlfriends, working on scrapbooks, drinking wine. Having pets was named as a source of stress relief and enjoyment, playing with them and taking them on walks. Watching comedies, just sitting and talking, playing pool, listening to music, cooking, reading for fun, and getting on a bike. Dr. Foster at HBCU talks about using yoga meditation, breathing, and trying "not to let myself get stressed out." However, with "time" being of such crucial importance in their lives, multitasking has seeped even into recreational activities. Dr. Whitehead, for example, likes to take her daughter to swim practice at the YMCA and use that time to exercise herself.

Constructive self-talk gets used as a coping strategy by Private Comprehensive's Dr. Pryzinski. She tells herself that "it's all going to work out because it always does." By now, she says, she has so many experiences with panic attacks based on not knowing how to get through all of her work that she has been able to benefit from that history. This is what she tells herself:

> OK, your job asks you to do this about four weeks every semester, about eight weeks out of the year. You are so busy with your job that you can't sleep, eat, talk outside of the job. And the rest of the time is pretty much yours to manage as best as you can. So give yourself over to these eight weeks, . . . don't fight it. Just give yourself over and know you can do anything for four weeks, or you can do anything for two weeks, you can do anything for three weeks, and then you're done, and the system will shoot you out, and you will recuperate your balance. But for these four weeks, it's all about the machine. It's all about cranking it out. Don't worry about it, don't panic about it, just get it done and get out. So that is how I do it now.

Dr. Pritchard at HBCU uses sheer willpower and determination to cope with her work. Others make peace with what is possible and cut their losses without too much worry. Dr. Whitehead has decided, for instance, that cleaning house cannot be a priority in her busy life, and she will not let it bother her too much. "Something's gotta go," she declares, "because you want to spend time with your family, and with three kids, and one a teenager, and a five-year old, there is stuff all over the place, and it's hard to maintain order." She tries not to rank a clean house too highly, she says, because "if I were compulsive about that, I would not be very happy."

Dr. Jacobs at Private Comprehensive sounds similar. She insists that she is not "a homemaker," and having a nice home "is the one thing, the one ball that's been completely dropped." She would like to have aesthetic surroundings, she insists, but being a single working mother, "something had to go." Dr. Littlefield at HBCU simply says, "I can't get the house cleaned often enough. . . . I hate to be around clutter."

Dr. Schumacher at Metropolitan can fully relate to the challenge but employs a distinct coping strategy. She learned to authorize herself to hire help, quite an accomplishment for someone not only raised a woman but a "Calvinist backgrounded western pioneer stock girl."

> I mean my grandmother would turn over in her grave if she knew I was hiring someone to come in and help me clean. . . . I've gone through these waves. Hiring someone, and then they go out of business, and then I think "oh, we can do it." Then I realize six weeks into it, we can't do it.

Dr. Schumacher strongly advises women to authorize themselves to "get help any way you can get help" and to "enjoy that gift every week." She also wanted to live in a condo, she explains, and not take care of any grounds. "But unfortunately my voice was not supreme in that," she says, "and I had someone who thought he wanted to be Mr. Greenacres. Now I'm the first one on the phone saying 'hi Bob's landscaping, would you come and cut our lawn and do the trees and get our leaves up. . . .'"

Turning to more esoteric topics, faculty found their passion for their disciplines to be inherently enabling. Community College's Ms. Ehrenreich says "I absolutely love my job. I love the discipline of. . . . I think it's fascinating. I love being in the classroom. I love teaching." Dr. Pritchard at HBCU expresses the same sentiment: "I love what I do. . . . The fact that one is engaged in work that brings you so much inherent joy enables you to continue." She also mentions "success" as an enabler, and the affirmation that comes with recognition by others.

Along similar lines, Private Comprehensive's Dr. Pryzinski explains how, in order to cope, she focuses on her research, her readings, her theory building. Keeping *ideas* at the core of her identity, she says, makes her a "really happy person." She talks about being in love with what she reads and writes, respecting it and nurturing it like a child, a person. But to sustain a creative life, she emphasizes, she cannot be a machine. In fact, she has seen many leaders in her field burn out because they behaved like machines. "They just weren't able to sustain," she says. "They were like these supernovas, and then they just burned out." To prevent burnout, she knows just what to do.

> I absolutely have to have other creative outlets, and spaces away from those ideas, so that the ideas can breathe, and grow and be left alone for a little bit to do their own thing, and then I can come back to them.

Everything about Dr. Pryzinski's life is geared toward supporting her writing, her home office, the flow of her home, her garden. She purposefully takes time away from growing her ideas and grows her garden for a while instead, describing it as a "huge life resource itself."

Dr. Jacobs at Private Comprehensive talks about the importance of space as well. She escapes to coffee shops to write, away from both her office and her home. In her office she could do "busy work," she explains, but not create. And her home would just distract her with its myriad reminders of the housework waiting to be done and rendering it impossible for her to be comfortable or calm enough to write. She is hoping that her partner's impending move into her house will help create a more peaceful and orderly environment where the couple and her two children can live together harmoniously. Protecting times to write might be a challenge though, she anticipates, and while his move will be a help, it will also be a disruption. "Figuring out, melding this, figuring out how to all live together . . . ," she muses.

Knowing yourself well enough to structure life in such a way that you can capitalize on your most productive times seems to be a skill many academics hone. Dr. Pritchard at HBCU carves out blocks of time to write, something her style dictates she does. Her best blocks of time, she says, tend to be Thanksgiving week, Winter break, and the summer. "I've learned to hold my summers sacrosanct," she explains, "because it's the only large block of time I have to do all of this work." She says she is purposeful about how she chooses to spend her time, and lets her body be her guide.

> I'm not sleepwalking; I'm making decisions. So I will decide "no, I will not work on that article right now because right now I wouldn't do a good job on that anyway. . . ." When you reach a particular point, you reach a point of diminishing return. . . . Sometimes it's better to step away and come back later.

Dr. Pritchard prays a lot, she says, and there is a discipline to it the same as in taking care of yourself, writing, or engaging in the many demands on her time. In fact, prayer is her greatest, most significant coping strategy: "It centers you. . . . I quiet the noise and the demands which will never stop, and I purposefully stop."

Friends are also mentioned as enablers. Dr. Jacobs at Private Comprehensive speaks of her nourishing social life.

> I'm a very social person, probably almost excessively so. . . . for me I couldn't live if I didn't have some time to hang out with friends and have get-togethers to have food and wine.

People are so busy though, she explains, but she does organize weekly chess nights at her house and invites people for dinner. Some people cannot believe that she, a single mother of two, can be simultaneously productive and have so much fun.

> She [a colleague] sees me, all alone with these two little kids, and, on top of that, having an active social life, and I think she just thought there is just no way I could get tenure.

Well, Dr. Jacobs did get tenure and reiterates what has been stated by Dr. Pelletier before, namely that friends are a needed resource, especially once her children get older.

HBCU's Dr. Littlefield finds friends who "help me vent, . . . allow me to vent." She sits with colleagues and "just moan and groan for a couple of hours. Then laugh it off and go home and start over again." She also copes by "just doing it," she says, and being extremely organized. She has her laptop and cell phone with her at all times and has "the tenacity that I will just do it until the job is done."

Private Comprehensive's Dr. Pryzinski talks about friends as well, and how they serve as an enabler of balance. She is friends with a woman who is not an academic and who fights both poverty and isolation. Dr. Pryzinski shares with her the struggle with isolation and "not having a family, not having relationships that are even present to us, let alone healthy." She, however, in contrast to her friend, has this "viable employment, and it makes me respect so much the life resource of my job." She tries to live with "grace, respect, and humility" in the "gift of that employment," she elaborates, and "all of those things are enablers for me."

Whereas Dr. Pryzinski uses creative alternatives to work to refuel her energy and focus, other mid-career women use the explicit communication of their needs, wants, and boundaries as a coping strategy. Dr. Pritchard at HBCU has decided that *she* decides. There will never be an end to the demands people place on you, she says, and she chooses which ones to honor. Some people say they want to collaborate with you but . . .

> . . . what they really want is to suck you dry. What they really want are your ideas, your work, and your energy. And they are not willing to collaborate and bring something of their own to the table.

Dr. Pelletier at Private Comprehensive says that while women are not very well socialized to set boundaries, she is slowly getting better at it. Dr. Whitehead at Metropolitan describes how she has gotten better over time not necessarily at saying "no" to professional requests but at least at giving herself permission to have family considerations enter her professional decision making. She was just asked to serve on a grant review panel, an activity that would necessitate overnight stays out of town. She reacted differently to the request than she would have in the past, she says.

> So it's like, well, I can't really say "no." I did tell [the person who asked] I have to go home and check my schedule and see if I can meld it with my personal

schedule, and he seemed, well he seemed to be understanding of that. And this is maybe where I differ from
what I used to have done. Probably earlier I would have
been reluctant to say anything about that.

Flagship's Dr. Seidman has similar experiences. She says she
is still learning and "coping with coping." "No," she has come
to understand, is a viable word in the English language, although
women have a more difficult time saying it than men. Both
personally and professionally, she is "learning the power of saying
'no'" and taking care of herself first, getting her nutritional, exercise,
and health needs met. "I can't cope unless I feel good," she says.
In addition, she echoes Assistant Professor Yong's practice of using
both professional and personal writing as a vehicle for coping. "I'm
currently helping two children publish a book," she says. "I find
that very validating."

Dr. Sikka at Community College is learning to work econom-
ically by collaborating and sharing projects, as well as activities
and materials for students. It keeps her from constantly having to
reinvent the wheel, she says. She is also revising her classes less
than she used to.

> I used to try to start every semester with a different
> outlook and change things around. For the past few
> semesters I'm happy to repeat what I'm doing. I've
> found things that work, and work well, and I am happy
> with that. I'll make a few changes, but not extensive
> changes, so it's useful to have that degree of experience
> . . . that makes it possible to do that. So that's helped
> quite a bit.

She does not always feel good about the limits on the quality
of her teaching her workload imposes. She teaches five classes,
she says, and "the grading is tremendous." She let papers and

grades slide, and for the first time this semester did not give a midsemester assessment in two classes simply because she had not finished grading their papers in time. "That's something I feel terrible about," she admits, "but I need to sleep too. . . ."

Drawing boundaries is something Flagship's Dr. Newton is learning as well. She talks about "coming to terms with what's important and not having it all." She is trying to let go "of that achievement of having to be the absolute top of the heap, the superstar," a tendency she shares with other female academics and an issue further explored in Chapter Three. Although her marriage once suffered from tensions because of her unavailability on evenings and weekends, she now tries to work smarter and more effectively, and structure her time as well as she can. She calls it "sort of psyching out what does really count and reconciling that with my own values and priorities." She skillfully walks a fine line. On the one hand, she allows herself to engage in certain professional activities such as service, teaching, and working with people, despite the fact that they are undervalued in academe. On the other hand, she strives not to get sidetracked but say "no" to certain projects so that she is able to carve out time for her family. This is how she captures the balancing act:

> I am someone who grossly overcommits on service, and it's why I am [in my field]. . . . That doesn't really yield much in terms of rewards in this business. It's much more about the publications. I often say to people that I write to teach. Unlike some of my colleagues who abso- lutely love research and love writing and sequestering themselves to produce the next book. . . . My first love is really working with people, promoting people. . . . So I get sidetracked, and it really requires a lot of discipline to try and say "no" to some of these projects. . . . It's a constant challenge. Trying to be emotionally available

for my family on a reasonable basis ... and really shoehorning my work into [certain] hours.

Dr. Newton employs very practical coping techniques that help her define boundaries and avoid being exploited by those who might have come to expect her to take on disproportionately high shares of service work. Being a visual person, it helps her to make lists of dissertation committee she serves, for instance, and to use these lists as a basis for her decision making as to whether or not to agree to a student's request for service.

> But given that I'm going to be working 50–60 hours in a week, how much can I possibly handle? I've come up with all these ways to visually organize so I can sleep nights. . . . I really try and plan ahead and plug things in. When am I going to do what and get started on projects ahead of time, and pace myself so that I'm not scrambling at the last minute, not going into my bedroom for a whole week to finish something up. I brute force scheduling, departmentalizing, and shoehorning into spots and giving myself deadlines.

Dr. Newton has come to realize that she is unable to devote excessive amounts of time to such things as grading papers or working on dissertation proposals, and she therefore sets herself time limits for these kinds of tasks. The imposition of artificial deadlines, she says, is the only way she can "sort of keep it all reasonable. . . . Am I going to spend eight hours on it, or am I going to say 'This person is getting three hours of my time, max. That's it. No more.'"

Things are working fairly well for Dr. Newton, who says she feels far more relaxed since she received tenure, and has a much better relationship with her husband.

I don't know, it's in better balance now. It's much more manageable. I'm sleeping better, and I have a sense of peace about all of this, and I seem productive more than enough.

Whereas Dr. Nelson has learned to be assertive about protecting her time, her colleague Dr. Sutherland describes assertiveness as a powerful coping strategy she employed even at the very beginning of her career. As a brand new Ph.D. she had gotten to know a world-renowned scholar who proclaimed he wanted to diversify his male-dominated profession. His research field was different from hers, but she was eager to switch, given that such a move would open up entirely new opportunities. He offered her a post-doc, but when she took him up on the offer he reneged on financial grounds. She did not give up.

I wasn't happy with that response. . . . So I contacted him again and told him I'd come work for free if he'd just hire me. Or I'd teach classes, or I'd do whatever was necessary to get the funding if I could come work with him. . . . About two days later he called and said "Okay, I found money, you can come." I feel like I kind of played hard ball with him, and I won. It was an amazing opportunity. I learned so much, and I totally switched my research field [to] . . . an evolving field with a lot of research funding and a lot of universities looking for people in that area. It opened up tons more opportunities.

Dr. Sutherland's assertiveness continues to serve her well to this day and is reflected in one of her current coping strategies. Working in a male-dominated field ("I was the only woman for about eight years"), she feels it is necessary to educate her male colleagues about her home situation:

I'm very quick to talk to them about what's going on in my life, and about my kids, and about how I'm trying to cope and deal with stuff. That's probably a coping strategy—educating people and letting them be aware.

Dr. Pryzinski at Private Comprehensive uses a different version of assertiveness. When her department chair makes "girly references" to her, she simply calls him on it. "Do you realize the feminization of my identity that you just performed here?" she would ask him. "Do you realize you just did that? Is it funny that you just did that?"

Her colleague Dr. Pelletier uses assertiveness as well and cultivates "the skill of having a very controlled and very targeted meltdown." She would not do this in her personal life, she emphasizes, because it is manipulative, but she does do it to her dean, whom she tells that "I have to have these resources if you want me to do this job, or I'm going to just scream or something until this happens." She does have the standing to do this now, she points out, and lists "throwing my weight around and learning how to do that" as a pretty recent coping strategy. Says she:

> I'm at a point in my career where I won't just be given a bad reputation, and denied tenure or denied promotion or something. What can they do to me? Furthermore, people know that I know so many people because I've been here so long, and I know people outside the university. . . . If someone tried to reprimand me or promote an image of me as unstable, everyone would know it wasn't true. So I can get away with these little fits every now and then.

Her illustration of a "controlled meltdown" is a recent situation in which she demanded secretarial help for her program and told the dean that if she did not receive what she asked for, she would "punt, and they were going to have the program back in receivership and would have to use their own secretarial staff to do it." Dr. Pelletier issues a note of caution: "This is the kind of stuff you don't say to the dean unless you're me, unless you're in a position like mine." Furthermore, she warns, it has to be done very carefully, and if you do it too many times, "it ceases to be effective and people do think you're crazy."

All in all, mid-career faculty in this study certainly encounter obstacles and barriers to balancing their professional and personal lives, just as their early-career colleagues do. After all, they are all operating in a system of "domesticity," which Joan Williams defines as a gender system built on the ideal of a full-time worker who takes little or no time off for childbearing or rearing. The ideal-worker norm may not define all jobs, she argues, but it does define the "good" ones such as professional middle-class jobs. In this system, the argument continues, caregivers tend to be unable to perform as ideal workers and are often marginalized (Williams, 2000, p. 1).

Not all female academics decide to have children, and this study includes many who do not. They are nevertheless caretakers of others and are struggling with trying to balance lives in an occupation that can be all-consuming. In addition to obstacles in this quest, however, the faculty introduced in this study also learned to capitalize on enabling conditions, often informally created, and use a wide array of coping strategies to deal "with it all." In many cases, they thrive, are successful, and serve as inspirations for their professional communities, as well as the people they love.

3

Late Career

"This Is Who I Am, and I'm Going to Be Who I Want to Be"

Compared to their early- and mid-career colleagues, most late-career faculty in this study have reached a point at which they seem relatively happy with the balance between their personal and professional lives. They describe their current situations as "suiting very well"; "very healthy"; "a good life"; "gotten to the point now, where I would say yes, [there is a good balance]"; "a delightful position to be in"; "gotten to that place in my life where I really do [find it possible to have both a satisfying career and a fulfilling personal life]"; "having control over my life"; "feeling very balanced"; "do whatever I want, and it is a really good life now"; "overall my balance is good"; "much easier, much happier"; "I do what I want to do which is really nice"; "I have control over my life."

There are, certainly, challenges that come with this career stage, too, as well as losses, costs, and regrets. Just like their colleagues at earlier career stages, these faculty members tell stories about it all: barriers to success, enablers, and the coping mechanisms they developed over time.

Defining the Relationship: "You've Reached That Level of Self-Actualization"

By no means do late-career faculty members agree on how the relationship between their professional and personal lives ought to be defined. But the majority is able to define it in ways *they* see fit.

127

Some have come to merge these two spheres of their lives, while others have finally reached a point where they can separate them to the extent best fitting for them.

The participant who perhaps spoke the most passionately about merging her life in and outside of academe is fifty-year-old professor at Flagship University Dr. Cohen. She is married to a fellow academic, and she describes her blended life in glowing terms. For her, life integration is not only a matter of taking work home, but skillfully weaving together work and play, time and space, as well as her marriage and her job. It is important to her that her spouse shares her philosophy of life integration and gladly works with her to blend their careers, their relationship, their children, and their pastime activities. This is how she sees it:

> One of the real delights of our [her husband's and her] partnership is that we work on a lot of the same ideas and issues. . . . Much of what we do overlaps. This is something that suits me very well. There are a lot of people who want their work life and home life to be two very separate things, and the circles of people they move in personally and professionally are very different. But both of us are of the persuasion that we like it all blended. I feel like it's a very rich life that remains the same when I walk out of the office door and go home. It's a pretty seamless thing. . . . We usually accompany each other when we're going to various professional things. It's been a really enlivening and intellectually rich partnership. . . . For me and him, it's very much who we are to have our life and work merged. In a sense we're kind of on duty all the time. It's something that we really like, and I don't think it looks excessive to people from the outside, although it may for some. Very seldom do we take, say, a vacation that doesn't have elements of

our work as a part of it unless it were just a family thing, like we go to the beach with his kids and grandchildren.

Fifty-one-year-old Professor Posan at Metropolitan makes similar comments. She talks of a "very permeable membrane" between her professional life and her life outside academe. They are "deeply interwoven," she says, "because my professional and personal life cover the same territory in terms of my interests, in terms of my community involvement. . . . There is no real stark distinction between my work and my private life in many ways." Her life is a "continuum," she elaborates, "rather than a separate category of boxes." And so she has gotten to that place in her life, she insists, where she finds it possible to have both a satisfying career and a fulfilling personal life.

That, she points out, has not always been the case. During her thirties she struggled, particularly when she found herself between academic jobs. Although she loved to freelance, she missed the security of an academic appointment. Now she has learned to combine her professional engagement in her genre outside of the university with her academic work inside, both of which she finds highly rewarding.

Retired professor Dr. Wiley's story about the relationship between her personal and professional lives once again reverberates with themes of merging the personal and the professional. Sixty-five years old, she just returned home after retiring from a deanship at a university in another state, where she served for about a decade after leaving her faculty position at Metropolitan. Her son is grown, and she recently lost her husband. As a dean it was hard in some instances, she says, to separate the professional from the personal.

There are so many parties and there are so many, what I refer to as "command performances." There is something going on, and you have to be seen. It is important. There

had to be times when I had people at my home. Potential donors and advisory boards. . . . Well, fortunately
[my husband] was very good at being a part of all of
that. . . . He didn't mind going to the events that I had
to go to. So there is a blurring of lines in some ways. The
other thing that blurred lines professionally and socially
[at her former university] was that all of my good friends
were [university] people. So whether it was tailgating
for a football game or having a progressive dinner, no
matter what it was, we did it with other [university]
people. . . . So our personal life revolved around the two
of us and the friends we made as part of the [university]
community. . . . It was very positive.

Now that she is retired, Dr. Wiley reports she has a good life,
doing a "little bit of consulting" and "thoroughly enjoying other
things." She trains her dog to be a therapy pet; she reads, knits,
and spends time with her son and his family, who live in town.
Dr. Wiley moved to a community of people at a similar life stage
where "everybody knows everybody." They have social events in
their clubhouse several times a month, started a bridge group, and
"there is no stress, there is no pressure." She concludes:

I'm finished with that part of my life. I like being
involved with Higher Ed because I think Higher Ed is
interesting. I can do it from a perspective where I don't
have to have an impact on anything, and I don't have
to be responsible for anything that has happened.

Associate Professor Saltmarsh at Community College draws
similar boundaries now. While her children were growing up, she
says, the only thing that was neglected was herself. Now, at age
fifty-eight, there are no barriers anymore to balancing her life. She

does not "want people to infringe on my free time. . . . That makes me feel more relaxed."

A colleague at Metropolitan echoes Dr. Saltmarsh. Not quite retired yet, Dr. Velvarde is finishing her thirtieth year at the institution. She is sixty-one years old, married, and the mother of one grown son. She recounts that for a long time she did not focus as much on her personal life as she would have wanted to, but began to change some years ago. It was then, she recalls,

> I just sort of thought to myself "what you see is what you get. This is who I am, and I'm going to be who I want to be, and I'm not going to try to be what other people want or do things to please others." And it was sort of like you've reached that level of self-actualization. I remember just saying "what you see is what you get." And it was so liberating and so affirming, but it took a long time to get there.

Now, she says, she is able to have a "pretty good balance" in her life, and for her that does not mean merging work and personal spheres but separating them. "I try really hard to leave my work at the office," she says. "I try really hard to be able to separate." She takes time to do the things that are important to her, and works on being able to "say 'enough!'"

Instructor Monet at Community College agrees. She is the sixty-year-old married mother of three grown children, and does not leave her office on Fridays until her desk is cleared off. She wants more free time over the weekend and no professional work on Saturdays. Conversely, by Sunday evening "my clothes all have to be washed, my house cleaned, and the grocery shopping done. I don't want to think about any of those things until the next weekend." She sums it up by saying, "At home I like to try to concentrate on home things, and when Monday morning comes,

I want to concentrate on my job Monday through Friday. I don't want things at home to drag me down." HBCU's Dr. Marx also takes an unequivocal stance in favor of separation. She says:

> I try to keep my social life separate from the university even though the university has a lot of activities. I find that professionally it is better to maintain a professional status and a personal status. And that's simply the way I am, not necessarily the best way. I do a lot of personal things outside of the university.

Sixty-two-year-old full professor at Private Comprehensive Mendelas has always made attempts to keep her professional and personal lives separate from each other. Her professional life revolves around her students; she maintains her relationships with them and watches "these people grow as my children would grow had I had children." Dr. Mendelas is not married and has many interests beyond "just family." Posttenure, she "never felt like I had to give up aspects of my personal life for my job." This is how she describes her history:

> Well, right now I certainly have jumped through the hoops. I have moved myself through the ranks, and I suppose I have done something right since I have gotten to where I am. . . . I feel as though many of the relationships I have made with my students have continued on over the years, and that has probably been one of the most important things to me. . . . I just love teaching, I really love being with young people. . . .

As illustrated here, several late-career women are happy to merge the different spheres of their lives, and others are finally able to separate. Some women, like Dr. Velvarde, allow themselves to scale down their workload and focus on those activities they find most worthy. Others, however, do the opposite and finally work as much as they want.

Dr. Kasper at Flagship, for instance, no longer feels the same tension she used to experience when her children lived at home. She is now free to pursue her work as passionately as she wants. This is how she tells it:

> To be honest with you, and this is interesting. I used to worry when the kids were at home. I used to say I have these two infinitely expandable things going on. Family life, which could take up as much time as I wanted, and work, which could take up as much time as I wanted. And so, once the kids both left, when the second one went off to college, work just sort of took over. While before I was trying to balance, now I could allow work to expand. So I would say, I am much more of a workaholic now with a small social life. I've been married so long, frankly that's not as big a part of my life. We both seem to do our own things much more than we did before. . . . I see myself much more as just a career person.

Dr. Kasper is "not unhappy" but is also not sure that she would describe the balance in her life as "healthy." She grapples with what she calls a "problem of opportunity":

> Healthy balance? I'm not unhappy. Do I think it's healthy? It's probably not healthy. I think I lost the capacity to create the other part in my life. But I'm not unhappy. I think it's OK. It's an odd question at this point in my life. Like I said, I'm not unhappy. I like being able to work and have this impact. And I do work long hours, but I don't mind it.

According to her, she has reached a place where she thinks she can have an impact both on her department and her profession at-large. She helps both men and women with their careers, she says, and she likes being asked to do things and to go places. "So there is travel, and there is impact at the level of discipline, field. So, feeling the reward is part of it." She nevertheless says "this is insane," but then adds "well, I say it's insane, and yet I told you I liked what I do. I just keep busy. It's very rewarding, I don't know how to cut back. . . . It's a problem of opportunity." Just like her colleagues in earlier career stages, she concludes: "I don't know how to say 'no.'"

Ms. Monet at Community College echoes some of these sentiments. She remembers that when her husband and she became "empty-nesters," not only did the relationship between her professional and her personal lives become "even easier," but she also found herself devoting more time to her work.

> When the children all left home, and it was just my husband and I, it became even easier. I found that because it was easier to be here, and I didn't feel the need to go home because there wasn't anybody at home that needed me, I found myself spending more and more time at the college. . . . I could come in early. I didn't have to wait for the school bus. I could stay late, attend meetings, and meet students later than I had felt comfortable doing because now I didn't have to rush home and cook for my family or anything like that.

Part of the general contentment of the late-career women in this study stems from their ability not only to craft the balance they prefer, but also to make peace with unfulfilled dreams (the issue of unfulfilled dreams is further explored under the heading "Regrets and Sacrifices"). Says Dr. D'Enbri at Private Comprehensive: "I do whatever I want, and it is really a good life now. I have accepted, although it still hurts, that I will not be promoted, and that I will retire as an associate professor. . . . It is a very good life. Yeah. I'm very happy with where I am right now."

Even though their journeys may not have been easy, in short, and plenty of bittersweet feelings are mixed in with their contentment, by and large late-career faculty in this study sounded positive not only about the relationship between their personal and professional lives but also about their more general state of being.

Such culmination of one's life journey in a relative state of acceptance can be interpreted within theories of adult development, as summarized by Bee and Bjorklund (2004, pp. 35–57). Erik Erikson, to name one influential theorist, postulates that a person has to resolve a series of crises or dilemmas over the course of his or her life in order to reach a stable identity. Once all prior stages of identity development have been dealt with successfully, adults culminate in a state of acceptance of self. A similar framework is psychologist's Jane Loevinger's theory of ego development. She believes that, in order to move to the next stage, one must complete the current stage, but she realizes that, at any age, people may vary widely in their ego development. Advanced stages consist of the conscientious, autonomous, and integrated stages at which people are able to spell out their own ideals and standards, take broad views of life, see the complex nature of things rather than seeking simplistic answers, and integrate central concerns of their own lives with those of society at-large. Adult development pioneer Daniel Levinson talks of "seasons of adulthood" and, once again, emphasizes that while people change, their development is not necessarily one from less to more advanced. Nevertheless, each period in life does build on the previous one. Other theories of adult development abound, and many of these abandon altogether the notion of stages as a basis of analysis (Bee & Bjorklund, 2004, pp. 35–57).

This study hardly claims to make a contribution to the literature on adult development, given that it did not follow a cohort over time to assess how individuals deal with the challenges of balancing their professional and personal lives during the course of their career spans. Suffice it to say that most of the women at the late-career stage in this study seem to have reached a point of relative peace and acceptance regarding the structures of their lives.

It is prudent to remind the reader once more that this study is one of relative *success* and excludes women who left academe, very likely at least in part because of difficult life balancing issues. And yet it should be encouraging to women at earlier career stages to know that happiness and contentment with the relationship between one's personal and professional lives are not only possible to find but were indeed found among the large *majority* of the diverse academics in this study. More research, preferably quantitative in nature, is needed to ascertain whether this phenomenon is generalizable and holds true for large numbers of late-career stage faculty.

Providing Elder Care: "Those of Us Who Are the Sandwich Generation"

While women at the late-career stage in this study tend to have a greater degree of agency in determining what choices they are able to make than their early- and mid-career colleagues, some nevertheless encounter significant restrictions and demands on how they allocate their time. Ms. Monet at Community College, for instance, brings up elder care, and the expectations directed at what she refers to as "the sandwich generation." She explains: "I think [institutions] also need to be aware of those of us that are the sandwich generation. We're getting our parents."

Ms. Monet is sixty years old, has been married for thirty-six years, and mothered three children who are now grown. Officially, she says, her husband and she became empty-nesters nine years ago. After her children left home, she experienced a period of relative freedom and was able to structure her days the way she saw fit. She spent more time at the college without the pressures of having to rush home and care for her family. Once she was able to take a summer off and do some traveling with her husband, something she calls "a dream come true." Those times, however, came to an end, and now "it's more like we're being tied down more because of my parents." A few months ago she moved her parents from another state to an assisted-living facility in town. "In the last two months I have picked up new responsibilities," she says. "I feel almost like I have two small children again." She provides more detail:

> Now that my parents are here, I've noticed . . . there are a lot of demands on my time. . . . I'm trying to get them established with a new cadre of doctors that they need to see here in town. I'm trying to help them adjust to the loss of a car. They're no longer living independently. They no longer have a car. They can't go places. They don't know their way around the area. There have definitely been days where I had to leave much earlier than I used to do. Maybe even cut short on office hours or something because I had to take them to a doctor or something like that. I'm hoping to find the right schedule for office hours and other demands so it'll be smoother next semester.

While she cares for her parents, Ms. Monet and her husband also continue to care for their children. They are literally "sandwiched" between two generations' various needs and, occasionally, things become overwhelming. Ms. Monet describes how during a thirty-day time span, she not only moved her parents but also helped her youngest child who got married. In the end, all she wanted to do was "cry, cry, cry."

> In a very hectic thirty-day period, we moved my parents. We actually moved them the day my mother got

> discharged from the hospital. I moved my parents, got
> them into assisted-living, emptied their house, put it
> on the market. In the middle of that thirty-day span,
> my youngest son got married. We had those demands
> too. At the end of the thirty days, I was extremely
> fatigued. It knew it because I was snip-snarling with my
> husband. . . . I felt like I wanted to cry, and I'm not a
> crier. I told my husband one day, what I want to do is go
> upstairs and crawl in bed and just cry, cry, cry. I wanted
> to have a personal pity party.

The adjustment to her parents being in town is one part of the
problem, Ms. Monet says, and her anger at her brother is the other.
"What are you doing?" she asks him.

> You're not here. You're not having to run down to the
> assisted-living and check on them, and see what their
> needs are. You're not the one getting the frantic phone
> calls "we need more 'Depends'; go get us some right
> away."

Her brother, she admits, has an adopted twenty-year-old daughter at home and, in addition, he deals with their parents, too.
Consequently, she says, "he feels he's sandwiched."

At HBCU, fifty-four-year-old associate professor Beseley echoes
Ms. Monet's sentiments. She is divorced with a twenty-year-old
daughter attending college and "aging, ailing" parents to take care
of. In order to live next door to her parents, she commutes about
an hour and fifty minutes, and that she finds challenging.

Ms. Monet and Dr. Beseley, of course, are not alone. According to the popular magazine *Newsweek*, some twenty million
baby-boomers (persons born between 1946 and 1964) are caring
not only for their own families but also for their aging parents

(Raymond, 2007, p. 62). Some of those boomers are faculty members in the nation's colleges and universities; and although maternity leave or child care are topics that begin to attract attention in academe, elder care and other forms of family care are rarely discussed.

Elder care is certainly not an issue confined to higher education but poses a problem across professions. According to a survey by the National Family Caregivers Association, a majority of its members indicated frustration, depression, and a lack of help from other family members (National Family Caregivers Association, 1997; quoted in Folbre, 2005, p. 358). The Brandeis University's National Center for Women and Aging and the National Alliance for Caregivers report that caregivers pay not only an emotional but also an economic price because they are losing out on promotions and training opportunities. About 75 percent of home caregivers for the elderly, furthermore, are women (Rimer, 1999, p. 9, quoted in Folbre, 2005, p. 358). Folbre argues that, given demographic trends, namely the relative increase of the elderly proportion of the population and an increase of the neediest population group consisting of people eighty-five and older, the need for elderly care will become more urgent. Unpaid labor to do so, however, is likely to decline, given that women are increasingly tied up in careers and often geographically removed. Therefore, she concludes, time has come to think differently about the "larger social organization of care" and address not only the special needs of children and the elderly but also the ill and disabled (Folbre, 2005, p. 359).

The Family and Medical Leave Act makes some provisions in that it allows faculty to care for a family member in case of an acute illness or emergency for a limited amount of time without risk of losing employment. Effective long-term care options that take into account the various obligations faculty may have toward aging family members, however, have yet to be designed and effectively implemented.

Regrets and Sacrifices: "There Are Always Costs"

Despite the fact that the late-career faculty members in this study talk almost unequivocally about the good balance they were able to craft in their lives, it is clear that the road many of them traveled to get to that point extracted its toll along the way. Several participants mentioned, for instance, that they scaled back their professional aspirations, mostly because of family obligations. Others made sacrifices involving their personal lives, and although in most cases they made peace with their compromises, in some instances hurt and regret linger on.

Scaling Down Professional Aspirations: "When I Should Have Been Working on My Career, the Demands of the Family . . . Were a Barrier"

Ms. Monet at Community College recounts how, early on in her career, she got hired at the lowest level, as an instructor. She was unable to attain the credentials necessary to work herself through the ranks because, initially, she took care of her children and, later, her children's college education depleted her financial resources. She explains:

> Early in my career I was hired as an instructor. . . .
> I knew what I needed to do was take more courses and get promotions, and so forth. Because of my children's demands, I didn't have the time to do that. I didn't feel like I could do that. Then I went through a period of time when we were educating these three children, sending them to college; and they all went out of state. There wasn't the money to pay for the graduate courses. . . .
> Through that time, when I should have been working on my career, the demands of the family financially and time-wise were a barrier.

Now she would have the financial resources to advance her education, she says, but, at age sixty, she is thinking of retirement instead. "I've reached the point where it's really not worth the effort to me."

Private Comprehensive's Dr. D'Enbri also looks back at a life punctured by events that cost her dearly. Sixty-one years old, she divorced a man with whom she once adopted two siblings who are now in their twenties. In response to my question of how long she has been divorced, Dr. D'Enbri replies that her standard answer is "not long enough," and then specifies "about twelve or thirteen years. . . . I got rid of him about four years before we got divorced. That was a very hard time. We lived in the same house for a year without speaking to each other; he wouldn't leave." The divorce made her life easier, she says, because he had been so unreliable concerning the children. Her divorce also made her a single mother, and that meant not only freedom to make her own decisions, but that "you have to take care of everything."

Dr. D'Enbri describes the stresses of the adoption process, and her disappointment with her husband's behavior once they had become parents.

> When you go through adoption, you go through this series of interviews; it is very intense. You talk about ways that you might parent or be good parents, and what a family blend looks like. After we went through the adoption interviews, we didn't get the children for four years. That was very hard because they called us, and I don't know how many social workers went through because they keep changing jobs. . . . That was a very difficult period, too. When we did get them, I guess I thought how hard we fought for them we would be more devoted to them. [My husband] thought his life would be exactly the same, and he would go to work at seven

> in the morning, and come home at six-thirty or seven
> o'clock at night. So, they were apparently my children,
> and my thought was that if they were going to be my
> children, then what did I need him for?

Before having children, Dr. D'Enbri explains, the only thing that mattered was work. Your career is who you are, she says, "but children really do put a monkey wrench in that." That was especially true in her case, given that the siblings had many special needs. Her daughter suffers from bipolar disorder, and both children are learning disabled and have attention-deficit disorder. Her daughter, furthermore, spent her high school years in mental institutions, and has since lived in a series of group homes. "She figures out enough ways to get enough attention to get herself kicked out," explains Dr. D'Enbri. Her daughter will always be dependent on her in some way, she says, and "I have a lot of ghosts who live with me."

Dr. D'Enbri describes some of her struggles in the past, such as the one that involved her efforts to get her children to graduate from high school. It took all her willpower, she says.

> Let me tell you, it took a lot. For my son to graduate
> from high school, I talked to his English teacher every
> day for a week before graduation. . . . And my daughter,
> my daughter graduated from high school I think mostly
> because the teacher wanted to make me happy. . . . just
> the stint of my will, I think, got her through school.

One day, Dr. D'Enbri made a mistake. At a vulnerable time in her life, a man became department chair who could not be trusted, she says, and she forgot that. When he came around to ask the faculty about their goals, she told him that her children had to be her priority right then. She had "no choice, whatsoever. I was a single mother, and I was raising two extraordinarily challenging children." This is what happened:

> I should have never told him that, but I did. So, I will never be promoted. There are other things that I have done not to get promoted, don't get me wrong. I'm stuck in the job where I am. I will always be an associate professor. While that is kind of an embarrassment to me, and a failure of sorts, I also made choices that I had to make, and I can't say all of that is due to the children.

Dr. D'Enbri is quick to point out that her children's need for her attention was not the main reason for her lack of advancement up the career ladder. A lot of that, she says, is due to the fact that "I do things that I want to do." Those things consist primarily of working with students, and that, she says, is what she was hired to do. Expectations have changed toward increased scholarly productivity, however, and she just does not fit that model because doing research never really interested her. She teaches students to do research, and she likes to work with them, but she does not publish herself. "That is largely what does it," she says, "that is largely what contributes to me not being promoted." There was a time, she points out, when she tried to do everything right, but she was already perceived in a particular way, and "it wasn't going to change. . . . So I stopped trying."

Professionally, she has come to accept her position, and she enjoys her students, their mutual projects, and her activities at home such as playing bridge and tennis with her friends and going to the gym five days a week. In short, she concludes, "I do what I want."

Other female faculty mention the costs of parenting. Metropolitan's retired full professor Dr. Wiley describes her career path as "not linear at all." She is convinced she would have been an administrator much sooner had she not been a single mother. At this point, however, she appears fully content and has "a good life."

Associate professor and administrator Ms. Saltmarsh at Community College also cut down her professional ambitions. The fifty-eight-year-old married mother of two adults used to find it difficult to find a healthy balance between her professional and personal lives because she always put the latter, particularly her children, above her professional life. Consequently, there were times she had to forgo career opportunities such as assuming administrative work full-time. She purposefully arranged her schedule and worked around her children's sports and school activities, something the flexibility at a community college allowed her to do. Still and all, she felt torn.

> You really do feel torn between your family and your profession because you want to do a great job. I'm sure one or the other gets slighted. It has to. I don't think you can give 100% to being a wife, mother, all those things that go with that, and to your profession. Physically and mentally, I don't think that is possible. There were lots of nights when you were pretty worn out and drained. You just wanted to jump in the bed, and everybody leave me alone.

Despite the struggles, Ms. Saltmarsh was always afraid to give up her profession altogether. Growing up poor, and being a first-generation college graduate, contributed to her determination to be a "professional woman, . . . able to take care of myself, no matter what might happen down the road." She wanted to prevent being in a situation similar to the many women who gave up their professional lives, and are now facing the difficulty of having to reenter the workforce because they are finding themselves divorced. Although she would have liked to stay home full-time with her children, in other words, she never considered doing so an option.

At this point in her life, she feels very fortunate and reports that she has gotten great satisfaction out of both realms in her life. She is, in her own words, "OK with not having advanced," and with her career path having been "pretty flat."

Torn Between Two Lives: "You Can't Have It All at Once"

Ms. Ketzel at Community College did not just reduce her career aspirations but also the number of children she allowed herself to have. She is of the opinion that "for many working mothers, life has to be sequential, and you can have it all, but you can't have it all at once." The fifty-three-year-old faculty member and administrator has been married for thirty-three years and is the mother of a twenty-five-year-old son. She felt torn working when her child was young, and describes the situation as follows:

> I guess I can say that's why I have one child. I felt very torn while working. . . . Not that I didn't have an ideal care situation. I just felt like I was missing out on so much by working, with him being young.

Ms. Ketzel taught high school before she entered her employment at Community College as an adjunct professor. It was the latter position that finally allowed her to find an acceptable balance in her life, yet at that point, she felt too old to have another child. "It was the conflict I felt between having a career and raising my son," she concludes, "that led me to have only one child."

Although there is nothing that lends itself better to a balance between home and work than a teaching career, she says, it was nevertheless difficult to balance her responsibilities to her son and to her students. Particularly as a high school teacher, it seemed to her that "some of my best energy went to my students, and I wasn't the energetic person that I wanted to be when I went home to my son. I always felt conflicted about that." She does not belong to the traditional generation of those who never expected to work outside the home, she emphasizes, and she enjoyed several sources of support. In addition to a "wonderfully supportive husband," she had a "wonderfully supportive principal," and, at Community College, she experienced enabling conditions as well: "if my child was ill, and I didn't come in, no eyebrows were raised. I never felt like my career was jeopardized." Despite these favorable conditions, however, her internal struggle continued. "I always felt like I was shortchanging my students. I always felt like I was giving short shrift to my own child or to my students. It was really a major conflict for me."

Ms. Ketzel did not just decide to have only one child because of an internal conflict she was unable to resolve, she also turned down professional opportunities. She was offered several administrative positions years ago but decided not to accept them because of her young son. Despite these professional sacrifices, Ms. Ketzel is highly satisfied with her decisions, and she does not think she gave up any opportunities permanently. This is how she sees it:

> If I chose at this point, I could pursue all of those things. I'm still only fifty-three. I still have time to earn a Ph.D. . . . For me, I didn't feel like I could have that high-powered driven career while, at the same time, being the kind of mother I wanted to be, and having the kind of family life I wanted to have. I know you can't go back and pick up and re-mother them once they've left for college. Once they're grown and on their own, you can't say "I wish I had spent more time with you when you were younger." And go back and recapture lost time.

Though she could have picked up her career once her son left for college, Ms. Ketzel explains, she decided not to pursue a Ph.D. or other professional options because, at that time, she was "so committed to the classroom." She had planned on possibly pursuing a law degree, but "I found to my surprise that when it was my turn to go back to school, I was too happy in the classroom, and didn't want to leave."

Ms. Ketzel sums up her story by emphasizing that higher education has not posed boundaries or barriers on her to find a balance. Any barriers she encountered have been of her own making, she says. "My own sense that I wasn't doing enough, as teacher, wife, and mother. I wanted to be 100 percent of all three of those things, which is an absolute impossibility. The only barrier I've felt is my own stress in trying to be a pretty high achiever in all three areas. It's difficult."

Other women did not opt for "sequential lives," but did try to do it all at once. They, too, paid a price for their choices. Flagship's Dr. Kasper says that before the children were of high school age, her life compared to running a marathon. Unlike some of the women she knew, Dr. Kasper never cut back. Over the course of her career she learned that she was a "super-ambitious person" who did not just want to succeed but "succeed big." And the more she succeeded, she more she "upped the ante." In comparison to other women who "weren't going there, who were happy just sort of to have gotten tenure and just sort of settling into that level," she found herself "going all the time." The cost was her life becoming a race, and sleep the only reprieve.

> I was just going all the time. And if I didn't have this mindset of just "keep going, no matter what happens, just keep going" (I now think of it as a kind of stupid mindlessness), but I probably wouldn't have gotten through without it. So I just never stopped. Kids get sick, you just keep going. You get sick, you just keep going. It's a marathon. . . . I think of the early days when the kids were babies, as dramatic. As they got older, it got easier, but oh yeah, pretty dramatic. I still love getting into bed, and just being able to go to sleep. Because that was the only reprieve I had then.

Now her children are grown, and Dr. Kasper has her "fair share of regrets" about not being able to do certain things with her children, or not paying enough attention to certain things. "I was sort of managing things, and I was dealing with things quickly that they needed." She thinks she spent enough time with her children, she emphasizes, and they themselves even think they were lucky because their mother was not as attentive as she could have been. And yet, she may not have given them enough attention. These are her feelings:

> It's hard to explain because it's not that I think I didn't spend enough time with them, it's not quite that. I guess it's more that I thought that the energy I had wasn't the best. Or there were times I remember when they would be talking to me, and getting my attention was difficult because I was thinking about all that other work stuff.

Dr. Velvarde at Metropolitan is similarly regretful. The sixty-one-year-old full professor thinks her son suffered because she was not quite available enough. He did not, for example, participate in after-school activities to the same degree as his friends did, a factor that may have contributed to him being a "loner" today, according to his mother. She tried, however, not only to meet his needs as best she could, but everybody else's as well. In the process she was careful not to commit "time theft," meaning she got up very early on weekends to do work while everybody else slept so she would not have to "steal time from the family." All this was done, of course, to the detriment of meeting her own needs. Now Dr. Velvarde is finally able to say, "'This is what I need, this is what I want.' When I get home in the evening, if I'm tired I'm going to put my feet up and just veg out, and my knitting has really become something that is just very relaxing for me, and I've found things that I want to do. And part of it is building toward transition as I think about retiring."

Guilt was certainly an issue for Flagships' Dr. Cohen. The fifty-year-old associate professor was a single mother for a long time during her career and remembers "that you just learn to live with a certain amount of guilt about not being able to do it perfectly on either front." She remembers bundling up her son who had strep throat, and letting him sleep on her office floor while she attended a meeting "conscious all the time that I was not the best mother." She felt "on duty twenty-four hours a day, seven days a week" in addition to having "that sense that your job is terribly important because you're the only supporter. There are high stakes all the way around." In addition to her struggles as a single working mother, Dr. Cohen reports having had to temper her professional expectations:

> I have a number of friends who stayed single, didn't have children, and have been single-minded about their careers; they've been able to accomplish a lot. The choices I made . . . the fact that my path to where I am now wasn't as straight as the paths of the guys who were my contemporaries, and not the paths of a lot of the women . . . I work with now, who went straight through, all these things combined means that I had to temper my expectations.

Now Dr. Cohen says she has "a dream job" and is married to a man with whom she was able to craft a life she thoroughly enjoys. She sounds as if she has finally "arrived."

Unbearable Costs: "It Is Possible . . . to Just Give Up"

Dr. Witherspoon at Private Comprehensive University does not draw happy conclusions now that she is at the end of her career. "I would never do this again," she says simply, and "I'm just waiting to retire." The fifty-seven-year-old full professor has been on the faculty of her university for almost thirty years; she is married and has a grown daughter. Up until three years ago, she felt she could have both a satisfying career and a fulfilling personal life. Three years ago, everything changed. Her eighteen-year-old son committed suicide.

Before that, Dr. Witherspoon recounts feeling very proud of her ability to manage and balance things, and her students thought of her as a model for the possibility of having both a family and a career. At age seven, she had already thought about becoming an "efficiency expert" because she loved multitasking and seeing how many things she could cram into an hour, "and never watch TV without a book open and six things going on." Yet life was difficult.

In her third year on the tenure-track she got pregnant with her daughter but did not feel as if the university environment would be supportive of her. So she hid her pregnancy.

> Back in those days, 1980, 1981, I didn't feel that pregnancies were necessarily welcome, and I wasn't going to take a chance of letting it interfere with tenure. I was very fortunate because I didn't show until June, and my daughter was born in late August. So, nobody even knew I was pregnant. . . . She was born August 12th, and I was back here at work the final week of August. Needless to say, I didn't breastfeed her any longer than the first couple of weeks. She remained pretty invisible here on campus. . . . That gives you an idea how I fit into the women in academics chronology.

Dr. Witherspoon tells the story of a colleague who was not so lucky. An Ivy League graduate, "she was very, very good," but became pregnant the same year Dr. Witherspoon had her second child. Although Dr. Witherspoon's department was supportive of her, the colleague's department did not react favorably to the woman's pregnancy:

And they literally told her they never wanted to see any kids around the office; and they were very upset, and she was denied tenure. That was the atmosphere at that time that I was afraid of.

Once her kids were born, Dr. Witherspoon continued to struggle. Her home is one hundred miles away, door-to-door, and for many years she has had to manage a grueling commute through dense traffic. Looking back, it was hard, she says. She worked all the time, dropping one by one all the things that could be dropped, "paring back my life to bare bones."

Her life was compartmentalized geographically, which made it difficult to have friends at work or at home. She was cut off from the network of women in her neighborhood, and unable to have friends where she lives because "there wasn't any time." She had no personal life, no hobbies or loves of her own, and was "just working around the clock." She recounts how she stopped reading the paper in the mornings, adopted a low-maintenance hairstyle, paid no attention to how she dressed, never put on jewelry. The description of her life resembles the description of a race:

> Bare bones. Get the kids in the car seat, and off to child care, and race the hundred miles down here, and race through my day here. I seldom took time out to have lunch with anyone because I was eating yogurt at my desk while I talked to former students. It was the feeling of the juggler of having a dozen balls in the air at one time. Everything was on high speed. I remember one of my colleagues saying to me early on that I never had the time to smell the roses; that was true. . . . My husband accuses me of being a workaholic, but that is not really true. It just was the only way to do it. I loved both things, both family and college teaching; and I was an absolutely determined person to hold on to both.

Dr. Witherspoon describes in detail how much she was invested in her work; she loved teaching and learning, loved the feeling of competence when classes went well, the feeling of her mind continuing to grow. Clearly, she was also a devoted mother, and tried to manage both. But her son's suicide changed her perspective entirely and, in retrospect, she would do things differently. "I would have left academics when my daughter was born," she says, but perhaps she would have considered teaching high school. "I really did love to teach," she says, but that has changed since her son's death, and now she is just waiting to retire and does not "intend to keep my hand in it at all."

Dr. Witherspoon tells the story of her children. They were both highly talented and promising young people. Her son, for example, is described as "the perfect kid. . . . Cute, loveable, outgoing, empathetic, compassionate, had zillions of friends, popular, straight 'A' student, a fine athlete. Perfect eyesight, the only one in our family. He was everything." What nobody knew was that he suffered from severe depression, an illness running in Dr. Witherspoon's family. During the course of her life, Dr. Witherspoon herself went through several bouts of it, but eventually she was successfully treated. She says she went from "a world without colors to feeling normal," a state that continued for a long time. When her son left for college, she even felt she was "on cloud nine." She had two wonderful kids, both enrolled in good schools, and "everything looked as if I had arrived at everything I had worked for. I told [my husband], I was so happy. It was so easy to balance that year because suddenly we were empty-nesters. . . . I was on top of the world." Shortly thereafter, she received a phone call from her son's college informing her that he had taken his own life.

Prior to his death, as a college student, Dr. Witherspoon's twenty-five-year-old daughter was also diagnosed with depression and anxiety disorder, among other things, and she has been hospitalized and medically withdrawn from school several times since. The young woman went from a "tremendously successful person to being someone who feels like a complete failure," Dr. Witherspoon says, and "we have no assurance that she will ever have a job because she needs to sleep very long hours, and she is up and down with all of the medications she takes." Perhaps because of his sister's medical problems, Dr. Witherspoon's son may have felt he could not tell his parents about his own battle with depression, she speculates, but "we will never know that." Their life experiences have led Dr. Witherspoon and her husband to a complete reevaluation of what is possible:

> So things have changed a lot for us, and our perspectives have changed, and our aspirations have, let's say, vanished. We don't see the world the same way. I think because of that I should have never become an academic, and I wouldn't do it again. Of course, I don't burden students with all of this, but when I talk to students about career choices, I don't take an optimistic, chipper, naïve approach of "sure you can do it now, and there's a lot more support now too." I think the costs are too high, and I don't say that to them. I just tell them, that it is very difficult to do everything, and there are always costs, and each person has to weigh those things very carefully herself or himself, because I think that is true for men too. Frankly, if you want to know how I feel, I think academics takes a 24/7 [commitment] unless you are at a very small college where there are no research demands, and you can live locally. . . . I just think it's hard to do everything. I guess I'm not sure anymore that it is good for kids to have mothers that work, which is odd for me.

At this point in her life, Dr. Witherspoon is determined to fulfill her remaining obligations to the university but, in general, she just wants peace. "I don't want to have to cope anymore," she says, "I'm really tired. It is possible for women like me who are extremely intense and not willing to give up anything, and who are just determined that they are going to fight the whole world, to finally just give up. That is where I am."

In conclusion, late-career faculty in this study may have been successful in their careers, but their testimony reveals a shadow side to their accomplishments. In some instances, they feel regrets about the compromises they needed to make, either in terms of their career paths, family size, or quality of time spent with important people in their lives. In other cases, the sacrifices were more profound, even leading to the conclusions that an academic career was the wrong thing to choose and, despite heroic efforts, trying to have it all, careers and families, comes with horrendous costs.

What these stories have in common, certainly, is that they shed light on why women continue to be underrepresented in the higher ranks of academe, in general, and in prestigious institutions, in particular. As feminist scholar Judith Glazer-Raymo observes, "the more prestigious the university, the fewer the women faculty" and "[w]omen remain mired in assistant professor, lecturer, and instructor slots, but men dominate in full and associate professor ranks" (Glazer-Raymo, 1999, p. 196). The costs and sacrifices academe demands of those who aspire to be successful *and* fully engaged in rich personal lives may simply be too high.

About Pioneers and Outsiders: "Nobody Is Going to Give a Five-Year Grant to a Seventy-Five-Year-Old Woman"

Dr. Amici has spent fifty of her seventy-five years as a scholar in her field. She holds a full professorship at Metropolitan University, but her native country is Italy, where she received her Ph.D. at age twenty-five, having skipped several grades in high school during World War II. She worked in places that were at the top of her field at the time, such as Oxford University and the University of

Milano. In 1960, she met an American scientist at an international conference. They got married, and she emigrated to the United States in 1961, where her husband had a university appointment. She was thirty-one years old.

"At that time, there were no women in [my field] in the United States," Dr. Amici says. "There were some in Europe, because Europe was about twenty to twenty-five years ahead of the United States in so-called women's rights." She was completely ignored, she recalls, and yet she wanted to keep working. So for fourteen years she worked as an unpaid post-doctorate at her husband's institution, doing research and helping him. She worked essentially full-time, she says, but she did not have an academic appointment. The couple wrote books together that gained national recognition, but she was never granted a position at the university. When their youngest child was about two years old, Dr. Amici's husband intervened. She remembers:

> My husband said if you wait any longer, it will be too late for you to start a career again. So, he said, I will spread the word, because he was very well known, that I will move if they give you a position. So he was willing to give up his very well established situation so that I could get a chance. He did get offered an endowed chair at a university, and they offered me a position as a full professor, because I was qualified. Even though I had stopped working, I had papers published and books written.

The couple moved and stayed at the new university for a few years before her husband, fifteen years her senior, retired. Then she took a position at Metropolitan where Dr. Amici continued her work for another twenty-five years. Her husband died a year ago, leaving behind his wife and three grown children.

The scholar talks about times past when she worked in her profession and had children at home. Not possessing an academic appointment for a long time was, in one respect, an advantage because she did not have commitments to the university. And yet, she recalls that even "under these so-called easy conditions, . . . I would remember when the children were just toddlers, I would go take a shower and would get the hot water coming over me; I felt like I could just collapse. It was an exceedingly difficult time." During those days, women's rights were just entering the picture, she remembers, and several of the more traditional men were not ready to accept women in academe.

Overall, Dr. Amici says that Metropolitan University has had tremendous potential, and she is grateful to have been able to contribute to a department that has made a name for itself on both national and international levels. Referring to her current status, she says, "the department has not asked me to retire as long as I am productive, and I work very hard. I'm still happy to do my job." Dr. Amici lives alone now, and even though she does have a loving relationship with her children and visits them, "we don't live in each other's pockets."

Her scholarly field is like a person to her, Dr. Amici says, and 95 percent of her life is work "because I don't have anyone at home." Her husband had been ill for a long time, and taking care of him was demanding, especially during the last year of his life. "He needed a great deal of care," she remembers, "but did not want a full-time person taking care of him. He wanted to have his own independence, and when I asked whether he wanted to employ a full-time person, he said, I don't need to. I have a wife."

Her department was very understanding while she cared for her husband, and during the last three months of his life, "I would just come here to give classes, and except for my classes, I didn't do much of anything else. I would rush back home, or to the hospital, or back to the nursing home, whichever. Now that he's dead, I work about twelve hours a day."

Dr. Amici insists that working so hard is not entirely her choice. She has to continue to fulfill her duties, she says, or she has to retire. When I remark that working twelve hours a day seems a lot, she tells me "you don't understand."

> There is a tremendous demand for creative work with a high recognition level. At my age, I can no longer expect to have large financial support from national agencies. Some of my colleagues here have between $500,000 to $1,000,000 a year in grant money. It is almost impossible for someone my age to get such a support because it is extended in the future. They give money for a five-year grant. Nobody is going to give a five-year grant to a seventy-five- or seventy-six-year-old woman.

Financial support, she explains, is given to younger people who can progress and have years ahead of them to do successful work. This is not anything hateful, she emphasizes; it is reasonable, and she completely understands. Someone looks at the age of her degree, which she received in 1954, and thinks she is eighty years old, she says. It is not unfair, it is not strange, and so she pays for her research projects out of her own pocket. She buys the materials she needs, and pays the salaries of the people who help her. "I have a fund I put money in myself; I call it a research fund, and I pay for it myself." Though her research may not be at the same level of intensity it once was, she nevertheless wants to continue doing it; she may not be able to hire a post-doc but she can hire undergraduate students, or someone with a graduate degree rather than a Ph.D., who can work full-time. "It costs me about twenty-five or thirty thousand a year," she states, and "I will show you now what I've done the last couple of years to support my idea that I wanted to continue. We teach a course called . . . , and I wrote the book for it."

Although witnessing resources being given to younger colleagues instead of to her presents somewhat of a downside to being a seventy-five-year-old scholar in her department, Dr. Amici reiterates that she is not the future of the department; she is its past; perhaps its present, in a way, she says. Her department acknowledges that she did a good job moving it to its current state, and so she does not feel shut down because of her age. "This department is good from that viewpoint."

Her colleague Dr. Witherspoon at Private Comprehensive University is not as much at peace with having become somewhat of an outsider in her department. She is planning to retire as soon as possible without any plans for future involvement in her college. When she was hired, the teaching load was 4/4, she recounts, and the people in her department were not very research oriented. Tenure was granted "for as little as a couple of articles. We weren't expected to write a book. Some people on campus even felt at the time that research was taking away from teaching. That was the kind of environment that we had." All of that, of course, has changed dramatically and, at this point, she is convinced she needs to get out because she is pulling her department down. This is how she sees it:

> This department has hired the very top [scholars] from Harvard and Princeton and all the top schools in the last dozen years. We have a terrific department now, and I feel that I pull this department down. My research is not up to their caliber; my teaching is not up to their caliber. They live in a different world, and they are very career oriented, and they will build strong academic careers, and I admire them tremendously.

Dr. Witherspoon questions her own qualifications and doubts she is still up to par. Down the hall, her colleague Dr. D'Enbri goes beyond that. Not only does she feel she may not fit the new model of a scholar anymore, she also views it as a model not worth emulating.

Current developments at colleges and universities are not positive, according to her, and many of the changes under way she resists. One of those concerns values, and who the university wants to be, which, to her, is becoming increasingly unclear. She does not approve of the growing emphasis on research to the detriment of working with students; in fact, she says: "This whole movement of universities to less teaching and more research really scares me. . . . Especially when you think about the people who cared about you when you were a student, and how important they were to you."

The "corporatization of the university" has been critiqued by feminist scholars because, among other things, it defines "expertise and the reward system in terms of scholarly rather than pedagogical expertise" (Glazer-Raymo, 1999, p. 202). Dr. D'Enbri despises the notion that universities are to be run like businesses because one of the fallouts of the business mentality is a loss of community. To be sure, these trends are national, she acknowledges, "but it doesn't mean I like them any more." Academe's increasing accountability mentality also bothers Dr. D'Enbri a great deal. "The big thing is to have absolute numbers," she says and elaborates:

> How many publications do I have to have to get tenure? I
> must have two this year; they must be in A1 journals, you
> know. This kind of thinking isn't looking at the quality
> of the questions being asked. Instead it is whether they
> can be published in top notch journals.

She would rather have faculty be able to live a good life, serve as good role models, and be able to have intellectual exchanges and investments in students than counting how many students they have seen during the last hour. Dr. D'Enbri provides a specific example for the unfortunate trend toward increasing accountability that has changed the culture of her college, and higher education in general. The professor used to belong to a support group whose members' sole mission consisted in being around one another. Then, as younger faculty came aboard, things changed.

> They are all so into the bean counting; we had to be doing something. So we had book groups, and we had a feminist theory class, and we had these things that we did so that it counted. . . . It was productive, as opposed to just listening to each other and being able to say "oh, what a lot of crap you carry around with you, and what can I do to help you?" Which is what I get from my friends outside of the university, the ones who accept me for all my flaws. There is an atmosphere in academia that if I admit my flaws, somebody will know, and it will count against me. I don't think many people let down their guard; they can't afford to.

The support groups she once knew would be very important to younger women today, Dr. D'Enbri argues, because many of them do not see that the burdens they carry transcend disciplines and life stages. "Sometimes, just coming together and talking really helps you," she says, "to be able to do something that isn't productive, and just being, I think, is really a good thing."

All of these developments currently under way led to an increasing sense of marginalization for Dr. D'Enbri. They are barriers to her happiness, she says, "because I have to sit around and think 'am I resistant to change, and therefore, ornery, and stuck in my ways, or will there ever be a return to the kinds of things that I value?' " Certain initiatives by younger faculty went on without her consultation, she relates, despite the fact that she had once done pioneer work in that area. That, of course, contributed to her feeling like an outsider. "I've always been out of sync with anything that is going on," she says, and "I'm definitely marginalized, oh yeah." There are advantages to being marginalized, she emphasizes, "everyone leaves me alone. It's very nice. . . . I do what I want. It is really quite good."

Late-career faculty members, in summary, experience the last years of their careers in diverse ways. Some seem to "have arrived" and exude an aura of seniority and competence, cherishing the impact they continue to have on their profession. As portrayed in this section, however, other late-career faculty have slowly gravitated toward the margins. Dr. Amici's status is simply a result of her age and the associated difficulty to secure the necessary grant funding. A pioneer in her field who had to work for free as a young woman solely because of her gender, she once again finds herself literally paying the price for her desire to perform her scholarship. Whereas institutions of higher education once let her down as a woman, they now let her down because of her age. She sees the injustice of what happened in the past but is entirely at ease with the situation at present.

In other cases, scholars began to feel on the outside of their departments or universities because of value changes over time, and yet others realize that their qualifications are no longer sufficient. The latter is one of the reasons for late-career faculty to consider retirement, a topic explored in the following section. Whatever the case may be, the outsider-status of some late-career faculty is a telling cultural phenomenon, and might not occur in places in which age and experience increase rather than diminish a person's status. Flagship's professor Koshino from Japan makes that point; she says, "I come from a certain country where age is revered . . . , and the longer you stay and the longer you remain more or less successful with what you do, people finally leave you alone finding fault with you or trying to play some tricks on you."

Whatever the reason for their marginalization, it stands in contrast to how faculty members tend to describe their general state of being late in their career. In particular, it contradicts their feeling of well-being and their satisfaction with the fact that, finally, they are able to balance the different realms of their existence.

Thinking About Retirement: "I Just Hope I Know When It Is Time to Leave"

The concept of retirement is relatively new, historically speaking, and yet many people do retire nowadays, and often spend many years in retirement (Bee & Bjorklund, 2004, p. 262). It is not surprising that the topic is on the minds of quite a few late-career faculty members in this study, but how they approach the issue varies. Seventy-five-year-old Dr. Amici at Metropolitan tries to avoid being forced into retirement, even if it means paying out of her own pocket for the support necessary to keep up with younger scholars, maintain her productivity, and thus be able to do the work she loves. Dr. Witherspoon at Private Comprehensive seems to be counting the days until her retirement but knows she has certain obligations to her institution she has yet to fulfill.

> The sabbatical next year should help me finish the book. That is an obligation, of course. I have a lot of people who helped along the way, financially and academically; so I intend to finish the book. And I will owe a year to the university after the sabbatical, and then I will be qualified to retire, and unless I feel differently, then I would probably retire at that point. It wouldn't be worth it for me to do a little teaching because of the commute with the gas prices. It wouldn't pay for me.

Dr. Witherspoon is not only eager to finally retire but also feels that it had been wrong to stay in academe once she became a parent, a decision that, in her mind, cost her dearly. She had tried very hard to make it all work and pursue both a career and a family but, after her college-aged son's suicide, decided that nothing had been worth the effort, and she should have left academe after the birth of her first child.

Others felt neither as passionate about staying nor as determined about leaving as Drs. Amici and Witherspoon, respectively. Dr. Mendelas at Private Comprehensive, for instance, is calculating carefully when she might be able to retire but views the act of stepping down not just as a practical but also a moral problem. She needs to figure out not only when she *may* retire with benefits, in other words, and when she *should* retire because it would be best for the students. This is her story.

At age sixty-two, Dr. Mendelas is faced with a dilemma she did not anticipate when she left her former institution. At her current university, she says, it is irrelevant how many years of service total a scholar has invested in academe in general. What counts in order to pick up a retirement package, instead, are the years of service spent exclusively at her institution. If she were to retire at age sixty-two, she elaborates, she would not have a retirement plan. She needs to reevaluate the situation and is unsure as to what to do.

Dr. Mendelas does very much like her position; in fact, she calls it "delightful." The older she gets, the more excited she is about being able to connect to younger generations. Being able to interact with them, have the young students' respect, kid around with them, and learn from them about what is important to them in their lives, is invigorating to her. She is not sure whether there is any other job besides teaching where one can maintain that connection, she argues. "I stay here, the kids go on, but there's always a new crop coming through to learn from." She also maintains her interests outside of the academy such as playing the piano, gardening, athletics, and social interactions with people who are not part of the university. All of those things are important, she stresses, because it is not healthy to be on your job around the clock and only know people with offices on your floor. At some point, you do not have that job anymore, she says, and it is important to explore other interests. Once she retires, she is determined to avoid becoming like some people she knows.

> I have certainly known people in academia who retire, sometimes they wait too long to retire. They become less effective in their professional lives. They don't have anything else going on in their other life, so they can't imagine not coming to work every day at a university, or wherever they may be employed. So I feel very confident that I think I have the balance, so that when I do eventually leave academia, I'm not going to be sitting around twiddling my thumbs.

One of the stresses she faces at this time, she says, is to make sure not to stay in the classroom too long but "leave when it's time to leave." Her field demands that scholars constantly update, and she enjoys that, but she sees new hires coming in who perhaps very legitimately should soon take her place.

> I . . . see the new faculty coming into the department. We've made five or six hires in the last five or six years, young people at the assistant and associate level. I see how inspiring they are; they are very frisky, they're very excited to teach. I see myself moving out of that. So, one of the things I have to do for sure is make sure I don't stay too long in the classroom, regardless of what happens with health insurance and all that other stuff. I have to leave when it's time to leave; so that's one of the stresses I'm facing right now. It has nothing to do with anyone else deciding when that time is because I do not want to be here unless I'm being as effective as I've been in the past. As you know, being a professor, nobody is going to tell you what to do in the classroom.

You have to make those judgments, and I just hope I know when it is time to leave.

Dr. Mendelas emphasizes that it is easy to stay and "collect that big paycheck." But, she says, that is neither fair to the university, the department, nor the students.

Dr. Witherspoon at Private Comprehensive shares the fear of no longer being good enough. Her institution has changed totally, she says, "its aspirations are sky high." She observes faculty coming up for tenure, "and they are extraordinary. I don't think you could get any better classes at Williams or Amherst or Yale or Harvard." She, herself, used to get extremely high teaching evaluations for many years, but now the students "have a whole different yard stick for comparison. . . . I never had aspirations to be at these heights." For her, it is simply time to retire, and so she sums up her feelings: "Ten years ago, I myself was eager to see some of the dead wood retire; I would be unrealistic to read things differently."

Retirement poses yet different questions for Ms. Monet at Community College. Her concern is less how or when to leave her position than what her life will look like once she does. For one, she witnesses her husband's health declining and is worried that the couple may not be able to find activities they will both enjoy during retirement:

> This year, my husband has had some health issues. I see him not being as interested in doing some travel or getting involved in, let's take some dance lessons, doing things. Now that we're empty-nesters, we have to rediscover each other. We need to find some activities that we can plan for retirement. For example, a couple at church talked about getting into fly-fishing, so they're both taking lessons and learning. This is their goal when they retire. I've mentioned some of those

things to my husband, but he . . . doesn't find the energy
for it.

She has a list of things lined up for herself to do during
retirement, she says, but worries about her companion. He is sixty
years old, has had a new job for only three years, and is apprehensive
about what would happen were he to lose his job again. In that
case, she may have to work longer, and that, too, worries her
because "what is he going to do down the road? I'm not going to
run out and do all these activities or try to get involved in things
and leave him home alone."

In addition to her insecurities about her husband's role in her
retirement, Ms. Monet is unsure about what kind of a retiree,
exactly, she will be. "Are you going to become one of those adjunct
teachers, or are you going to become one of those who turn their
backs on teaching?" she asks herself. She has given a lot of thought
to the profession lately, she says, and wonders: "What are you
going to do when you retire?" One of the defining factors, she
knows, is money. If she is financially needy she will teach as an
adjunct professor because "to be an adjunct is probably the best
money I can get." At the same time, though, she always wanted to
engage in adult basic education and may do so as a volunteer. At
this point, she does not seem entirely decided.

Sixty-five-year-old Dr. Wiley, in comparison, has been able to
craft her life as a retiree in ways she thoroughly enjoys. After a long
career as a faculty member at Metropolitan University, she had
left the university to assume administrative work at a university
out-of-state. Recently she retired from that job and moved back
home, assuming part-time employment at Metropolitan.

She stays involved in higher education because of her own
interest in it but without feeling responsible for it. Though she
used to merge the personal and professional aspects of her life
when she was employed full-time at her previous university
out-of-state, she now keeps the two realms much more separate. Her

personal friends used to be the ones associated with the university, but now they are not. Dr. Wiley still teaches a few classes for the university and engages in some consulting work, but everything is done on her terms. She also enjoys her family and various pastimes. In addition to her sporadic professional activities, in short, she is "thoroughly enjoying other things."

In conclusion, many late-career stage faculty in this study tend to think about retirement, yet it is worth mentioning that not *all* of them do. Some scholars seem to continue to be engulfed in their work, and did not mention the topic of retirement much in our conversations. The oldest participant in the study, Dr. Amici, even actively fought it.

Higher education faculty are unique in that their profession does not mandate retirement at a certain age. Institutions may entice faculty to consider attractive retirement packages, but they typically do not force them out of their jobs simply because of their age. Faculty are therefore able to decide for themselves how they wish to design their "golden years." Naturally, these designs differ widely according to myriad factors such as personality, financial means, life partners, family constellations, and the occurrence of traumatic life events, to name a few. Some faculty members cannot wait to get out of academe and are preoccupied with strategizing about how to work out the logistics. Others seek to exit gradually, with some adjunct teaching or consulting work during the transition. Although some tend to be primarily concerned about their own needs, others also consider obligations they have to the institution and the profession at-large. Along similar lines, several of the women in this study appear convinced that they continue to have a lot to give to their students and their field, but some colleagues are beginning to consider themselves "deadwood," unable to offer the profession all that their younger colleagues do. Be that as it may, retirement happens for most academics at some point, and for the women in this study it tends to conclude rich careers and fascinating professional histories.

Making It Work and Dealing with It: Enablers and Coping Strategies

Late-career female faculty possess a plethora of experiences that have translated into a rich arsenal of coping strategies. Over time, they have also benefited from myriad enabling conditions aiding them in their quest to establish balance between their personal and professional lives. Their accounts speak to both enabling conditions and coping strategies of the past and the present. The following section is structured accordingly.

Past Enablers: "The Flexibility"

Late-career faculty mention many people who served as enablers in the past. Some are significant others and family members; others are intimately connected to the family. Dr. Amici, for instance, raves about the full-time babysitter who helped her and her husband raise their three children for thirteen years. "She was so wonderful, intelligent, and caring that I owe to her about half of the success that I've had in raising my children." Ms. Monet looks back at the time her children were still at home, and she had a housekeeper who enabled her to have more free time and do things with the family.

HBCU's Dr. Marx talks about her son and how, as a mother, she felt she was actually better balanced in the past than she is today because she had to focus on somebody else. She engaged in activities with her extended family, her sisters, and their families, who also kept her son while she was in the library on weekends.

Dr. Noah remembers how her supportive husband was a major enabler to her. In addition, she mentions an enabler that is often seen as a disadvantage for women, namely nonlinear career paths. She explains that she was working in the field rather than academe when she had her children, and that was a distinct advantage because she was able to focus on her family once she was at home rather than having to extend her professional obligations into her personal life. This is how she sees it:

I always say, when you work in the field, when you're done, you can come home. As an educator, you're never done. So you're bringing work home to grade, work to read; you're writing lesson plans, you're making tests. . . . So I would say the big difference is being in the clinical setting as a provider, unless you're taking call, . . . when you're done, you can come home.

Mid-career faculty member Dr. Seidman at Flagship University expresses a similar sentiment. She, too, finds having taken a nonlinear career path inherently enabling. Nonlinear career paths mean, according to her, that you enter academe not only at a later age but, more important, with more life experience than someone on a traditional path. She did exactly that, and began her career as a faculty member eight years ago after many years as a K–12 educator. She is fifty-seven years old, and perceives herself as having a "balcony view" of her job. She is now better able to prioritize and "blow off" some of the things that might be major stressors and disablers for her more traditionally aged peers. She elaborates:

For example, worrying about annual reports and not getting a maximum raise. . . . I think I'm able to look at criticism more constructively than destructively. I think that's a result of where I am in my life, both professionally and personally. The daily details now aren't big priorities for me. I'm able when I finally leave my job, if I haven't done all my e-mail for the day, or I have a phone call that I didn't return, I know that it's not going to stop the world. If I get a paper rejected from a journal, I know that there's another journal out there. It's just a question of trying again. I really don't let little things tax me as much as they did when I was first beginning.

As a student she was older than many of her professors, she says, giving her a certain confidence she would not have had at a younger age, and a certain sense of humor. She elaborates on the "balcony view of her job":

> In order to climb the steps to get to the balcony you have to have certain successes and probably certain failures along the way. You can look at those constructively and with a sense of humor and say: "Oh well, I'm not perfect, but I'm not going to take a step down either. I'm just going to keep on going." I'm fifty-seven, and I'm still learning it every day, how to do that. I'm much happier, much more productive, when I keep the little things the little things. . . . I finally realized the academy may or may not validate you in what you do. You have to find your own validation. . . . It's OK not to be successful in one area, because life is too short to be unhappy. Either in your personal or professional life.

Sixty-seven-year-old, retired professor Wiley looks back at a nonlinear career path as well, due, mostly, to being a single mother. Although she does not comment on whether or not her career path was inherently enabling, she recounts many enablers that helped her along the way. This is her story.

When Dr. Wiley was in high school, she always wanted to go into journalism. The only place nearby to study journalism at the time, however, was a large university, and when she visited its campus, she was daunted. "I was a kid from a small town in middle Wisconsin, and it was just so overwhelming; it was so big." So she went to a small liberal arts college instead, and was very comfortable there. At age eighteen, she fell in love, got married, became an English teacher, and then worked for a publishing company. She put her husband through medical school but he left her after he finished his internship. Their baby was eighteen months old at the time, and Dr. Wiley's journey as a single professional began.

She moved back to her hometown so her parents could take care of the baby, and began graduate school, which, she explains, was highly unusual for a woman at that time. "Being born in 1940 is different," Dr. Wiley says. "When I look at my friends that I had in college, very bright women, and very academic, and very accomplished, nobody went to graduate school. It wasn't something we thought about." And yet she did, commenting that "most of what I had done hadn't occurred to me before I did it." Not only did she get a master's degree but also a doctorate, enabled by her parents and later a supportive environment with married students who had children. One of the things that helped her also, she said, was that "there were always people around, and none of us needed anything. I mean our social night was Saturday night at someone else's apartment, and you brought your own popcorn." Wives of other doctoral students were happy to baby-sit, she remembers, and it all worked out well.

Her support network continued to grow beyond graduate school. When she received her first faculty appointment, a friend moved in with her and helped her raise her child.

> I was talking to my friend who was very depressed about where she was and what she was doing. In fact, she was in a PS some number in the Bronx, and it was a very difficult environment, and I said "I know they're looking for teachers; would you consider coming to [my town]?" She applied and got the job late in the summer, and she came down here, and I had a small house, and the intention was that she would move in with me for a month or so until she got acclimated. . . . Well, we got along so well. . . . She didn't leave for four years.
>
> . . . It was absolutely wonderful because she liked her job, she liked [the city], she fell in love with my kid, and

she took responsibility. . . . We shared the experience of living almost as if we were a couple of some sort. It wasn't designed that way, and we weren't, but she loved being with my son, he loved being with her. She took responsibility for cleaning the house and cutting the grass as much as I did. It was a wonderful sharing, and this was the first four years I was an assistant professor.

Dr. Wiley served as a faculty member for seventeen years, being a single mother the entire time. She was approached frequently with questions as to whether she would consider moving into administrative positions, but repeatedly decided against it. A major reason was the flexibility she enjoyed as a faculty member, something she experienced as a major enabler. She remembers:

People approached me about administration, saying "have you considered, have you thought about it," and every time I said "I thought about it, and I think sometime I would like to do that, but I'm not doing that until my child is out of school because I want the flexibility.

Once her child was grown, Dr. Wiley got married and became a successful university administrator. She remembers an extremely supportive environment as her main enabler when she faced new challenges; she had breast cancer and her husband died unexpectedly. Through all of this, she kept working the whole time.

I had a provost and a circle of deans who were incredibly supportive. The provost put a spider communication thing on his desk, and the deans' meetings I went to even if I were in bed. . . . I knew these people so well, I could do that because I knew who was speaking. I knew what their agendas were, and I knew what to expect from them. And they were all very supportive of me. Both through cancer and through my husband's death, that community was what made me whole.

Her support staff, too, was extremely cooperative, she recalled, and helped her so that she would not have to deal with certain business related things. "I didn't have any trouble delegating," she remembers. "I trusted them." Dr. Wiley calls herself "incredibly lucky," but when I say, "It had something to do with you, too," she responds, "I don't deny that it did."

Dr. Beseley at HBCU echoes the sentiment. "I've been fortunate," she says, "because at all the places that I have taught, I have had people who understood. I'm not sure what the university policies were, in terms of what was written down. But I've always worked at places, taught at places where the department chair, the dean, or other people understood other obligations that I had. So I didn't have a time when there was some demand placed on me that was in conflict with what I needed to do at home."

Individual administrators were enabling for Dr. Velvarde's career, who describes her dean as "really believing in family." What impresses Dr. Velvarde so much is how her dean models an understanding that "there is life beyond this university." The administrator herself had disappeared one day because her brother was ill, and she felt the need to be with him. Likewise, Dr. Velvarde's mother got very ill one day and, on top of that, was concerned that her daughter might lose her job because of the many emergency trips she took to be with her. So Dr. Velvarde sent an e-mail to the dean, who responded: "Tell your mother I believe you. Why would you need to be here; just telecommute."

Along similar lines, Flagship's Dr. Kasper calls her former department chair a "major enabler."

A woman. I could always pick up the phone and say "these people are pissing me off," and that was that.

That was fine. And we had a deal; we could come to each other's offices that way. The deal was you could just walk in and say "so and so . . . ", and then she didn't have to say anything. I could just close the door and go back out. She retired but . . . I talk to her frequently. As I was moving up the career ladder, "what shall I do? So and so did this, how should I approach this?" Somebody to talk it through so that I could then present myself and be confident about how I was presenting myself. Without having to rely on the guys for advice, major enabler.

Out-of-towner Dr. Witherspoon at Private Comprehensive talks about an enabling department that helped her schedule her classes during three days of the week so she did not have to commute every day and could do part of her work at home, and Dr. Posan remembers a wonderful mentor program at a previous university that supports incoming women faculty. Junior faculty are paired up with senior colleagues, typically from another department or college. In addition, the institution provides grants for women to do research or creative projects. She describes the project simply as "very critical in the early 1990s when I was getting back into academia."

In addition to enabling conditions, late-career faculty members in this study remember strategies they employed to deal with their lives in the past.

Past Coping Strategies: "I Have a Very High Pain Tolerance"

"It wasn't a matter of coping or not coping, I think I just felt this is what I had to do," says Ms. Saltmarsh at Community College about her younger days. "If I wanted to have a somewhat successful professional life, and be a somewhat successful mother, I had to have a very high pain tolerance." Thinking back over her thirty-some years in the profession, she reaches the conclusion that most times she did not have time to think about coping. Her attitude was simply, "I just had to do it," but, fortunately, "it takes a lot to get me rattled or for me to have a meltdown." What she did do, however, when things were hectic, was "go to a quiet place" when the kids were in bed. "Maybe I had to grade papers, who knows, but still just being by myself." She also liked to spend time with friends, and doing "fun things." In order to cope, Metropolitan's Dr. Velvarde learned a strategy during her doctoral program.

> My son was four years old. And I would try to lie down with him; he was the kind of kid who wanted someone to lie in bed with him while he fell asleep. So I'd lie down with him, he'd fall asleep, I'd get up, and I'd be a zombie. So I started going to bed at 7:00 when he went to bed. And I got up at 1:00 or 2:00 in the morning, and I worked from 1:00 to 6:00 or 2:00 to 6:00. Even the dogs slept. No one would bother me, and I had my time alone.

Community College's Ms. Saltmarsh mentioned the design of her schedule as a coping strategy. Because she performs administrative functions, her teaching load is relatively light, something that allowed her in the past to participate in many of her children's activities.

> I had to do work at night sometimes that I could've done during the day. When [the children] were small I would teach night classes, so I could be home during the day, so my husband could watch the children at night. I purposefully arranged my schedule so I could have as much time with my children.

Dr. Cohen at Flagship thinks back to her coping strategies when she was a single mother, trying to juggle her professional obligations and raise her child. "I learned that things work really well when you have a whole routine down," she says, and "whenever one element of that routine changes, you've got to engineer it all over again." She remembers having a reserve of strength she tapped into a number of times. "I ended up feeling I had a really good life," she concluded, "very rich. I loved my friends. I had a good supportive environment where we were living." Neighbors functioned as surrogate grandparents to her son, and as parents to her. She had a good church community; so the only thing that was missing was a partner for her. Friends recommended she should move to a bigger city so she could meet a lot of people, but she had her own way of coping.

I thought, "Why would I do that when my son is in a good place? I'm in a good place, I have great job. Why would I pack up everything on the off-chance that I might meet some really great person? For several years, I just thought, 'This is just the way my life is. It's full enough; it could be better, but OK.' Once I met [my husband], my life got all the way good."

Despite the fact that quite a few of the enablers and coping strategies described here persisted over time, late-career faculty members also went through change and encountered new conditions. Accordingly, they found new enablers and developed new coping strategies "to deal with it all."

Present Enablers: "Experience Is a Big Enabler"

One of the enablers late-career faculty in this study mention is what they don't have and do, or no longer have and do. Ms. Saltmarsh at Community College responds to the question as to what helps her balance with these words: "Today is actually pretty easy. Not having the children at home. I don't do the kinds of things I used to do. I don't cook like I used to cook. I'm not as much of a mother today." Her colleague Ms. Monet sounds similar when she says, "For many years I got by on five hours of sleep. . . . I don't have to do that now because the children are not around." Dr. Koshino at Flagship says she has no children, and because her husband is very like minded and compatible, she can more or less successfully balance her life. She remarks that her personal life is so positive, it does not invade her professional life. Dr. Noah at HBCU also employs a negative definition of enablers: "For me, by everyone being grown and me not having a spouse, that has enabled me to make decisions independent of what somebody else would want you to say or do. . . . Because my children are grown, and my husband is deceased, I have control over my life in comparison to someone who perhaps does not."

"Experience is a big enabler," insists Flagship's Dr. Kasper, and she explains how knowledge and know-how have accumulated. It sometimes surprises her, she says, that she "just sort of knows" how to do things she did not know how to do when she was younger. And knowing who you are makes things easier, too. "When you're young, kids and career, you sort of struggle for your identity."

Significant others and family members are also identified as enablers. Dr. Beseley at HBCU lists her family as a "big coping strategy" because she is close to her brothers, sisters, parents, and daughter. Dr. Marx at HBCU mentions her sisters, extended family members, and friends as enabling, and she talks about her adult son who helps her create a balance between her personal and professional lives. This is what he does:

> He decided, "Mom, you're working too hard. This isn't working for you." He got a sheet, and wrote things to say "no" to, things to say "yes" to. . . . He would give me motivational speeches. I should tell you he's a doctor. "What are you doing today?" On the weekend, he would say "Are you working? Please leave it and come out, and let's have lunch." That kind of thing. He really helped me.

Dr. Koshino describes herself as very fortunate; her husband and she work so well together, she emphasizes; they carpool, he serves as her courier in case students need to get something to her, and he is generally of enormous help. Dr. Posen at Metropolitan talks about her husband in similar terms and, all in all, describes him as an enabler to her. He takes care of things at home, she says, doing errands, shopping, and cooking, thus enabling her to focus on her work and get more of it done. Yet he moved to town reluctantly when she accepted her position, and is still resistant about being here, she says. "That lack of enthusiasm or negative attitude on the part of a spouse or partner about what you are doing when you are getting an academic job, can be a real liability, on many levels."

Dr. Kasper at Flagship mentions a husband who "now instead of being a support with the kids is not as demanding. He is OK with me going all over the world. That's an enabler." In regard to housework, she notices an interesting irony:

> He does his share of housework; it's sort of ironic. You struggle over it with kids, and by the time the kids are gone, you worked it out. So he now routinely does the laundry and changes the sheets, and all that stuff, while getting him to do that twenty years ago was really hard. Of course, it's easier now because it's only the two of us.

Another enabler is making enough money to hire someone to clean the house, to do this and that, she says, and yet here lurks another irony. "When you've got the kids and the job you're also not making as much money, the money that helps make your life easier."

Further enablers mentioned are support groups and close friends who work in the same field, as well as collegiality among faculty and staff. The support of women was highlighted, especially. Dr. Beseley at HBCU believes that it "is important for women to become part of a community. . . . to have some sister circles, and for women to mentor women." Women tend to form communities, she says, and her community of female teachers, professors, and students help each other. This is how it works:

> We do support each other, and that I think has been one of the greatest things to go on. As a matter of fact, you heard the phone ring a few minutes ago. That was one of the people that I talk to probably three or four times a week, to say "how is it going, what's going on?" There are probably four or five other professors; we get together for lunch, we talk in the afternoon. We are able to cope that way. It helps having a community of people.

Dr. Beseley finds the academic community can become very alienating for women because of its supervisory and administrative nature, male orientation, and male domination. It can become stressful. Therefore, she says:

> One thing I try to do, since I have been doing this for about thirty years, I really try to talk with . . . any new female who joins my department or close department. I make a connection with that person to say "you won't find this in the handbook, but I know that you can do this.". . . So I think sister circles are important for women.

Flagship's Dr. Kasper found that, although men have helped her as well, "having women at various points in my career is absolutely key." She interacts with female colleagues outside of academe as well, emphasizing that "having women around is very important." Twice a week, she works out with a group of women. "And when we work out we chatter, vent, and that's a major thing. Having lots of female friendships, having time to go out for lunch." Particularly enabling, she says, is a mixture of social and professional camaraderie.

Dr. Posen describes, as well, how female support helps her deal with many things, some of them particularly relevant to women of her age group, such as menopause.

> I think [menopause] is starting to have an impact on how I feel, and you do bring that to the work place. The positive thing is that our front office staff is heavily female, and there is a great relationship between the female faculty and the female staff in our department. On the whole, it is a very comfortable, friendly atmosphere. So there is that kind of sharing of those of us in our fifties with the younger women, about menopause stories, that kind of thing.... We are very close. There isn't that kind of separation between staff and faculty that you see in other departments or places. So, people bring their children in.... Children, dogs. So I think that helps, to be in a fairly positive atmosphere in the workplace.

Chronic or serious illnesses are starting to affect her age group now, she says, and her husband had lung cancer last year and surgery two weeks before classes started. That was very difficult, but because of her great support system at work she was able to get to the hospital three times a day. Epilepsy prevents her from driving but, she says, she had three different drivers every time she went. "Just enormous, enormous, support, and it was mostly from the people in the department, not my friends from outside."

When asked about institutional support during these difficult times, she replies, "beyond the department, I don't even know what that is or would be." She does not find it inconceivable, however, to obtain a more flexible schedule if she needed to in order to be able to function as a caretaker. She is also grateful for the health coverage she has, which compares favorably to her situation years ago when, as a freelancer, she had only minimal coverage and was scraping by. "Yeah, I was . . . having a great time, but fortunately I didn't get ill during that time period."

Metropolitan's Dr. Amici, who defines her life primarily around her work, also sees her department as enabling. She describes it as "absolutely wonderful to me. It has given me all the support and all of the acknowledgment that I needed to feel fulfilled, and all of the opportunities to do the things I wanted to do." Ms. Monet at Community College credits her department as an enabler as well; during the times she had to take care of her aging parents out-of-state and miss several days of teaching, her colleagues covered for her so classes did not have to be cancelled. Software that enables her to craft assignments online is also helpful, she says, when you cannot physically be present in class. The same point made was made by others, who mentioned Blackberries, e-mail, and technology in general as enabling faculty to do work independent of place. Furthermore, Ms. Monet is grateful she is in charge of designing the teaching schedule in her department; and while its creation involves all faculty, she is nevertheless able to largely control when her own classes take place. That, in turn, allows her to carve out blocks of time dedicated to the care of her elderly parents.

Although late-career faculty certainly mentioned many enabling conditions, much is up to them. They had to develop coping strategies to deal with the aspects of their lives that were not, in and of themselves, enabling.

Present Coping Strategies: "I Reinvent My Courses to Reinvent Myself"

Dr. Kasper at Flagship finds it difficult to talk about or even think about obstacles that are in her way of establishing a healthy balance in her life. She does not think, she says, that the world ought to be structured in a certain way and then complain about it when she finds that it is not. "I know lots of people complain about the way it is, but I don't think that way," she says. "I just try to be strategic given the way it is." This section addresses strategies like hers.

Late-career faculty cope in practical ways. HBCU's Dr. Beseley likes to read and practice positive affirmations. Her colleague Dr. Noah parks far away from her building and walks to work and up the stairs. Dr. Marx at HBCU gets up from her desk and walks every few minutes to rest her eyes. She and others exercise, go to church, explore the state, talk on the phone, read, and take care of their health.

Dr. Koshino at Flagship tries to maintain good working relationships with her colleagues to prevent trouble. For the sake of her personal balance, she treats herself to massages and tries to take care of her body and her mind. She also keeps her office clean, she says, and does all sorts of practical things to balance. It seems as if she copes by controlling those things she can, because she mentions that "there are some things there is nothing you can do to change."

Travel is listed as a strategy to get away and remove oneself for a while. HBCU's Dr. Noah says, "You're always on call," and recommends that "people pull away, and just have time to yourself or your family or your spouse." Otherwise, she is afraid, one might burn out.

There is talk about surrounding yourself with family and people at work you know are not going to pass judgment but are available to talk things through. Ms. Monet has more free time at home now that her children are grown, and uses it to be with her husband. In addition she likes to cherish an hour or so every day that is just hers alone, whether it is to watch TV or read a book or paint her fingernails. "I've noticed that if I have a day when I don't have that hour, I'm cranky and crappy the next day." She also copes by keeping her personal and professional lives separate in the sense that she devotes weekends largely to personal activities, and keeps the week free of housework.

Private Comprehensive University's Dr. D'Embry considers herself "a great coper." She copes best in crisis, she says, and "I just do what I have to do." She cites a psychologist who states that home and family are always seen as being in conflict when, in fact, conflicts arise *within* these realms as well. Conflicts at work, conflicts at home, and "so you choose whatever is most pressing at the moment." She has been accused of putting out fires rather than anticipating them, she says. "But at least you put them out," I respond. "Yes," she says, "I generally can put them out." She is also very good at a lot of other psychological mechanisms, she explains, "like denial. This is not happening to me. I'm very good at that. I excel at that." In addition, she is learning to take care of herself; she goes to the gym and gets massages and manicures. "I take care of me first. Always," she concludes.

Some coping strategies are entirely focused on the self and derive from individual strengths. Retired Dr. Wiley, for instance, has never been bothered by breaks in attention, she says, and she does not have to close the door to get something done. She can be distracted from what she is doing, and yet come right back to it without difficulty. "I am well organized mentally," she says and elaborates:

> I work very fast, I write very fast, and I've known that since I was in graduate school. I had several professors who said "you really turn it out in a hurry.". . . I love to collaborate and can divide things up and can say "you take this, and you take this, and you take this," and we'll get it all back together again and put it together. I'm always the one done first. Always the first one finished. So, I think that kind of personality helps. I work well under deadlines, and I've never missed a deadline. In fact, when I was writing the textbook that I wrote, the publisher jokingly asked, "Can we hire you to go around

and teach faculty how to write books?" Because I never missed a deadline, and I always had it on time, and I always did what I said I was going to do. . . . Deadlines are important to me. I'm never late either. If there is an appointment, I'm there. I think that was my mother's teaching. You were never late for anything.

Dr. Wiley served not only as a faculty member but also as university administrator for many years and recalls that "getting the right people around me in the office was incredibly important." She needed to work with people in such a way that they could arrive at consensus about most things, she says, and have fun with them at the same time. She wonders whether she is "a Pollyanna by nature" because she tends to gravitate toward people who support her. "And I want to support them, and feel supported by them. When there are folks who are incredibly difficult to deal with, I tend to ignore them. Unless I absolutely have to interact; then I find a way to do that as minimally as possible."

An essential coping strategy late-career faculty learned over time, and continue to use, consists of making choices and setting priorities as to what they are willing and not willing to do. Ms. Ketzel at Community College mentions, as many participants before her, how difficult it is for women to say "no," something she learned to do when her son was young. "I've learned how to turn down things that are flattering when I think about them, and think this is just going to be more stress," she says.

"A bit of a maverick" is what Private Comprehensive University's Dr. Mendelas calls herself, and this is why:

I have always felt that everyone, while they are in the work part of their lives, should devote 100 percent of their energy to do that, whatever their expectations are, in the classroom, the research sphere, community service. However, I have never been a person to do things just because the administration said I should do them. I make a judgment for what I think is 100 percent, for me. I do that, and then I go home, or to the gym, or whatever. . . . I'm willing to take whatever penalty the external sources might impose on me for that behavior. Actually, I've not had any penalties imposed on me. For that reason, I think it is possible to achieve a balance, but you've got to know what you want that balance to be, not have somebody else tell you what it is going to be.

Dr. Cohen at Flagship sets physical boundaries and maximizes her time at home. Over the last few years she set herself a schedule that allows her not to come into the office until about ten-thirty in the morning. This is how she sees it:

I love the house. There's a lot of glass; it looks outside. I'm there with the cats, and I can putter in the kitchen while I'm working. It gives me more time at home, and I can go out and walk and do some things. I don't like feeling that home is where you show up at eight P.M. at night.

She also enjoys travel with her husband and, once again, arranges her schedule in order to be able to do so as much as possible. "Often we see more of each other if we're on the road together," she says.

Late-career faculty do not only insist that others accept their choices and limits; they have also learned to accept many things themselves. "Well, I would say accepting the situation the way it is," responds Dr. D'Enbri at Private Comprehensive to my question as to what helps her establish a balance in her life she just described in positive terms. She now accepts her children the way they are, although she admits to feeling a twinge because "they are not perfect children," and will never be academic, intellectual, or achieving the way their mother is. In addition, Dr. D'Enbri has learned to accept herself.

> I think there is also just an acceptance of me. That I am who I am. I always knew that but I think I used to feel a lot more cocky about it. Then I went through a very insecure period about it, and now it is "que sera"; it is the way I am. . . . It is wonderful. I realize that I talk to my friends, and my sister, and my students all in the same way. I just don't change.

Always being the same person, no matter who she talks to, she says, may account for what stymied her career. There is a concept in psychology called self-monitoring, she explains, and being a low self-monitor has been very dangerous for her. Not only is she not good at playing the game, "I'm not even aware of the game most of the time." I tell her at this point during the interview that not playing games makes her authentic, to which she replies: "Maybe authentic but not well loved. . . . I can be very irritating." So she tries to find the people who like her the way she is as a person and accepts the fact that she is not a politically savvy person.

Her friends, she says, tolerate her for the way she is and love her despite her flaws. She elaborates:

> I think that with age does come, I hope for most people, some level of acceptance of things the way they are, whether it is the situation at work or the situation with children. Who you are. . . . It is not giving up. I have decided that I can't change things here. I cannot change my children. I could change me, but I probably won't. . . . There you are.

Using past experiences and learning from mistakes prove to be valuable coping strategies as well. Dr. Posan at Metropolitan, for instance, tells how she learned from mistakes she made as a very young and "very green" beginning professor. Her first job she remembers as extremely difficult because she was not prepared for the politics of academe. She left academe, worked in the practical, professional side of her field, built a reputation, and then reentered the academic world better prepared.

> I learned to pay attention to the workings of a depart-ment and the administrative relationships. . . . I learned that you have to document everything from day one of your first appointment even if it looks like it is a wonder-fully perfect situation. You may still find that you have to protect yourself. . . . It took me leaving academia for a while to do professional [work] that gave me the experience I needed to reenter academia. It gave me the credentials and professional credibility and author-ity to reenter. Having some kind of . . . notoriety; people knew me and knew my work because of the work I did outside. . . . I gained a lot of professional experience and a lot of writing experience, and it prepared me to reenter the academy. Better armed in a better place with a kind of wisdom that I think I can impart on my students; and the stories you tell your students I think will really help prepare them to be in academia.

In terms of influencing students, Dr. Mendelas at Private Com-prehensive has learned over time that the true impact on her students cannot be found in the information from the courses she teaches. Rather, it is moral in nature. "It has to do with the virtues of honesty and skills that go way beyond knowledge transfer." Therefore, she has replaced "studying for the test," and instead sends her students away with problems to solve. That, in turn, relieves pressure and stress on her. "And it's not because I'm not doing the work; it's just that the kind of work I'm doing is much different than what I used to do."

Ms. Ketzel at Community College copes by rekindling her excitement about teaching through various means. She learns new technologies and applies them, such as the development of hybrid classes that are taught partly online. Her textbook editor purchased the course from her, she says, and put it on the publisher's Website so that other faculty could use it. She likes to mentor and present at conferences, all activities that account for why she feels so "refreshed and excited about being in the classroom." She is also one of those teachers who never use the same syllabus, she says, and never use the same test. "I reinvent my courses to reinvent myself; it's always been a strategy for keeping this interesting to me."

In summary, late-career faculty members in this study recount many enabling conditions that helped them balance their lives over the span of their careers. Enablers ranged from supportive individuals—be they at work or at home—to learned life lessons and skills to such inherent features of the academic profession as flexibility and control over one's schedule. Sometimes it helped to just grow older and out of a certain phase that proved to be more stressful than the one to come.

It is significant to note, however, that in no single case were institutional policies mentioned as enablers. Flagship's Dr. Kasper sums it up:

> There is a lot of talk about institutions changing to be more friendly or comfortable for women, but it seems to me interacting with administrators and those higher-ups hasn't changed that much. . . . I think academe is a more comfortable place for me mostly because I have established myself but also because there are more women around, and also more awareness. But I can't think of many obvious structural changes that have occurred that enable me.

Even though colleagues, administrators, students, and, in some cases, special programs greatly supported the women in this study, built-in structures geared at systematically enabling faculty women were conspicuously absent. For the most part, the women managed despite university policy, not because of it.

And just as they had to fend for themselves when they were younger, trying to gain access to the profession, carve out identities, start families, and manage it all, "women of a certain age" do without institutional support now. Neither reliable policies nor an institutional culture void of ageism aid them at the end of their careers. Some women do not seem to need much support, or at least they portray images of themselves as being on top of their game, having arrived, and being in almost perfect situations that finally allow them to balance their lives, enjoy the impact on the profession they have had, and harvest the fruit of their long-term labor. Most no longer care for small children or struggle to make a name for themselves in the academy, and they generally made peace with who they have become.

Yet others are being called upon to assume new roles as care-givers, for instance for their aging parents. In addition, they face illness and impediments, either personally or occurring in their immediate families. They are dealing with marginalization and unanswered questions regarding their status in their depart-ments and their schools, regarding retirement, and, more generally, regarding their present days and their future lives. They, after all, live in a culture where age is not revered, and they are not nec-essarily cared for, despite the considerable sacrifices many of them have made to be able to contribute to higher education and to get to where they are now.

Perhaps it is at least partly due to the lack of formal support structures that these women had to be so creative in developing coping strategies that would aid them in navigating the waters of academe, which one might not call particularly stormy, but treacherous nevertheless. Of course, they also had to find ways to effectively deal with the many challenges life outside of their professional spheres would toss their way. And so they did, leaving behind incredible lessons on how to cope, how to deal with adversity, capitalize on one's strengths, and build supportive structures where there were none. Their stories teach the younger ones among us, and are testimony that we have reason to believe that things can happen against all odds. After all, the women prevailed, some having arrived in happier places than others; and they leave us touched by their memories and inspired with hope through the stories of their lives.

4

Comparisons

Women in this study speak to several issues that transcend their particular career stage. They compare themselves or their female colleagues with men, and address how men affect the balance between professional and personal lives. They speak of how previous generations compare with younger ones. And they talk about change itself, comparing the present with their past and their future.

These comparisons lend additional depth to the study as the women situate themselves in relation to others across gender and time. As observed by feminist Joan Kelly-Gadol: "The activity, power, and cultural evaluation of women simply cannot be assessed except in relational terms: by comparison and contrast with the activity, power, and cultural evaluation of men, and in relation to the institutions and social developments that shape the sexual order" (Kelly-Gadol, 1987, p. 21).

I was surprised to find that the scholars' disciplinary background did not seem to make much difference. I did not discern any trends, themes, or patterns across the diverse fields and departments the participants represent. Some of the most egregious stories of discrimination happened in a women's study department, and a School of Engineering has the most progressive policies and practices. Although male-dominated fields pose special challenges in terms of women's isolation and blatant sexism, female-dominated schools and departments are just as difficult to navigate for balance, and are not at all devoid of discriminatory behavior.

Men: "I Still Experience a Lot of Male Privilege"

"Being a female is a barrier," says HBCU's Dr. Nelson. Twenty-eight years old and with a brand-new Ph.D., she is the only woman in her department, and she feels exploited. Not only is she teaching five classes per semester, which truncates her time to engage in scholarly activities, she is also expected to do things she finds inappropriate.

> To prep everybody's lab, that's not part of my job description. . . . I told the dean; the dean said I was overreacting. . . . Every little thing like cleaning the lab, they would call me up to come up and clean up. Initially I did it because I thought I'm helping out, but after a while you go "why is it always you?" When we have the department meeting, after it's done, if they eat, they would say "Kendra, why don't you clean up?" . . . There's something wrong.

Dr. Nelson took her complaints to the provost, and will move to a different department. However, "the bad thing is, it exists everywhere," she says. "[Members of the new department] are not doing it to me, but they are doing it to the other female. . . . Whenever she wants to voice her opinion, they go 'if you don't like it, get out of the meeting.'" Though she says "it's hard, being a female," Dr. Nelson also describes how her experiences with her chauvinistic departments make her "want to be a better person, work harder, and do better than the men." She is competitive, she says, and strives to excel to prove not only to them but to herself that she can do just as much as they can. It's a shame she has to go to that extent, and she should not have to prove anything to them, she surmises, but "in this game, you kind of have to.

I don't know how it is in other fields, but I think pretty much in [her field], you're constantly fighting to prove to somebody that you're capable of doing what they do."

Dr. Nelson's experiences are not atypical in male-dominated fields, as indicated by research on women scientists and engineers. Despite the fact that the most pressing concern was identified as women's difficulty in balancing family and career, overt and subtle harassment were also found to be issues women encounter (Rosser, 2002).

Mid-career Dr. Newton at Flagship addresses similar concerns and argues that, whereas women are much more accepted now, at least in fields that are not men-dominated, they face new challenges even in those disciplines. There are males, she says, who perhaps unconsciously expect women to pick up the slack on the "service end of things." She warns "not to be flattered by that, and resist the temptation to save the day, and push back and say 'I've got to have time to get this accomplished.' And set some solid goals for the writing and the research that needs to be done." Just as Dr. Nelson describes how the environment at work makes her want to gain a competitive edge over her male colleagues to prove herself, Dr. Newton says:

> I think women outperform the men in terms of produc-
> tion, would be my guess. Currently, and if you go back
> say ten years, I think it was probably the case then too,
> that women had to do it better, faster. Just do more in
> every regard to earn their place at the table.

Dr. Newton qualifies her statement by stating that she does not feel the pressure that much anymore today, except when it comes to service related activities, "some of the scutwork that exists in higher education." She elaborates:

> It's not all about teaching and doing research, which
> is what a lot of the male colleagues see it as. There's

advising, and also doctoral committees where they
just don't take the time with the advising that's
appropriate, or with program advising. They'll send
[students] to colleagues or the admissions office and say,
"just go ask them." And not bother and try to assist.
I don't think there's a bias about being capable, but
women sometimes get sidetracked with strenuous work
that doesn't pay off.

She has no doubt that the "old boys network" continues to
exist, and "they still assist each other in access to goodies, benefits
of some nature, whatever it is." Discrimination nowadays is no
longer as explicit as it used to be in the past; it is much more
subtle, almost subconscious or subliminal. She likens it to "de
jure" versus "de facto" segregation, meaning legal segregation as
opposed to segregation by custom that happens *despite* the law. The
same is true for gender politics in higher education: "it's hard to
fight against; there are no policies or rules that you can attack. . . .
There's nothing on the books, nothing explicit that we have
to fight against like in the 1970s when people were really trying to
fight laws that prohibited women from being hired."

Many men support women, Dr. Newton says, and yet there
are some who still "subtly 'zing' women by sidetracking them into
activities that are not rewarded by the system." It is hard to put
your finger on, she says, but "guys may be better negotiators when
it comes to contracts, better at demanding higher consulting fees,
better at making sure they get teaching assignments that pay better,
better fringes, whatever. They're pretty good at working the system,
and we've got to get better at working the system. Open your eyes,
and realize what's going on." Her accounts serve as examples for
what Holden Rønnig calls the cultural barriers and entrenched
attitudes that need to be eliminated if a gender balance in power
sharing in academe is to be achieved (Holden Rønnig, 2000, p. 99).

HBCU's Associate Professor Foster would agree. According to her, male colleagues have opportunities, particularly financial ones, she is denied. Be it grant, administrative, or teaching opportunities that are financially lucrative, men are much more likely to get them, and if women do, then it is because they were able to "penetrate the old boys network by being friends with those who are the old boys."

She concludes: "there is definitely a difference between me and my male colleagues." Dr. Marx at HBCU agrees: "I really hate to say this, but if the administration is male, you have a very hard time. . . . That is an old boys network. That's a fact." Many women cope, she observes, by "adjusting to the male persona" because if you happen to offend, "you could be cut off at the knees." When she feels isolated in male-dominated environments, she copes by writing. "So I've done quite a bit of publishing because of that."

Her colleague Dr. Kohn, also at HBCU, voices similar concerns; standards are higher for women in academe, and they also get less support and less mentoring unless they mentor each other. She says about her male colleagues: "they make more money, and they have life a little easier." She recounts how she was affected by the gender wage gap, and being told that a single female does not need as much money as a male head of household. Her bitter conclusion: "Men have views of women even with doctorates that you're second class."

At the core of it all, according to Private Comprehensive's Associate Professor Pryzinski, is misogyny, and she has seen plenty of it at her institution. This is what she has to say about gendered interactions in her professional life:

> I think one of the issues of having a healthy balance
> between me as a woman, and me as a professor in the
> academy, is how, in a mundane way, at the level of

the department meeting, how men interact with me, and how I interact with them. I would just say that I still experience a lot of male privilege in those speech situations. Where men's voices just get attended to more quickly, more readily than women's. I think that does identity damage that leaks into the personal, me.

Dr. Pryzinski tells how men want to "typecast" her in a very feminine category perhaps "because I am an academic woman who does her nails, and wears low-cut shirts, and make-up, whatever, you know." It is those types of casts, she says, she is trying to navigate. "'Are you trying to put me in some kind of feminine girly category who can't speak on the same level as you, or think on the same level as you?' I experience those things on a regular basis, and I'm always sort of working to try to manage, but I'm not sure that I do a very good job." She uses humor, sometimes, to cope with situations: "So I'll make people laugh at themselves for saying things that are goofy, so it just gets deflated, 'oh, you busted me, well OK, let's talk about the schedule.'" She acknowledges, however, that her technique does not resolve the core conflict, "and the core conflict is misogyny, bias against women."

The most egregious example of misogyny Dr. Pryzinski experienced consisted of sexual harassment over a time span of six years by a senior colleague who was eventually dismissed from the university because of it. Everybody knew it, she says, it was public. It began even before she got to campus because he had interviewed her at a convention and gone back to the department arguing they needed to hire her because she reminded him of his wife when he first fell in love with her. "That was how I was introduced to the faculty," Dr. Pryzinski shudders. These are examples of the harassment she endured:

He would tell me I'm his beautiful Queen in front of students. I would come out of class, and he would be standing at the end of the hall, and he would be like "there is my beautiful Mediterranean Queen," and he would walk up to me and put his arm around me and try to give me a hug in front of my students. He was always making comments about how I reminded him of his wife; it was just creepy and gross. . . . He would break into my office, and we caught him breaking into my office. In a faculty meeting, I would make some kind of comment like "I think we need to reallocate the special topics courses because they are all going to one person, and they are never going to me . . . , and he would look at me and smile and say "you are just so cute." You know, little dismissive comments like that that are huge dismissive comments.

For a long time, Dr. Pryzinski was too fearful to confront him because of the power differential between them, and continued to be stunned by the treatment. "I couldn't believe this was happening; it just paralyzed me in the moments. And I would go home, and just be like 'what am I going to do?'" At some point, however, she reported the behavior to her dean, and the harasser was dismissed as chair. She wanted to see him gone altogether but was pressured not to file formal charges. Instead, she filed informal charges, and protective procedures were put in place. The harasser could not serve on committees with her, nor review her for tenure. The latter disadvantaged her because she lost someone who could have reviewed her from within the standards of her discipline.

The harassment continued despite these steps. The behavior would go underground for a while, she says, and then resurface. Every time it did, she went back to the dean, who would meet with the harasser, who, in turn, was claiming a right to protection because of a mental disability. "At least that's what the dean was telling me," she says. "'We can't fire Frank because he and his lawyers were claiming that all this was part of a disability.

He has OCD [obsessive-compulsive disorder], and part of his obsession is you.' This is all really, really real." The dean left the institution, a new one assumed office, and he resolved the situation within two weeks. At the end of the year, the harasser announced early retirement, "and I think the university strong-armed him into retiring early." Nevertheless, he could not leave without one last twisted statement: "The very final thing he said in class when my second dean said we're going to end this behavior once and for all, . . . he announced to his classes that 'for years, Dr. Pryzinski and I have not been allowed to interact based on university dictate, but as of today we are finally divorced.'"

Dr. Pryzinski is hugely relieved, and feels like "a newborn woman in that space. . . ." When you have those kinds of traumatic experiences in the workplace, she says, and then they go away, it is really easy to achieve balance. "Now I don't have that monster on my back, now I can actually breathe."

Less openly sexist, but nevertheless powerful in its consequences, is another topic women across career stages discussed: the persisting privilege men enjoy because they are less encumbered by domestic duties than women. Slight changes are under way in younger generations, it seems, yet even the early-career faculty in this study had plenty to say about continuing gender inequalities.

Early-career faculty Ms. Young-Powell at Community College, mother of two young children, compares her situation with that of a male colleague, a parent just like her: "He's got that network at home of mom being there where he's got flexibility to come and go." Private Comprehensive's Assistant Professor Rossi states: "There is a difference between women with children and men with children. Most of my male colleagues have wives who take care of the children, and many of my female colleagues who have children are also the primary caregivers. Their job is perceived within the couple as the secondary job. I think that would be really tough." Full Professor Mendelas at the same college describes how increased professional expectations affect women more than men.

It is more difficult at small institutions to obtain grant funding, she says, and yet scholarship expectations have been ratcheted up. It creates stress, and "I've seen it time and time again. It does not seem to affect the guys. I guess mom is at home taking care of the kids while the guys are here working nights, writing grants, and that sort of thing. But I have seen [the stress] in women." Her younger colleague, Assistant Professor Calhoun, contributes her own observations:

> It does seem awfully easier for men. I have this one colleague who has three children, three children under the age of nine. His wife is a lawyer; it's not like she doesn't have a career, but I was once chatting with him and a female colleague who also has young children, and sort of inadvertently comparing how much they were talking about how much they had to do around the house, because the issue was having kids this age. What she was describing was all about picking people up, and taking them places, and dropping them off, and making lunches. What he was describing was all about, you know, interacting with them when he got home at seven-thirty, in the hour before they went to bed. I was sort of thinking at the time; he has got a good deal. It is kind of a nice little setup. He comes home at seven-thirty and plays with the kids for an hour and a half, and then they go to bed. My poor colleague Cathy was talking about all of this stuff, and it just seemed very poignant.

Pregnancy and young children pose particular challenges for women, as Flagship's Associate Professor Seidman describes: "I have one colleague who has now had two children in probably the last four years. I've seen her kind of struggle at the end of her pregnancy just to be here and put in the time. Obviously I don't see that physical challenge for men. I think sometimes women have more on their plate." Dr. Carver at Private Comprehensive addresses how difficult it is for her not to engage with her infant even when her husband is at home. She calls it a "cognitive difference," a feeling of being in charge even when both parents are physically present. The phenomenon leads to her inability to focus on anything else but the baby whereas her husband seems easily able to concentrate on something else. She calls it "a real asymmetry."

And again, men often benefit from this asymmetry. Flagship's late-career Professor Koshino says: "Most of my colleagues' wives are housewives because they have children. Here and there, they do this chore or that chore, but basically domestic life is managed by the wives. So here you are. They can really concentrate on what they do professionally." In her case, though, things are different, because her husband is "extremely proficient" domestically. Flagship's Assistant Professor Miller sounds similar. She says about the men in her department who have children: "in many of the cases, the wives take the primary role in raising them." Yet the situation is different for her and her husband. He has the same priorities for family life and personal life as she does, but because he has not yet been able to secure a tenure-track position, the pressure is even greater on him than her. Her early-career colleague Dr. McLeod echoes her description; she says she "seems to know of more men here whose wives don't work, and so when you have that situation, I think that obviously can lessen the burden." Yet she, too, perceives change in her generation. At her child's day-care center, for example, children are dropped off and picked up by both women and men. She elaborates:

> If there's going to be a cohort of people that thinks seriously about evenly dividing household tasks, it's sort of this classic overeducated white middle class group of people who are populating the faculty ranks. I don't think men get off easy at all.

Associate Professor Schumacher at Metropolitan would agree. Her husband engages in child rearing to the same extent she does, and he, too, is "stretched tight like a drum. . . . You just can't do both," she says, being a full-time employee and a parent, and that is the reason almost all of the successful women she knows are child-free. As far as men are concerned, many still do have stay-at-home partners, but those who do not are beginning to wrestle with the same problems associated with dual roles as their female counterparts.

Community college's mid-career Ms. Ehrenreich, however, does not perceive much change and finds it "unfortunate" that women have to engage in negotiations of work and home, while men do not. Says she:

> If a man wants to pursue a high-powered career, and he wants to be married and have kids, he does not have the same kind of struggle and dilemma issues. Until we kind of work to equalize that in society, and have it change where men are seen as responsible for those kinds of things, I don't think things are going to change much for the women.

Mid-career faculty Dr. Foster at HBCU reports how she had to choose between her profession and men not because *she* was unable to deal with both in her life, but because *they* were unwilling to accept her as a professional. "I had men who were in my life I had to let go when I was writing my dissertation because they couldn't understand why my dissertation took up all my time." Along similar lines, retiree Dr. Wiley was surprised to find that some men with whom she had serious relationships felt that they were competing with her. "I had no idea," she says. "I didn't even know it." When her first husband left her, she was totally surprised:

> I said: "What have I done?" Because it came out of the blue, I had no idea. He looked me straight in the eye

and said: "You didn't do anything wrong; that is part
of the problem, you never do anything wrong." Which
was more a statement about him, and his level of self-
worth, than it was about me, and I went, huh. There is
something wrong with doing it right! . . . After that relationship ended, and I was slapped in the face with that
relationship ending, I didn't know what was happening.
A friend said: "Did you have no idea he was competing with you?" I wasn't making more money, but it was
something else.

Although some women's relationships ended, in other words,
because of their partners' inability to deal with their professional
lives, sixty-one-year-old Dr. Velvarde was able to change her husband's ways of thinking. The senior faculty member remembers
how her husband, having grown up with a stay-at-home mother, had
very different assumptions about how their lives would play out once
they had children.

It's sort of a funny story because I didn't realize that we
were on different wavelengths at that point in time. He
was presuming that once we had a baby, I would become
a stay-at-home mom, and I was presuming that I would
have a career. We had neighbors, our dearest friends,
and I was talking to my friend one day, and told her
that I was thinking about looking for day care. . . . She
said, "It's really interesting; your husband was over here
last night, and he was talking about how you're dropping out of school when the baby is born." And that
night, I said, "You know, that's not fair. I'm not going
to ask you to stay home to take care of the baby. I don't
think you should ask me to stay home to take care of the
baby." And he said: "But that's a woman's job." And I
looked at him and said: "There's only one thing I can

do for the child that you can't, and that's breastfeed, and I won't let you do that. Anything else, there is no gender requirement for." And then I thought about it for a minute and said: "OK, I'll do the first nine months, you get the next nine." And he just looked at me, and ever since then it's been pretty egalitarian.

Fifty-eight-year-old Ms. Saltmarsh at Community College regrets not having done something similar in her younger days. She wanted to be a traditional mother and establish a career but did not communicate clearly enough to her husband that more of his involvement in domestic affairs was needed. She now tells her daughter not to repeat her mistake.

> I tell my daughter all the time now, have expectations of your husband early on . . . and don't think you have to be wonder woman and try to do it all. Then you end up getting mad. Down the road you especially get mad. It's partially my fault because I think people do what you demand of them. . . . I regret that. I really do regret that. I think it could've been an easier time had I expected more help or assistance from my spouse. That's my fault. . . .

Though Ms. Saltmarsh wishes she had insisted on more help from her husband, she does not harbor any illusions that it is possible for both members of dual career couples to pursue their professional aspirations with the same degree of intensity. "I think when two people in a household both have careers, one career has to take a little bit of a precedence over the other. I don't think two people can devote 100 percent to their career and still have a healthy family life," she says. She was willing to let her husband further advance in his career than she did because "I knew if we both advanced, the children would suffer. I wasn't willing to do that."

As a consequence of their division of labor, Ms. Saltmarsh suspects her husband would say today that he got slighted in the process, often feeling on the perimeter. "Of course my answer to that always is, well, you have to engage yourself. As a father, you shouldn't expect an invitation." She thinks feeling left out when the children came is probably "pretty universal for most men."

Now that they are empty-nesters, they spend more time together than they used to, but probably not as much as other couples, in her estimation. There is a certain "it's about me" attitude now, she says, and they both feel that "we're old enough now that I'm going to do what I want to do. I'm not going to do it because I feel that I have to do it." It is "a little sad" they both feel this way, she finds: "you think as your kids leave the house you are going to do more together." She is curious to see how their relationship will be affected once their grandchild will have been born because "our common thread was our children. . . . We both loved our children, and our lives revolved around the kids when they were growing up. It'll be interesting to see when the baby comes if that changes the dynamics of our relationship." In the end, she concludes, "life is too short; I try not to sit around and analyze it."

Going back to the realm of the institution, participants at all career stages brought up the continuing fallout of a system that, although it may be slowly changing, is nevertheless mired in a history quintessentially patriarchal in nature. Dr. Amici's story described in Chapter Three (under the heading, "About Pioneers and Outsiders") serves as a dramatic illustration of explicit gender bias in the past. The scholar was not given an academic appointment during the 1960s and 1970s because she was a woman. Dr. Ingersen-Noll at Flagship, along similar lines, describes how her university did not even admit women until the 1970s. The women in this study were hardly deterred by the barriers, however. Retired Dr. Wiley remembers serving as the first female president of the faculty senate at her institution during the

1980s, and how she tried to introduce a new leadership style and different ways of doing business.

> I tried very hard to kind of loosen up the senate a little bit and try to move away from everything having to be parliamentarian into much more open discussion. Parliamentary procedures to me are designed for situations where there is bound to be conflict. I mean, that is what they use in Congress, and it is formal, and it does not encourage creative thinking. It doesn't even encourage listening, and I broke some of that down.

Dr. Wiley decided to do something "very female oriented," namely making sure that when she was in front of the senate, she dressed in a feminine fashion. "And that wasn't a black pant suit, it was a silk dress." "Silk dress" is a metaphor, she explains, but she felt she was much stronger if she came across in ways the members were not used to, instead of trying to "play a boy's role." She later became the first female dean at another institution, and while she had emphasized her femininity in order to protect her authenticity, and made it a point to look different from her male counterparts, she says that when people ask whether she was treated differently from men, her answer is "No. I didn't perceive that I was treated differently."

In conclusion, not one of the women in this study categorically vilify men. In fact, and as described in earlier chapters, many saw the men in their lives as major enablers and supportive partners. Male colleagues were mentioned as effective mentors and as "incredibly helpful." Despite the positive experiences many women have had with the specific individuals who mattered so much in their own personal and professional lives, however, there was also an unequivocal realization of continuing male privilege. The female faculty members, in other words, carried two seemingly contradictory notions in their heads, that of enabling individual men, and that of institutional as well as societal structures, customs, and practices that continue to systematically advantage men at the expense of women. The question then is: how do we capitalize on the existence of the former and eradicate the latter?

Feminist Allison Jaggar aptly observed that as human knowledge of nature, including human nature, grows and develops, we gain insight into possible human goods and how to achieve them by means of controlling both ourselves and the world around us. She gives the example of drought no longer being seen as an act of God but as a result of the failure to effectively preserve water. Malnutrition is not perceived anymore as inevitable but as a consequence of bad social policy. Constraints that once were viewed as unavoidable, in other words, are now recognized as acts of oppression. Since oppression is a human construction, liberation can be, too. She writes: "the possible domain of human liberation is constantly being extended" (Jaggar, 1983, p. 7).

More than two decades have passed since her optimistic statement, and some of the testimony in this section leads one to doubt that we have come far since her writing. Still, some progress has been reported across generations, and this issue is further explored in the next section.

Generations: "We Still Have Strides to Make, but at the Same Time, We Have Come a Long Way"

Women at all career stages were asked to make comparisons across generations. Consequently, early-career faculty compare themselves to what they know about previous generations, and mid-and late-career faculty make bi-directional comparisons. They compare themselves to generations of women who came before them, and to new generations entering academe at the present time. The following section is a portrayal of the women looking back, looking around, and looking forward, reflecting on what is, what was, and what could be. They remember, assess, and imagine, comparing themselves to former selves and to others. The central question is that of progress, and how much of it has been made for women, if any, and in what ways. They talk of things getting better but also of stagnation, backlash, and new cause for alarm. The section is not of linear design but attempts to represent the rich tapestry of the women's thoughts, weaving dialectically their feelings of progress and recession, hope and disappointment that are parts of their experiences as women in higher education.

It is clear that women have gained access to institutions of higher education, and no longer need to establish their presence in academe. That fact alone accounts for significant generational differences. "I have more resources, in terms of I'm not a freak of nature because I'm a woman speaking in public, and because I'm a woman teaching, and because I'm a woman writing," says mid-career Professor Pryzinski.

Time and again women, especially mid- and late-career faculty and particularly in male-dominated fields, mention how they were the first or the only women in their fields, or that there were very few of them when they began their careers. Flagship's late-career Professor Cohen did not have many role models when she began college, she says, and her family gave her sister and her "almost no encouragement . . . to pursue professional lives." Her mother was a housewife who raised her daughters to be stay-at-home mothers. "We should have been, according to my mother, happy to stay home and tend our children and be supportive of our husbands."

"If you take this department and look at the esteemed colleagues who have served the department over the years as chairs, they're all men. . . . I think that it's not until my generation that you actually might see a picture of someone like me on the wall," says end-career Professor Mendelas at Private Comprehensive.

Flagship's mid-career professor Newton recalls an older colleague who served Flagship when the institution employed very few women in its faculty ranks. "She felt like she was under constant pressure because men were waiting for her to screw up.

Just waiting for an excuse to pounce on her and find fault with what she was doing," she says, and "I haven't really felt that pressure at all." No surprise, then, that faculty women of previous generations had to be single-minded to succeed. HBCU's late-career Professor Beseley describes female faculty who taught her as regarding them-selves as "these stern, educated women who had to spend all their time reading, teaching, research. . . . When I think back of some of the women professors that I had when I was an undergraduate . . . , most of those weren't married. They thought 'I don't have time for children, I don't have time for this.' . . . I think the ones who came before me did not have a balance." Retired Dr. Wiley thinks of academic women before her as having had "a very lonely life. That is just a guess because [women in academe of previous generations] would be so unusual."

Sixty-one-year-old Dr. Kasper at Flagship was one of those "unusual" women in her field:

> I remember in the early years I always tried if I had a conference to take the kids and husband with the idea that he would manage the kids while I was at the meeting. And I would be back and forth. That lasted for not more than three or four years, if that many. And then I certainly figured out that I wanted to go to those meetings by myself. Much better to leave the kids at home. And it served this dual thing; it was easier to manage the career stuff; and it actually gave me a little break. That seems to be something much more taken for granted [now] that women will go alone to conferences. Whereas for me it was very awkward; how to behave at these conferences because there weren't as many women. At [previous institution] I was the twelfth woman faculty; we were keeping track. And I remember one day there was a reception for faculty, an evening, and I went there, and I walked into this huge reception

room that had maybe eighty people in it, and there was not a single woman in this room. And I had to walk in alone, not knowing whether anyone was going to talk to me or acknowledge me, or whatever. I don't see that happening so much anymore.

At her first job, she recalls, there was a [university] women's group. "Well," she says, "it turned out that was the group of all the wives of the faculty. . . . They would invite [the few female faculty] to become members of that group. So there was this total ambiguity about where we fit in the institutional informal structure." Women of her generation, according to Dr. Kasper, were "moving into this world blindly. There was no institutional support for it. And we had to make it up. Now, I don't know whether you call it institutional support, but there's more of a network. The world is more used to women working."

Full Professor Pelletier, age forty-six, at Private Comprehensive, recalls slow changes:

When I was a graduate student, there were only four women students in the department, and there were no women faculty. Since that time, there have been a lot. I was among the first cohort where there was a significant number of women coming in. So I had companionship in ways that women who came before me didn't. We had a feminist reading group in graduate school that the students put together. This was the mid-1980s. There were men in the group, very open, very feminist men. I think that would have been unimaginable for my senior colleagues. As a consequence, I think I had a much easier time of it just in terms of preparing to be a professional person, and understanding my situation. I had a grasp of what was happening to me sometimes that wouldn't have been possible if I didn't have people to observe and talk to.

Given the relative shortage of women in her field, however, Dr. Pelletier mentions she always had to "contend with the claim that I was an affirmative action hire at every job I've had." She knows there is a way in which the claim is true, she grins, namely that the institutions would not have hired a woman if they didn't have to. What is not true, she insists, is the insinuation that she was not as qualified as men.

Over time, the number of female scholars increased, and late-career Professor Mendelas at Private Comprehensive witnessed a reversal of numbers in her field. When she started her education, women made up 10 percent of the class, she says, but now they outnumber men. She did not have many female peers or mentors, and feels fortunate to be able to serve as a model for some of her female students. Although she heard stories about women "constantly having to fight this business of being a woman" in her field, she personally never felt that her gender played a role in someone holding her back from achieving whatever she wanted to achieve. "Maybe I've just been incredibly fortunate in the people I have interacted with," she says.

Times have changed, indeed. Retired professor Wiley does not think that, at least in her female-dominated field, "women are being discriminated against in any way." Flagship's Associate Professor Sutherland points out that having a male stay-at-home spouse is a sign of this day and age. It would have been nearly impossible in previous generations, she is convinced. In addition, women are less questioned in regard to their skill level, especially in male-dominated fields where years ago women felt constantly criticized, evaluated, looked down upon, and perceived as the token. The provision of a one-semester maternity leave is only ten years old at her institution, furthermore, and Dr. Sutherland reminds us that "certainly women twenty years ago would have a much harder time having children and continuing on the tenure-track."

More people are understanding nowadays that faculty have to take child care schedules into account, says Metropolitan's forty-six-year-old mid-career faculty member Whitehead, and faculty, including men, are more willing to talk about their children. Working in a male-dominated field, she remembers her reluctance as a graduate student to draw attention to "female type issues," because it "made you look different." The person who used to schedule classes was a man without children, she says, and she avoided asking him for special consideration because of her children's schedules. Now she does:

> There are more younger faculty that come in and have children and share the roles; they have wives who work and share. And I can say "you know I can't do that because. . . . ," and there won't be any misunderstanding . . . whereas before there weren't a lot of us like that. I was the only one at the time that had young children, and the only female that had them.

Maternity leave or delays for Ph.D. requirements are granted more easily now than in the past, she says, and at national meetings nowadays you see more families, "and you can't just assume it is the male there with his wife and kids."

Further mentioned as examples of progress in higher education is the growing number of female university administrators and the pipeline for women this may create, as well as an increase in voice because women are now represented on and led by such bodies as the faculty senate. Says Metropolitan's Associate Professor Kaminski: "There are things coming forward that have never been considered in the past, . . . and I think that is a good thing."

The distribution of domestic labor was seen by some women as a generational difference. The so-called "double shift," with women being expected to perform all household and child-care related duties in addition to their careers, is waning, it was argued. Ms. Ehrenreich at Community College believes that women of previous generations had so much more pressure to fulfill all responsibilities at home, in addition to their jobs. She says she hopes that women of current generations are more likely to have spouses or partners who see household labor as the responsibility of everyone who lives in the house, instead of the woman's job alone.

According to Community College's end-of-career faculty Saltmarsh, women of younger generations are indeed more assertive and demand more of their partners in terms of participation in domestic duties. She says: "I think women today, . . . from the beginning, they expect more from their spouses. I think women today want more time for themselves." Their attitudes contrast with the ones prevalent among her and previous generations, which she summarizes as: "If I'm going to work, I still have to do everything else." Stay-at-home men hardly existed in her generations, she recounts. Instead, men were of the opinion that their jobs were important, and if women worked outside of the home also "you almost got the feeling 'that's your choice, you take care of it. You still have to do all this other stuff. I'm the man, I worked hard, I come home, I'm tired.'" She sounds a little cynical, Ms. Saltmarsh concedes, which she does not want because she considers herself the enabler of her husband's attitude. "I think today's husbands have wised up, and I think it's because women have demanded them to wise up. To me, that's very intelligent on the woman's part to say, hey listen. I had this baby, you participated in the process, now we both have to take care of it."

Despite the positive trend, however, Ms. Saltmarsh doubts the division of labor will ever be truly egalitarian. "It's still never going to be 50/50," she concludes, "I don't care what anybody says."

Flagship's late-career Professor Kasper is not convinced that domestic distributions have improved that significantly either but detects signs of progress across the generations. "We always hope that the next generation of men will feel differently about their wives working," she says. "We hope that the next generation is better. What I hear is it's not, but I don't really know." She does believe, however, that progress has been made over the generations. Women of younger generations "now have worked those things out before they got married or had kids," as opposed to her generation, when "we were winging it. We really didn't know what we were getting into. We just didn't sit back and become traditional wives, so we were like making it up as we went along. Didn't know where it was going. Now I think women have a better idea of where it's going. . . ."

End-of-career Dr. Velvarde at Metropolitan sounds similar. The expectations of the women's liberation movement have been that women are able to do everything, she says, and so women have taken on responsibilities, but not given up on the other end. Therefore, the division of labor at home is not 50/50 in most cases. The younger generation is different though, she thinks.

> I think people like my son who have had a mother who has been full-time in the workplace, and who realized that it has to be a partnership, maybe those are the people who will have some balance. And I certainly see people younger than me saying "I've got a life, and that has to take place," in ways that we weren't comfortable or able to do.

She explains that the current generation does not have the same work ethic as the one her "Depression-era parents beat into" them. People of her generation always thought they had to be responsible to their jobs, and did not say "no." "And I see young people now, when we come to them and say 'here is another committee, or here is another course, or here is another this,' they say 'no.' . . . I think times have changed, and I think that is good."

Whereas progress has clearly been made on some fronts, and in many ways younger generations compare favorably with previous ones, challenges persist. HBCU's late-career faculty Dr. Marx says succinctly: "[Women who are just starting out in their academic careers] are going through the same things. I've seen it. The workplace . . . hasn't become any more friendly anywhere." Essentially, in other words, quite a few women still view academe as working in much the same way as research described it twenty years ago, namely as "based on assumptions, attitudes, and policies which are more likely to benefit men than women" (Simeone, 1987, p. 133).

"I still see so much stress," says Dr. Posen, late-career faculty at Metropolitan. "I hate to say it but particularly on women. I see it taking a physical toll on their health." The young women she knows lack support systems, she says; they are not married and delay having families. "That is a choice they make." Some of those who are opting to have families, however, decide to teach at the high school level rather than in academe, according to her.

In addition to stress, isolation, and the curtailing of careers, women continue to be underpaid, as mid-career Dr. Ephron at Community College reminds us. The reasons are manifold, but she did not negotiate her salary when she was hired, "and I think a lot of women don't do that because we are not trained to do that. I think my salary, and a lot of other women's salaries, are probably lower than a contemporary male's with the same education and experience. That's a difficulty that I don't think is going to change until women change to some extent." Although she thinks it would be beneficial for women to become "harder" in some ways, she also says, "I'd hate to actually see it happen because I think we are the nurturers. . . . I'd hate to see us lose our softness to become very hard and negotiable."

Not only do salary inequities persist, women are also choosing to go into "lighter professions" relative to males, according to sixty-two-year-old Professor Mendelas at Private Comprehensive, who has seen generational change over her long career. Some of the young women she teaches tend to go into the health professions, medicine, dentistry, and so forth, and they choose specialties that allow for better balancing of professional and personal lives than others. "I want a nine-to-five job," Dr. Mendelas reports her female students saying. "I want the career, but I want a family too." And so they choose a specialty that will allow them to do that, like dermatology or radiology, and avoid surgery, cardiology, and other high-pressure fields with less predictable schedules. "Women are beginning to make choices, and they can make choices now," she says. "I have not heard any woman come back to me and say 'you know, I wanted to enter this profession but I couldn't because I was a woman.' I have not seen that, and I think this is wonderful." Although Dr. Mendelas's students' choices tend to enable them to obtain convenient schedules, however, they do not get the salaries and prestige that tends to come with high-pressure professions.

Late-career Dr. Cohen at Flagship also describes how students today insist on making choices. They are much more "explicit and insistent about how much they want to balance than their predecessors," she says, but she is not sure that they are going to be able to get all they're asking for, when they are tested with real children and real jobs. "I'm not sure institutions have changed enough to permit that," is her worry.

Her colleague at Private Comprehensive Dr. Witherspoon is similarly impressed by the assertiveness of her junior colleagues. "The expectations are so high. Hire my spouse, have on-campus child care, let me control all of the academic clocks and take time whenever I want. We really bend over backwards. I think it's much healthier. . . . I think academics have come a long way. I think society is much more supportive. . . . I hope they can get everything they want. Lord knows they want everything. Lord knows they are a lot brighter and better trained than I was, and they will never spend ten years in the wilderness with a 4/4 load and then try to come back to research and reestablish themselves as I did." Despite her optimistic portrayal of institutional support, she is also aware, however, that academics "at that top level is really cutthroat."

As far as new generations of faculty are concerned, Dr. Mendelas offers a counterperspective. She is convinced that things have not changed much for those who have children. Whereas men put their jobs first in terms of significance in their lives, she says, women still put their families first, and thus "the woman is bearing the burden almost entirely of that attitude of always being there for the kids and the significant other."

Though some issues, in short, improved, others simply stayed the same or changed only marginally over the generations, and new challenges arose. Sexism, for instance, has not disappeared but has simply gone underground. Dr. Pryzinski goes as far as saying that she would prefer outward expression of gender discrimination to the subtle and masked institutional sexism she perceives nowadays. She gives the example of a junior colleague who thinks she has good institutional maternity leave resources available, and yet fears the backlash that is now more hidden than it would have been prior to any institutional resources being in place.

> I've talked to other junior faculty women in my institution who feel that way too. Like, yeah, we have these institutional gestures toward us, but we are still wondering how that is all going to pan out. . . . I think their issues are unknown at this point, but they carry around this kind of lurking fear of the unknown. I just wouldn't want to be a junior woman coming up for tenure ever, ever again because it is horrible.

Metropolitan's Associate Professor Schumacher is similarly doubtful concerning progress toward gender equality, particularly in regard to women who are professionals and mothers. She is re-reading some of the earliest feminist writings about the complexity of motherhood and work; she says, "I think, oh my God, it hasn't changed in the slightest." In addition, she sees Metropolitan morphing into a "hatchet university" and expects that tenure will soon be granted on a more limited basis, especially to women. She had her children after tenure, and cannot imagine what it is like for new Ph.D.s who are coming to Metropolitan and may be thinking about starting their families. "I think I would be terrified," she says. Associate Professor Pritchard at HBCU harbors her own doubts:

> In some ways it's not different. The standard by which we are going to be held is still higher than men. . . . There's an expression in the African American community, you have to do twice as much to go half as far; I think that still holds for women. I think that the other thing that's the same is the perpetual need to juggle because society, we are evolving, but we have not changed so much that the primary housekeeping and childrearing issues fall equally to men and women. The most evolved of men backslide into more traditional roles.

Despite her reservations, Dr. Pritchard does observe her twenty-year-old daughter's generation to possess more of a sense of their own power and healthier self-esteem. She thinks they shed some of the angst her generation may have had. Though the standards are still higher, she says, her daughter's generation is "equipped for it, and ready to fight."

Other women join her in rejecting the notion that things have simply gotten easier for women over time. At the very least, they are ambivalent. Being asked how she compared to women of previous generations, Assistant Professor Calhoun at Private Comprehensive University captures her "double consciousness" in these terms:

> There are two answers to that. If I compare myself specifically to the other women at [Private Comprehensive], sometimes I feel a little bit resentful that they weren't coming up for tenure under these new higher

research demands. . . . It is resentment of all the people who have tenure in my department, none of whom had to have books for tenure. Now they are in the position of evaluating junior faculty who are required to have books. So the disconnect between what other people were expected to do, and what we are expected to do, feels frustrating. More generally, I have to say I probably have it easier. Trying to do this without having older women faculty to mentor me would have been incredibly difficult. There are plenty of women in the generation and a half before mine who had no women. So, I feel spoiled in some ways. There is a much better support structure, if not a better institutional support structure. I mean, the institution doesn't even have a maternity leave policy. Certainly, the senior women I know go out of their way to be helpful to the junior women, and that has been incredibly great.

At Community College, twenty-eight-year-old instructor Ohler feels the same way. On the one hand, she says, it is much more common for women now to break into the job market and pursue their interests. More resources are available to pursue careers in academia; grants, loans, and scholarships have become more accessible to people who seek them. On the other hand, the atmosphere is a lot more demanding, and expectations have risen. She brings up degree inflation, and how community colleges now tend to require doctoral degrees to fill positions previously held by people with master's degrees only. Even at the community college level, furthermore, where professional expectations used to primarily focus on teaching, scholarship is increasingly becoming an expectation too. "Pressure has been building," she says, and "the evolution of colleges and universities sort of demands that we're even more qualified than applicants had to be in a different generation."

Other faculty echo her assessment. They talk about the increasing importance of research, publications, and the ability to attract grant dollars. Processes are becoming more competitive, both grant writing and journal publishing. Not enough time is allowed to do everything, says Metropolitan's Assistant Professor Adams, and "the bar has been raised." Late-career Professor D'Embri at Private Comprehensive is stunned when she observes her junior colleagues: "They are here on weekends, they are here late at night. I never did that. Never. . . . They work all the time. They are just crazed. The demands are insidious." She describes a young female faculty with children whose every minute is scheduled, and another one who color-codes her schedule:

> I remember one of the times when we did have the
> support group going, and there was one woman, and we
> started to talk about our to-do lists, and she said "mine is
> color coded." And we were all laughing because she used
> different colored pencils depending on how challenging
> or how quickly she had to do it.

Her fear is that, in a way, history repeats itself, and the junior women in her school have to work just as hard as generations of women before her had to. It may not be because they are women and have to prove themselves because of their gender, however; it may just be because "that's what it takes to get tenure these days," she says.

Late-career Dr. Velvarde at Metropolitan confirms: "Faculty have it harder today than when I was starting out. I often think about the fact that I'm not sure if I'd even be hired today, given the criteria for promotion and tenure and what they're looking for in faculty. I just think it's gotten harder and harder, and women are having to do more and more. . . . As a woman, in order to be as good as, you have to be better than, I believe. I don't think the playing field is level." Mid-career Professor Newton at Flagship also perceives heightened standards for faculty, and describes how those with children are particularly affected:

> There are some faculty members who are childless, and probably will remain that way. They feel incredible pressure. It seems that every year the standards for tenure go up, up, up. Every year they just put the screws to these people. . . . There's a real competitiveness about how much people produce. And so everyone is sort of scrambling to meet that goal. There are some people who throw themselves into it completely who don't have children, and there's other people with children who look pretty harried because they're pushing, pushing, pushing. So it really depends. I think the pressure is greater than when I came through. I really do think the standards are higher. It depends on whether they have children or not. When it's a two person professional couple, a lot of times both of them are working nonstop. The ones with children get frustrated or mad at the system. . . . They either don't sleep or push themselves incredibly hard.

Despite the increase in pressure, Flagship's Assistant Professor McLeod reminds us again just how much easier it is for her generation to balance personal and professional lives, comparatively speaking. And whereas Ms. Calhoun talks about her resentment of senior faculty, Dr. McLeod wonders whether senior faculty may not harbor some resentments of their own:

> It seems like it's much easier. I mean, just the choices. The impression I get is that a lot of people felt there was an explicit need to choose between getting tenure and having kids. And so to imagine an environment where fairly reasonable people would feel that way, sort of, I

can imagine what a scary place it was. . . . Sometimes I wonder if there is a tension around that . . . where people who have gone through and have had a really hard time sort of feel like the younger people either take stuff for granted, or are getting way more and aren't really appreciative.

Addressing late-career faculty's attitudes toward their junior colleagues, Metropolitan's Associate Professor Kaminski distinguishes between two categories of late-career faculty women: "Some have made it, and are pioneers and are wonderful mentors and have been great trying to increase the ranks of women and have been more generative, but there have also been those women who I think have been very possessive of being in that sole position, and have not been very gracious and helpful.

Regarding unhelpful female faculty, late-career colleague Velvarde at Metropolitan talks about "horizontal violence," perpetuated by women, especially in female-dominated fields. She elaborates:

I see this in [my field] a lot; . . . where you don't have a lot of power in the environment, so rather you're powerless. You just lash out at each other; it goes laterally rather than vertically. And then the other thing is as a group that's been oppressed for so long, when you finally get to the point where you've reached some power status, the oppressed become the oppressors. As opposed to sitting there and saying "I remember how hard it was for me; I want to make it easy for you." It's like "Well, I had to struggle; you best do the same thing."

Be that as it may, Metropolitan's Assistant Professor McMillan insists that things are much easier today because women do not face the same resistance to them being in their positions. "The walls in front of them just to get through the days," she imagines, "I can't even conceive of how you could go in every day and deal with something like that." Women today are learning not to be oppressed, she thinks, and how to say "no," although they still take on jobs men don't want because it is expected of them as women. "We still have strides to make, but at the same time, we have come a long way."

Flagship's Assistant Professor Miller adopts yet a different perspective. In some ways it is a lot easier today for women to balance, she says, and yet in previous generations the situation was different because hardly any women made the choice to pursue both careers and families; thus they had less balancing to do. "Most of the women I know who are at least five or ten years older than me never had families," she says. Her statements are, of course, based on experiences with professional white women, primarily. Many women of color have always worked outside of the home in addition to raising families, and have thus always had their own balancing to do. Community College's Ms. Young-Powell's observations must be interpreted with similar caution. She says women are now getting into the workforce "a little more," and "generations before, I can hear my grandparents saying 'I can't imagine leaving my kids during the day, and not being that stay-at-home mom.'" Now, she emphasizes, society makes it easier for women to leave their children in day care and after-school programs during the day and she, personally, has very understanding supervisors.

Thirty-one-year-old Flagship Assistant Professor Ingerson-Noll brings up a generational issue not mentioned by any other woman, namely that of the discrimination against males. She came to the United States four years ago from the Netherlands and says she has seen the female population in her field increase drastically over the span of her educational and professional career of fourteen years, and believes that "people's judgment of work has become independent of gender, basically." However, there are still issues to be solved, she insists, such as the dual-career problem. This problem, incidentally, is one faced by both men and women, and they are "thinking about this in the same way, pretty much." Men and women of her generation, raised in the 1970s, 1980s, and 1990s, generally think more alike than in previous generations, she argues. Despite the fact that both genders face the dual-career problem in the same way, attention is primarily paid to women, and how to enhance their opportunities. She talks about this to her husband, who is from the United Kingdom:

> He tells me that in the UK this is leading to negative results because in schools, and also during childhood, women are continuously encouraged to the point that boys do not receive the same kind of attention. They are basically underachieving because they think they are stupid, because all the time the girls are being encouraged in everything. . . . That seems to be a problem right now. Apparently boys are doing worse in math and science than girls now. It is the exact reverse from how it was fifty years ago.

Dr. Ingersen-Noll believes that her generation is the only balanced generation, wedged in between previous generations that disadvantaged girls and a new generation that sees the pendulum swing the other way. "Now there are very specific events for girls, . . . like science days for girls," she says, and wonders: "Why would you want to exclude boys from going to such science days?" An overemphasis on girls is not right either, she argues, because it only emphasizes the difference between boys and girls. "You shouldn't do that," is her conclusion.

Dr. Ingerson-Noll is not alone in her worries about boys. Beginning in the 1990s, researchers have pointed out that after years of focusing on eradicating discrimination against girls, it is time to acknowledge that males, too, suffer from gender bias that needs to be addressed (Lesko, 2000). It will be interesting to follow the research in light of the topic of this book, and assess how young generations of males fare not only in terms of academic and professional success, but also in regard to how they square their professional aspirations with their personal lives.

Community College's Dr. Lilian, who is thirty-four years old, gives thought to the differences between generations. Her generation, according to her, enjoys a distinct advantage over previous ones because its members have grown up with technology and a fast pace, both of which make it relatively easy for them to meet the demands of modern life. Older persons may have to adapt, but "for me, this is how you operate," she says. If you don't have time for a sit-down dinner, you just grab something, and although this may violate the older generations' customs and "can be a big issue," flexible habits are not as stressful to her as they would be to her mother. Whereas her mother's life was neatly divided into work and family time, telecommunication makes it possible for Dr. Lilian to bring work home. "In my mother's generation, everything at work was in the file cabinet, and you couldn't put that file cabinet in the car. So you didn't take the things home; now everything is electronic, and I can get to it, and work more on it from home." While some may consider the development disadvantageous, Dr. Lilian thinks "it just depends on what kind of person you are." And for her, doing several things at once, mixing the personal and the professional, and constantly being on the move is not a problem but simply a way of life.

End-of-career Dr. Noah at HBCU provides the counterperspective. She views technology very differently, and indeed not as an enabler but a barrier to balancing personal and professional lives. It has made faculty members more accessible, creating "in a way virtual office hours now." Students are constantly e-mailing you, she explains, and awaiting an immediate response. You have to be very clear about the boundaries now, she insists.

Another generational difference was explained by mid-career faculty member Sikka, and may be particularly relevant for the community college context. Women of previous generations, according to her, tend to have children, and they took time out to have or raise them. They came into community college teaching after teaching high school, were never very focused on research, and did not have the aspirations to work at the four-year college level. They are different from her generation, which has to be more research focused, even at the community college level, and different from women like her who gave up hopes of being at a four-year institution because of family obligations. She explains:

> Generally speaking, the folks that have been here thirty years, they tend to have children. The whole generation had children. Their children are now young adults. . . . Most of them took time off. . . . They raised their families, then came back to teaching, or started teaching. I haven't got the sense that they went through what I went through because they didn't really go through it themselves in the same way. They didn't have the same sense of themselves in the context of their profession I think that I did, as someone who anticipated teaching at the university level, and making adjustments along the way. A lot of them were really happy that they're teaching at the community college; this was the pathway out of high school teaching. So, this was a new opportunity, and a good opportunity. It's a different approach.

At this point, community colleges are increasing their expectations for scholarship, according to Dr. Sikka. Consequently, more and more young faculty members do not find them to be the conducive places for balancing personal and professional obligations they once were. Rather, they face the same dilemmas their colleagues at other types of institutions face. As a result, some opt out of any aspirations to have a family and rather choose to be "child-free." "The term I've started to hear," Dr. Sikka says, "is child-free. I am child-free by choice. . . . They feel that they have so much going on in their lives that there is no real desire to have children."

Fifty-three-year-old Ms. Ketzel at Community College confirms Dr. Sikka's assessment of the situation and provided the counter-narrative from the viewpoint of her generation. She sees a real generational difference, she says, between women now starting their careers and her generation.

> I began wanting to live out my life as a high school teacher. . . . I've chaired the hiring committees for five new faculty in the last three years, and all of these women are here. . . . They've come to the community college with the idea that this is the starting point for their career. They mostly have aspirations to move into higher education or administration. I do think that's generational . . ., they see themselves on a ladder. I saw myself on a plateau. When I started teaching, I was doing what I dreamed of doing; everything else that's happened has been serendipitous and accidental for me, whereas the young women I see starting out have plans. That's not how my career worked. In part that may be me; in a large part I think it's generational.

The young women will have more conflict, Ms. Ketzel thinks. It will be more difficult to be at a "research one" institution, producing the research and teaching, and balancing family lives. "When my son was growing up," she says, "my summers were largely me sitting by the pool with my son where they'll have to be doing research and work over the summers in those positions. They're setting themselves up for a little more conflict in their professional and personal lives." She did not encounter the same conflicts that many dual career couples face, she says, "probably because of my lower aspirations." She then corrects herself and adds: "I don't want to say 'lower' because teaching is a pretty special thing. . . . That's what I wanted to do. People might see it as a limited aspiration."

Not only have institutions, structures, and expectations changed over time, individuals change as well, of course. End-of-career Professor Mendelas lets her career-stages pass before her eyes and says:

> The pressures are always there until you get tenure. It doesn't matter how great a teacher you are, or how much you publish, depending on the expectation of the institution, you never know. There are no rules on what it takes to get tenure. So you are always work-ing hard to achieve whatever you hope it takes. It's beyond your own personal expectations because there is a larger community that's going to make that decision. Once that first decision is made in a positive way, I suppose anyone could just say "OK, I'm here to stay, unless I do something really awful," and just float. Or you continue to work, but you work more within the bounds of what you consider to be a reasonable amount of time. Pre-tenure, . . . I have seen many, many women—not so much men—but many women, who have been very, very stressed because of the commit-ments they have outside of their professional lives, to maintain their lives while they are also trying to get through that tenure. I think once you begin to move through the associate rank, and then the full professor rank, you just by the very nature of these, you try to balance things out a little bit more, for your own mental health, if nothing else.

Her colleague Dr. Newton thinks about her career and considers herself lucky because she came to her institution with a good scholarly record already, and then was able "to ride the wave" by constantly being involved in projects. "It did build up to a fevered pitch right before tenure. Anyone who has been through it knows it's an incredibly anxiety producing, grueling experience." Since that time she backed off a little, she says, and tried to establish a more reasonable tempo. Now that she has these habits in place, she reports, she is "equally as productive, but I don't have the same tension and anxiety about it."

In conclusion, participants in this study share the acknowledgment that different generations faced and continue to face different challenges. Women across career stages point to improvements that have been made over time, but they also name realities that remain problematic, or got worse, and new problems that have surfaced.

Certainly access to higher education is no longer problematic for women, but especially late-career faculty remember different times. Dr. Kasper had to "walk in alone" and face the all-male convention. Others remember the loneliness and second-class status they themselves experienced, or that the women before them did. If and when these pioneer scholars made the choice to have families or a life outside out the academy in addition to their careers, they had to bear the burden and do the double shift almost without support. After all, their choice was socially constructed as luxury, not necessity.

Younger generations are much better off in many ways. They benefit from the work of those before them, the mentoring, the networks, and, however limited, the institutional support. Many have been able to grow into strong, assertive women, able to take for granted what their predecessors could not even imagine and demanding of the system things the older generations find breathtaking.

Still, most women across career stages agree: in some ways life is harder now for the young. Not only have many realities proven to stubbornly resist change but also new challenges have arisen, and they are hurting women, in particular. Access to all realms of higher education is secured, both legally and practically. But equal opportunities do not just revolve around access; what happens once an underprivileged or minority group has become part of the system is just as important. Process and outcome, in other words, are the problematic areas nowadays, not just in terms of gender, as in this study, but also in terms of race and social class. What Michele Fine argued in regard to K–12 education years ago still holds true nowadays: "Today questions of equity must focus not on educational *access*, but on educational *outcomes*" (Fine, 1991, p. 13). She uses high school completion rates as proxies for educational outcomes, and since dropout rates are patterned by race, ethnicity, class, gender, and disability, she sets out to explore the reasons behind the dropout problem that are systemic in nature rather than attributable to individuals. Likewise, in this study, my focus is on what happens to women once they are in the system (process), and how they fare in comparison to their male counterparts, particularly in terms of the successful navigation of the professional and personal spheres of life (outcome).

In terms of process and outcome, women still struggle, especially the younger generations. They demand and use available institutional resources but fear backlash. They learn to say "no" to excessive demands, yet labor to the breaking point under ever-increasing expectations. Sexism has not disappeared but gone underground, rearing its ugly head often enough as to not be forgotten. Women demand that men learn and share, but domestic divisions of labor are not sufficiently equalized in many cases. Older generations of women often see the plight of the young, but are not always equipped to be sufficiently supportive. The discourse across generations displayed in this chapter, in short, reveals that past generations have come a long way on the road to equality, yet the road remains one that future generations must continue to travel. As observed by other scholars of gender equity in academe, "The focus has moved from confronting gross manifestations of inequity to detecting and remedying the more subtle forms of gender inequity that permeate a range of domains relevant to life in academe" (Miller & Miller, 2002, p. 103).

5

Recommendations

Flagship's Assistant Professor Miller puts it straight:

> I feel as academics we are in a pretty privileged position.
> We make decent salaries; we have largely flexible sched-
> ules. Millions of women in much worse situations have
> raised families of five or six or seven in history, and they
> do it. I don't feel like I have much ground to complain.
> Except that the purpose of this [study] is to be proactive,
> and see what we can do that makes it better.

The goal, then, is to build upon existing enablers and, simultaneously, address the barriers to female faculty members' abilities to
balance their personal and professional lives in ways they define as
healthy. Women in Science and Engineering (WISE) conference
participants stated in 1998 that twenty-five years' prior "success"
may have meant obtaining a "measure of recognition from our
peers." When they met, however, they defined success as "'the sum
over a lifetime of our satisfaction in career, family, and personal
life,' indicating that balance has become much more of an issue"
(Baker, 1999, p. 210). I argue that is still true today; balance is still
an issue, and it has not been sufficiently addressed.

The women in this study generated rich proposals for institutional and cultural reform and also offered advice for their peers

in the interim—practical suggestions on how to cope while higher education embarks on the road to change. Some of these proposals are beneficial to all faculty members, regardless of the makeup of their personal lives; some are useful for men as well as women. The following sections capture them all.

I should point out that several of these reform proposals are no strangers to reformers of higher education; they have been made before, and are in no need of further elaboration. To avoid redundancy, therefore, they are listed without much discussion. Others may be new or unconventional, and thus in need of explanation; hence they are presented in more detail. It should be kept in mind, however, that whether or not a particular suggestion is only listed or discussed in length in no way correlates with its degree of significance. All of these recommendations are crucial; some are merely better known than others.

What Women Want: Reform of Academe

The following recommendations are general in the sense that they tend to apply to faculty regardless of their specific life situation, family constellation, or other variables.

General Recommendations

Time and again, faculty across career stages spoke about the need to clarify the tenure process and more clearly delineate expectations. It would be helpful, furthermore, to facilitate communication among senior and junior faculty and address common issues to help newcomers understand that they are not the only ones confronting challenges. Dr. Seidman at Flagship illustrates the point:

> Sometimes you feel like you're all by yourself out there. Your problems are very unique, and they're probably not. I think there's a certain professional paranoia about an academic's life. Maybe you're the only one who has

writer's block. Maybe you're the only one who can't get a research agenda going. Maybe you're the only one who doesn't know how to write a grant and get a grant. That's just not true.

Suggestions are to institute mentorship programs and aid new faculty in the design of effective research plans, teaching and assessment strategies, and how to generally organize one's professional life. Senior faculty may consider collaborative opportunities with their junior colleagues as ways to initiate them into the profession and share the social capital they accumulated over the course of their careers. Other nonevaluative groups such as "faculty clubs" were mentioned as greatly beneficial to newcomers. This is what Dr. Littlefield at HBCU has to say:

> One thing I have to give [my previous institution] credit for, they had a university club. It was the old white guys who retired from the university who came together each week and they want new faculty to come in so they can help mentor them and guide them. . . . Again I would be the only black female there. . . . The idea is a good idea. That's what new faculty need.

She advocates that such meetings include not just retired but current senior faculty and be held at times when the university commits to a "university hour" when no classes are scheduled. Networks for the purpose of information sharing and collaboration were recommended by Ms. Ohler at Community College as well. She thinks groups that encourage collaboration among peers would be helpful. After all, she emphasizes, "there is such a richness of experience, and there is so much useful information to be gleaned from the people around you." She is of the opinion that often faculty "don't really think about that" and, instead, "just try to do it on their own."

In addition, new faculty need reduced teaching loads to help them get acclimated, in addition to junior sabbaticals to foster their scholarship. A system should be put in place that disseminates information about available campus services for faculty and students, something that is currently often learned by sheer happenstance alone. As Dr. Pritchard at HBCU puts it succinctly: "Your best friend or your worst enemy is your own vitae. So you have to take ownership of that." Although institutions need not encroach on academic freedom and individual choices that are the faculty members' to make, she explains, they need to provide information to facilitate the process.

Dr. Whitehead at Metropolitan mentions a concern she considers "minor" but, nevertheless, thinks that, if it were addressed, it would help balance her personal and professional lives. She would like to be able to access the university's sports facilities free of charge, something she would perceive as a "family-friendly" gesture. Such benefit used to be available in the past, she says, and "a whole bunch of us would go and take aerobics, you know, and play. . . . But now, they start charging you. . . . So I don't go." It would help, she says, if you can eke out an hour to do something personal.

Workload issues also need to be addressed. Dr. Pelletier at Private Comprehensive advocates for "administrators to revaluate what they are asking their faculty to do." Fewer, yet more meaningful, student assignments would cut down on grading, she says, but students need to be appraised of the policy before they get to the college. Professional advising until students declare a major would address faculty workload, and so would the professionalization of dealing with student needs outside of the classroom in general, instead of constantly relying on faculty to provide advice and stimulation.

We are supposed to do a lot of class discussion, so we can't cover as much material in lectures. The reason is

they don't discuss with each other outside of class. They
have to have a teacher to stimulate a discussion. When
I was in school, we went to lectures. Then we talked
about them later.

She believes it is short-sighted for administrators to "try to
keep the students happy" at all costs. Being market driven,
she argues, the university attempts to retain almost all students
despite the fact that not all of them want to be there. "I'm supposed to shepherd them through the four years of their life and
keep them here," she complains.

Faculty in this study mention another market-driven problem,
namely the exploitation of adjunct faculty, a disproportionate
number of them women. "That needs to change," is how Dr. Witherspoon at Private Comprehensive puts it. "I think some schools
are really awful."

Above and beyond these general proposals, however, are
those that more specifically address women's needs in certain
situations, and thus they do not necessarily apply to all. They are
summarized here.

Specific Recommendations

The following are recommendations specifically geared to alleviate
hardships of certain faculty subgroups. They may not, in short,
apply to all faculty across the board.

Child- and After-School Care on Campus

High-quality, affordable, nearby child care with flexible hours was
one of the main issues mentioned by female faculty, even by
those who did not have children, or whose children are grown.
Included should be care options for children with special needs,
care for mildly sick children, and for school-age children after
school hours. At no institution was the child care, if provided at
all, seen as sufficient. Instead it was either altogether absent or

offered too few slots, resulting in prohibitively long waiting lists. Day care on campus would be a great benefit primarily because of its proximity to the place women work. Explains Dr. Carver at Private Comprehensive University:

> I really don't know what I would ask besides on-campus day care, which we do not have. That would be nice. It would mean that I could check-in in the middle of the day, and feel close to my child while I am still working. I think that would be the ideal. In my job, that is the one thing that is missing.

Support of Faculty Who Provide Elder Care

An increasing number of faculty, many of them women, are taking care of aging and ailing parents. The need for elder care is a trend projected to grow in the future as people's life expectancy increases. Faculty would benefit from increased institutional attention and flexibility, as well as release time and load adjustments for elder care.

Immigrant Scholars

Another faculty group largely unrecognized consists of scholars from other countries and cultures who may experience a sense of isolation little understood by their American colleagues. It is time for dialogue about what their needs are, and what it takes for colleges and universities to better meet those.

The Dual-Career Problem

An increasing number of faculty do not have "portable" partners who easily relocate either because of their flexible jobs or because they do not work outside of the home. Often, they are academics themselves and dependent on finding employment at the institution that hires their spouse or partner. "We need a lot more flexibility in some of the processes," Flagship's Dr. Cohen says. "We need to figure out better ways to hire people who have partners or spouses—if you only want to deal with people without partners or families, you run the risk of hiring only sociopaths. . . . It's become a part of the market now in academics and industry that if you hire one person, you're bringing a whole family on board, and you need to restructure in order to keep those people happy. . . . We can certainly do a hell of a lot more than we do now."

Counseling Opportunities to Faculty at All Career Stages

Faculty at all career stages, not merely during the early years, find themselves in situations that demand life-changing decisions to be rendered, and resources to aid in these decision-making processes would be helpful. Those might consist of mental health services or facilitated meetings during which more experienced colleagues counsel those with less experience. Dr. Sutherland at Flagship serves as an example of a full professor in need of support. She describes herself as "very successful" and "very career driven," and she is considering becoming a dean. Yet she does not know who to turn to for advice to better ascertain what such a move into an administrative post might mean for her balancing act. Married mother of two young children, she expects additional commitments on weekends and during evenings, as well as more travel, to come along with such a position. "While I think I'd really be good at this, I have people telling me all the time I'm ready for this," she says, "I'm really struggling to decide how much of a sacrifice with my family it's worth." She wishes more resources were available for people to help make decisions and learn to balance.

> I wish there were some place I could just talk to people about, OK, this is what it would take for a sacrifice, and how would you deal with it. The pros and cons of it. I don't think there's enough mental health type of resources available to faculty.

A Forum for University Parents

Especially early-career academics tend to be recent transplants from far-away places without established support networks nearby, family or friends. They are starting new jobs, new lives, and, quite possibly, families. Some are minorities in their departments and lack people to talk to about family issues. Assistant Professor Miller at Flagship says about her department: "There aren't very many women. The women that there are have almost exclusively put their careers first and not had families." Early-career women with children would, consequently, benefit greatly from organized ways of exchanging information. Dr. Miller relates how finding faculty with small children has been purely serendipitous for her, and yet she could use a network, a support group, even if it were online. "If there were an online site where people could recommend things or not, or ask questions, on how do you deal with this, or how did you maternity that. A network."

Redesigned Family Policies

The academic tenure system is based on the idea that the faculty member has a wife at home. Most female faculty, however, do not. They not only pursue demanding academic careers, but they may also bear children and play an important role at home. The current state of maternity leave policies at most colleges and universities is insufficient despite the fact that female faculty are investments academe can ill afford to lose. It is for that reason that colleges and universities might wish to consider looking at other nations, Western European or Scandinavian for example, to find models of more effective parental leave policies for which women *and* men are eligible.[1]

Dr. Ephron at Community College stresses the importance of both genders being able to take leave. It takes "the pressure off that if I get pregnant I've got to leave the job because I can't do both." Dr. Schumacher at Metropolitan suggests giving a year to every parent of a new child. Its purpose would mirror sabbaticals (or research leaves, study leaves, whichever they may be called), which are given with the purpose of increased productivity in mind. She explains:

> The history of sabbaticals is that we have discovered that people really needed to be given time to get away and think. The best thing you could do to people in order to help them be more productive, if that is what you want, is to give them time to raise their children. They will come back refreshed and are willing to work.

Well-Publicized Policies and Centralized Services

University policies designed to support parents are not only sparse, they are also veiled in a shroud of obscurity. Better advertising of what is available and an informed, helpful human resources staff would aid faculty who are attempting to balance both their professions and their families. Says Dr. McLeod at Flagship:

> Making policies explicit I think is nice. You never want to be the poor slob that just didn't get told you could get X, Y, or Z. Then you feel like you got screwed. It's bad for you; it's bad for the institution.

One suggestion made by Dr. Schumacher at Metropolitan is to institute an Office of Family Issues geared at supporting people in diverse life situations and stages to deal with having and caring for children, caring for elderly, and more. Institutions should change the rest of the world, she says, and such change ought to be made central to the mission of the university rather than be marginalized and outside its parameters. Right now, she explains, her proposal sounds like heresy, especially to a bastion of white men. "When you say that stuff, they really look at you like you are asking for strip bars in the middle of campus or something. They don't get it."

A Changing Culture

Along with policy changes comes a change in attitude toward what it takes to bring children into a person's life. Dr. Kaminski at Metropolitan argues along similar lines. She thinks it is essential to do as much as possible to help faculty members with new children to survive, particularly the first year after a child is born or adopted. A major enabler would be a change in academic culture so that new parents are relieved of the inevitable guilt if they are temporarily unable to pull their weight. Says she:

> I think that if there are things that can be done so that it is more of a celebration and a recognition that this is an important part of your life, and not to feel guilty because you aren't teaching as many courses or not publishing as much that year.

The Redesign of the Tenure Process

If female faculty desire to have children without being relegated to second-tier positions, the tenure system needs reform that enables women to effectively accommodate family needs without fear of negative consequences. Dr. Sikka at Community College gives her own story as an example of somebody who took time to have children, and now finds herself noncompetitive for positions in four-year colleges. She has "gaps" in her career, she says, and though she is now much better focused on her true research interests than she was years ago, she feels disenfranchised from mainstream academe. Gaps in women's careers need to be assessed for what they are, she argues, and a system put in place that allows for more flexibility. Dr. Cohen at Flagship University would agree with her. She says:

> Within institutions, a cultural change needs to happen now that there are more aspiring academics with

unconventional career paths; search committees should set aside some of their old assumptions when they sit down and interview or look at CVs. They can miss exciting candidates when they persist in looking for conventional trajectories with no gaps. Or when they assume that gaps, times away from the academy, are bad.

She also emphasizes the need for institutions to be more welcoming to people coming back to academe at midlife. "I believe that somebody can start a new phase of their career at midlife and do a credible job and qualify for tenure, even if they start at forty versus twenty-seven." She remembers a student at her university who enrolled in medical school at age forty. He had been a successful architect, but after taking care of aging parents with terminal diseases, recognized his calling was in medicine. "He's going to be a wonderful physician," she says, "and think of all the stuff he brought into his medical education which your usual twenty-two-year-old doesn't have."

Dr. Sutherland at Flagship reminds us that current academic culture is based on the assumption that progress is a "steady slope going up." It does not have to be that way, she thinks, and universities ought to allow people to back off and focus on other things for a while, such as having children. "Right now we don't have a venue for doing that," she says. "Perhaps the ten-year tenure cycle . . . where you're not tenured until after year ten may be more conducive to allowing women to go ahead and have kids."

Stopping the tenure clock is becoming more common, but it may not allow enough time to have and take care of children; nor may it be the best way to address the issues early-career women face. In fact, women worry it may lead to inflated expectations of tenure and promotion committees ("she's had an extra year, so why did she not produce more?"). As Jon Marcus in *Change Magazine* puts it: "It will take significant changes in America's higher-education culture so that women no longer suspect—regardless of what the faculty handbook might say—that they'll be seen as weak for taking time off to raise a child" (Marcus, 2007, p. 28).

A related problem is addressed by Flagship's Dr. Kasper, who recently attended a conference on women in her field. She remembers how the younger women opposed the idea of a women-friendly curriculum because . . .

> . . . they wanted it to be clear that they had succeeded in their careers via the standard rules. I realized it was like affirmative action. Tainting somebody, implying you couldn't have made it without the special program and, therefore, you aren't as competent. So, the pitfall is that programs designed for women may do harm to women. . . . The programs tend to stigmatize.

The task, then, is to design programs that are not specifically directed at women but benefit men as well—better still, to change academic culture and enable what Dr. Kasper calls "sustainable humane careers." At this point, careers are not humane, she says, for either men or women. Where better to start changing academic culture, therefore, than with its bedrock feature: the tenure process itself?

Instead of just giving candidates an extra year, the tenure process should be redesigned altogether in order to make it more flexible. A new system should also address the potential "unintended consequences" of a seemingly benign policy. The following proposal is based on a comment made by Dr. Sutherland at Flagship, but was otherwise not mentioned by the participants in this study. It is my brainchild, and I take full responsibility for its potential flaws.

The Exemplar Model

It has been argued before that there is nothing magic about the six or seven years typically defined as the probationary pre-tenure period. Some medical schools, for example, have begun to extend this time, several even indefinitely. For one, increased competition has made it more difficult for junior scholars to develop the necessary record of scholarship and, second, some junior faculty made it clear that they need more time to balance work and family responsibilities (Liu & Mallon, 2004, p. 210). Universities, such as the University of Michigan, offer extensions by one year for childrearing, dependent care, or medical leave (*University of Michigan Faculty Handbook*, 2006, 6.D.1). The University of California-Berkeley has long had family accommodation policies, among them the stopping of the tenure clock. However, as I have argued before, policies geared primarily at women are inherently stigmatizing. Therefore, the proposal here is to extend the probationary period for *all* faculty, either indefinitely or for a very long time (such as ten years), during which they have an opportunity to demonstrate that they are worth a life-long commitment by their institution. They could also come up for tenure at *any* time, even before the now customary five or six years have passed. Such an option addresses the realistic concern that institutions would be enabled to endlessly string faculty along without job security.

Along with an expanded time frame, expectations would have to be firmed up. In other words, tenure would become outcome based rather than time based. The danger, certainly, is bean counting. If institutions prescribe exactly how many papers a scholar has to have published to gain tenure, how many grant dollars are to be secured and books written, and what minimum scores on teaching evaluations have to be, professional discretion is forfeited. However, departments might be able to agree on a certain number of diverse portfolios of scholars they deem successful. Those exemplars would serve as guides and provide standards for early-career faculty to learn that there are different ways to be successful in one's field and to see concrete and realistic examples of what, exactly, scholarly success entails. The new model would allow people to scale back temporarily when necessary, work part-time, take time out for finding partners, plan and start families, and take care of small children, aging parents, or other personal needs. Institutions and their departments would communicate to faculty what it takes to succeed, but faculty would have the discretion to decide how to make the expectations fit their lives and how to reach their goals.

The exemplar model of tenure addresses the chronic complaint of junior faculty that expectations are vague and leave them stumbling through a jungle of ill-defined standards for years. Junior faculty, even graduate students preparing to join academe, would now be able to compare their aspirations with the work of a diverse group of exemplary scholars who were successful in the institution. The timeline as to how to achieve exemplary status themselves, however, is designed by them and custom-tailored to fit their individual needs and wants regarding a life that is healthily balanced.

The system would be flexible. As times, priorities, and demands shift, the portfolios of exemplary scholars would change, and new generations of faculty could see updated versions of work to orient themselves. In sum, the system makes standards more transparent. More generally, it preserves the bedrock of higher education that guarantees academic freedom, namely tenure, without shackling people, particularly women, by means of its rigid timelines.

Design Policies That Take into Account the Mutual Dependency Between Professional and Personal Lives

It seems almost too mundane to state the obvious fact that people do not live their lives in separate entities but rather move back and forth between different parts of their lives, and what happens in one realm tends to shape the others. One might call it an ecological relationship in which changes in one arena are likely to affect all others. A significant increase in salary, for instance, might enable a person to move to a different neighborhood, have another child, or retire earlier. Job loss may lead to depression, divorce, even suicide. It is hardly surprising, then, to find these same dynamics true for female faculty members. The following quote illustrates how the personal and the professional spheres are closely related, and how one aspect is seen as shaping the other:

> At least in my personal life I am more stabilized, and I also want to settle down and find a better living environment for my son. So that's another motivation I wanted to be good in my professional life. So my short-term objective is to get tenure so I can really make a long-term plan for myself. . . . So I want to make sure to be successful in my professional life to support my personal life.

Although the mere insight that the professional and personal relate in a qualitative sense is not in and of itself groundbreaking, the fact that this reality does not seem to get the attention it deserves from colleges and universities has important implications. One beginning faculty member serves as illustration.

Dr. Adams was hired as a tenure-track professor at Metropolitan University but decided to leave because it was impossible for her to find a healthy balance between her professional and personal lives. She moved to town with her daughter and had to leave her husband behind in another city due to his inability to find a job in the new town. She concedes that the university had told her about resources available in the human resources department to help spouses find jobs, but she thought they could do it on their own. Now she wonders whether it "would have helped anyway," given the challenges she encountered during her first year tenure-track. When asked whether her husband having a job in town would have made her stay in her new job, she replied: "Yes, but if I had to think about my first year here, I don't know if I would've had a marriage if he had been here." She found herself in a vexing situation because she needed for her husband to find a job in the new town, yet even if he had done so, the demands of the tenure-track position may have made it very difficult for her to combine her professional and personal lives.

Dr. Adams points to an interesting dilemma in the academy that makes it unnecessarily difficult for new faculty to manage the challenges of their personal and professional lives. Though knowing more about the life situations of new hires might enable the university to provide support geared at increasing their likelihood to succeed, the real issues are hardly ever addressed throughout the hiring process. After all, it is against most institutions' policies to ask questions about candidates' personal lives during job interviews. Metropolitan's "Guidelines for Lawful Interviewing," for example, prohibits the following questions to be asked: Are you married? Do you have children? When do you plan to have children? What child care arrangements do you have in place? Does your spouse mind if you travel?

Dr. Adams describes such a policy as a "Catch-22."

> This is sort of a Catch-22 you're dealing with. I think about people when talking about the search committee and the different questions that they can and can't ask people. And the things that most people tend to leave for are those questions that no one can ask them about.

Dr. Adams is hinting at an important paradox. The very concept that candidates interviewing for positions may not be asked personal questions is based on the *intent* of protecting the candidate. A person's personal situation is not deemed relevant to their professional life and ought not influence the minds of those who are to make decisions about whether or not to hire the person. Such policies, ironically, may have unintended consequences in that they do not permit a hiring institution to assess a candidate's life situation as a whole and make the necessary support available. This kind of omission, however, may well set the new faculty member up for failure.

The policy of "not naming" the issues is based on the assumption that a candidate's personal circumstances and possible plans are *liabilities* and, if brought to the surface, could potentially impede a person's chances at being offered the position. The underlying implications are illustrative of a higher education system that, to this day, continues to be based on male standards. The ideal candidate for a position is essentially *unencumbered*, if not supported at home by a devoted spouse. Asking questions about the scholar's personal life, however, could bring to light that she *is encumbered*, be it through children at home or plans to have children in the future. This would not be good for the job prospect, and so it is only fair to omit all questions about her personal life in order for such issues not to come to light. As illustrated by Dr. Adams, not naming what may need attention in a person's personal life, however, may well backfire and not only cut short an individual's career at a certain institution, but it may also mean that the institution wasted precious resources during the recruitment and search process for a person who was essentially set up to fail.

Colleges and universities should reevaluate how to deal with the interview process and early interactions with job applicants. To be sure, the issue of asking candidates about their personal lives is a precarious one, and they themselves are not free to share their life circumstances until entire mindsets will have shifted, and family obligations are no longer seen as distractions from work but rather necessary societal contributions. Until such cultural shift occurs it may be wise to consider that once an offer has been made and accepted, university administrators in conjunction with specifically trained personnel in Human Resources discuss with the new hire what kinds of personal support mechanisms are needed. These conversations ought to be routine parts of the hiring process, and need to go beyond a casual hint that "resources are available in the human resource department." They would center on whatever is relevant to the individual's circumstances and situation but might include such issues as finding affordable housing and high-quality schools, spousal hiring, child care, maternity policies, or elder care.

It is essential, however, that concerns with personal needs not simply be delegated and shipped off to human resource departments. Their services are certainly helpful and provide expertise and information on available resources that deans or department chairs may be lacking. However, new hires need more than a brochure listing available child care facilities. They need their individual situations considered by those who have the power to make a difference and adjust the new person's schedule to accommodate when children need to be picked up from school or work out a lighter teaching load during a pregnancy, to name only a few examples. As anyone who is new to a job can attest, the first year or so tends to be both stressful and demanding. Colleges and universities have a choice to become more proactive in addressing relevant issues early on and helping the newly hired person succeed.

Flagship's Dr. Cohen captures it succinctly:

> Only in the last four or five years has the . . . school here understood that the best way to take care and nurture and retain good faculty, especially younger faculty, is to really reengineer how we organize their jobs. The kinds of things we are willing to talk about with them on the job. Elder care, child care, allowing them to talk about some of the tensions and balancing acts, to really bring that conversation into the workplace and not leave it to everybody to figure out in isolation.

In conclusion, academe may well face a "problem of opportunity"; there is, in other words, ample room for improvement of the ways institutions of higher education aid their faculty, particularly women, to establish a healthy balance that enables them to pursue both productive careers and fulfilling personal lives. Much can be done, and the participants in this study make numerous proposals for reform. Some are systemic and require fundamental restructuring of practices and culture; others are detail-oriented, specific, and easily implemented. All are steps in the right direction.

While Women Wait: Advice for the Interim

The preceding section summarizes proposals for institutional reform voiced by women across career stages and presents a model to reform the tenure process. While academic women in the nation's colleges and universities either wait, or actively participate as change agents in reforming the academy, they may find it useful to consider the wealth of advice participants in this study give about coping with complex challenges on a daily basis. After all, even though ideas for systemic reform are essential for the fate of higher education long-term, practical suggestions are needed short-term because most female faculty members cannot afford to wait until their college has finally morphed into a qualitatively different institution. The purpose of this section is to pass along what was offered.

General Advice

"Say 'no' to some things. Say 'no' to a lot of things. I mean, just learn to say 'no'" is how Community College's early-career faculty Lilian puts it. Mid-career Professor Newton at Flagship sends a similar message; there is a real need for mentoring of women on how to play this game, she says, and although it may sound cynical, we are talking about gamesmanship. "On a bad day I feel like I need to be a little tougher and more strategic on how to allocate my time, and what duties I say 'yes' to, and how I'm going to organize my work and promote myself." Women should advise each other on establishing priorities, sticking to their guns, and not feeling guilty about their decisions. "The goal is to have a balance," she emphasizes, "not necessarily to break all records." Her suggestion is for women to take the long view and define what is important rather than engaging in the minute-by-minute prioritizing that is quite common. She, for example, does not take phone calls when someone is in her office, and is convinced that just because something is "urgent" does not mean it is "important." "Step back and have some perspective on what you choose to spend your time doing," is how she puts it.

Finding a mentor, particularly a woman, is a huge resource, echoes Metropolitan's Associate Professor Kaminski. "That is something I would tell younger faculty; to get that mentor. Someone you can really go to who can help you navigate the system. That is critical." Mentors in her life have pushed her not to back down on a number of things, she remembers. "I would like to give that message to younger women. Stand up for yourself; be comfortable being assertive. You don't have to be the aggressive woman, but to be assertive, to be aware of what the opportunities are, and to feel that you are entitled and deserving of as many opportunities as your male counterparts." Women, she thinks, are still very timid about asking for pay increases, for instance, or getting release time, graduate student support, and other means they need for their careers. She knows she has been guilty of reticence when it came to asking for things, and of feeling she did not deserve them. "Thank goodness there have been some mentors there who said 'don't shortchange yourself,'" she reports.

Late-career Dr. Posen at Metropolitan could not agree more with Dr. Kaminski's perspective on women's need to be assertive. These are her words:

> I don't think anyone should sacrifice themselves on the altar of someone else's ego. I think women do that. They do it for department chairs. They do it for deans. They do it for other people in their lives. They do it for men. I think that is one of the hardest things to learn. To really get the kind of self-confidence and agency is something some of us are not very good at. Being

assertive without being perceived as aggressive is always the challenge for women. Can you be strong without being considered being too much like a man? This has been going on for decades. That issue is still there. How are we supposed to dress? These issues are still with us the way they were in the 1970s when I was in graduate school, to a certain degree.

Repeatedly, assertiveness comes up as an essential trait for women to acquire. "You have to learn how to say 'no' to work," is the familiar-sounding advice, this time given by Associate Professor Seidman at Flagship. She recommends knowing what the expectations are and not getting sidetracked by "something interesting that comes along and you feel passionate about." In addition, it is important to find out how to cope with stress and to leave stress at work. Doing so will enable you to attend to yourself when you get home, personally, emotionally, and spiritually, as well as to those with whom you are in relationship, she says. Dr. Seidman has seen junior faculty who are able to do that, who protect themselves, and are then in a much better position to balance. Universities are tempting places, after all, where it is easy to get sidetracked.

When you get into a university setting, there's so many things going on, and there's so many people who have so many interests, and there are so many outreach opportunities that you just want to do them all. I think you have to attend to your own professional life, and what's expected of you, and then pick and choose very carefully beyond that.

She talks about committees all "wanting a piece of you," colleagues who are doing research in your area of expertise "wanting a piece of you"; and although there is a lot of pressure on you, these projects also promise to be fun. And "it's all positive, but I don't think you can jump into everything. I think you really have to protect yourself, and protect your time initially until you get your feet wet."

Dr. Seidman further recommends a focus on the self, and then those with whom one chooses to share one's life. They are the ones who help you balance, she found, and they are the ones that help you get along, not the job. After all, you will never get rewarded for all the things you do, and you may even get sanctioned for some of the things you do, according to her experience.

Community College's late career faculty member Monet stresses the importance of clearly understanding an institution's expectations; her college, for example, consists of three campuses, and faculty may be assigned to teach on all of them. In addition, they may have to teach at night, and there is currently a movement under way to require them to be available on Saturdays. Consequently, Ms. Monet thinks "people need to have a good vision of what's expected of them before they go in."

Her colleague at Flagship, Associate Professor Sutherland, goes beyond that. She thinks what is even more important than finding out institutional expectations is for faculty to define success for themselves, to compare that definition with the definition of success at their university, and to leave if the two do not match up.

> Well, there's a lot of pressure when you first get started to make sure that you do what's necessary to make tenure at the university you are at. I've seen people that were totally preoccupied with that worry. As a result, they stressed or were constantly worried, or sacrificing or doing things to make sure they made the tenure. My advice to young people, when they come in, is do what it is you think is necessary to succeed, and [according to] your definition of success. If your definition of success is different from the university's definition, then you're probably at the wrong place anyway, and who cares if

you make tenure. I try to advise them to stop worrying about meeting standards imposed by the university, and set their own standards. If they happen to be at a place where their standards don't match the university's then you just as well find out now and go some place else where you're going to be happy. That's my biggest piece of advice. As a result, I guess I've always been of the philosophy, like in my lab when I advise my grad students, that a healthy amount of play is necessary to efficient, good work. The lab that plays together stays together. To make sure people find time for other things, so they're happy and fulfilled.

Late-career Dr. D'Embri at Private Comprehensive could not agree more. She wants students to ask themselves what kinds of lives they want to have, and to make decisions accordingly. She reiterates advice given by others in this study, namely the importance of knowing what is important and recognizing that priorities can wax and wane, shifting between research and children, for example. A colleague at her institution, late-career Professor Witherspoon, simply states it this way: "People need to know themselves before they go into academics, and not be blinded."

"I tell my students, find a career path or find something that you feel passionately about. . . . Set priorities that are meaningful," mid-career faculty Ehrenreich at Community College says. And HBCU's Associate Professor Pritchard recommends faculty order their priorities and realize that "everything that comes across your desk is not a priority, no matter how it's framed." If women have children, furthermore, she recommends to give them their due time, and in addition "you need not neglect your health." She also insists that "you need not neglect your scholarship" and reminds us that what counts in our profession is "publication first, and interaction with your students second, and service third. We love service, and we want to do that, but if you want to get tenured, then

you need to understand the hierarchy." Metropolitan's Associate
Professor Schumacher puts it even more starkly:

> If I could tell any pre-tenure woman anything, it would
> be the thing they can't do. . . . If I was starting fresh with
> what I know now, I would never set foot on this campus
> except to go teach my class. [I would just stay home and
> write] . . . because the university will suck the life out of
> junior faculty. I see it happening all the time. . . .

Flagship's late-career Dr. Koshino warns junior faculty "until
you get tenure, don't worry about being nice and pleasing to everybody. Concentrate on two areas: teaching and publication. . . ."
Given that she works in a research-intensive institution, she
even recommends not going beyond the call of duty in regard to
your teaching responsibilities, either, because "publication weighs
more," she thinks and, as far as publishing is concerned, recommends: "concentrate on one manuscript, and really work on it."
She finds it important to get one's personal life in order, furthermore, because it affects one's professional life. Be careful what
kind of mate you find, and be communicative with sympathetic
colleagues and chairs, she offers.

Retired professor Wiley seconds Dr. Koshino's statement about
finding a suitable mate; her advice to women is to pick a good
partner, whoever that partner may be, share the load, and have
some understanding of one another. Young professional women
should also be advised, she says, to "be very alert to the men in
your life, and whether they are competing with you." And if they
are, she suggests, "find somebody who is not." Doing so does not
mean you are choosing down, she insists; it merely means you are
looking for someone who has the self-assurance that your success
is not perceived as undermining the partner's success.

HBCU's late-career faculty Beseley's advice does not concern
men. Instead, she urges female faculty to "form the community

of connected women where they have this connected knowledge, this connected being." At Flagship, Dr. Koshino is not so sure. She does not like to play the "gender card," she insists. Women being administrators, for example, "doesn't seem to do anything for women." Those females act like men, compete with them, and are part of the power structure, she observes, and "so gender goes down the drain, and I'm very, very concerned about that." Consequently, women have to be more conscious of their own gender without playing the "gender card," and rather than being needy ("I'm a woman, I'm a woman, so I need this, and need this") they "have to have guts, they have to have an active attitude toward improving things. . . . Without playing gender cards, women can accomplish more for other women and for society, as a whole."

Metropolitan's late-career Professor Velvarde has her own ideas about what female faculty ought to do. She does not think that competition with each other gets women anywhere but, instead, "we as women need to figure out if we don't help each other, nobody's going to help us, . . . especially at a place like this university where there aren't a whole lot of women in leadership roles."

Retired professor Wiley provides a concrete example of how women may do this. Junior faculty women at her former institution built a support system by forming a writing group and being faithful to it. Married or not, families or not, she says, about five women met for three hours every week.

> They had assignments for each other and critiqued each other's research and writing. Challenged each other on what they were doing, and I saw that as very healthy. They looked forward to that, and they developed friendships out of it, and they developed work out of it. They combined their career with a support system that understood them, although they came from different disciplines and had different kinds of writing

that they were doing, different kinds of research that they were doing, but they learned from one another as a result of it. It was like a really top notch graduate seminar that was productive. They held each other responsible. "You said you were going to get this done by such and such a date, where is it?" In a challenging but supportive environment. . . . Some of the guys started teasing about it and saying "can we come too?"

Advice to Graduate Students

If you are interested in a position in higher education, go ahead and get the Ph.D. right away, is Ms. Ohler's advice. She teaches at Community College with a master's degree in hand, and wishes she had made a different choice and completed her Ph.D. before she began her teaching career. Now she is planning to enroll in a doctoral program but is daunted by the prospect of having to balance her teaching job with the requirements of a Ph.D. program. "One thing I would have to say to someone who is looking for this sort of teaching job, I would encourage them, knowing the field now, to go ahead and get the Ph.D. right after the master's if you feel interested in that," she says.

In addition, she emphasizes the importance of making contacts and networking by attending conferences and taking advantage of people one knows who can help make contact with people at other schools. "Establishing that social network in the workplace is critical," and so is staying current in the field. She was able to get her instructor position after only a couple of years of adjunct teaching, she reports, and before she applied, she had gone to two conferences. "I think the [search] committee was really impressed with that. Not only was I teaching as an adjunct, but making an effort to be active in academia and in that world." She advises being active and going "beyond just your assigned platform, and making sure you take the initiative to keep up with your own projects at least to some extent, even if it is just one conference a year." HBCU's mid-career faculty Pritchard would agree. "Network, network, network," she recommends. "This is how you gain opportunities to publish, present scholarly work, and gain professional advice."

Early-career faculty member Nelson at HBCU believes it is crucial for young women to "have a good head on their shoulders." They are, she says, often not focused when they start out, but take the easy way out, and drop out. Most men, however, keep going because "they tend to be more competitive, and they don't want to drop out of stuff because they worry about the way it looks. I think girls need to have the same outlook, and say 'you know, I can do it although I'm failing; if I try, I might just make it.'" They must have a good sense of direction and know where they want to get, and work hard toward those goals. If those things are in place, "they will definitely make it because obviously that's what I did. There were many instances when I wanted to quit, but I didn't quit because of my support system," is the way she sums it up.

Thinking about graduate students, Flagship's early-career faculty member Miller's advises: "don't have children while you're taking classes," yet "having children while you're an advanced graduate student is probably not bad because your time is flexible." The same is true for post-docs, she thinks; they are flexible and may still be able to get a fair amount of research done even if they have children. Having a baby as an assistant professor is probably a "pretty stressful thing to do," she anticipates, and yet she is currently pregnant with her second child. "That's a choice," she explains. "I don't want to be having my children when I'm forty." Generally, she concedes, she does not live according to the advice she gives others:

> I don't know, the advice I've always given to my students
> is, they need to—and this is funny to hear coming out of
> my mouth because I don't live by this. I mean the advice

I give them is put themselves first, because if they're not happy, they won't be productive. . . . I wouldn't say, I'm unhappy, but I don't put myself first.

Advice to Faculty Who Are Considering Careers and Families

Ms. Young-Powell at Community College advises beginning faculty to know you can have both and balance both, a family and a career. However, you need to be able to plan and prioritize, she insists, and decide how much you are willing to give to your profession versus your family. "I know with me, if it came between family and career, it's definitely family," she says. "That has to be my #1 priority as mom. I chose to have them." She thinks the sequence of events is important, too, and that establishing a career before having children might be more practical than the reverse. "I see people I teach who have a family, and now they're trying to take classes and work, and they're mom and wife," she says, and perhaps it is better to first decide on a career, get established, and then add the family to it. "I think trying to jump too quickly and do everything at once can definitely throw you off. Planning, prioritizing, and saying 'I want both, and I know I can have both. . . . It's just balancing it,'" is her mantra.

Some faculty members give specific advice concerning the care of children, and how to raise them. Getting on the waiting list early for quality child care, for instance, is important. Assistant Professor Miller at Flagship University reports a two-year waiting list at her university's day-care center, which leaves as the only option sending her small daughter to a different facility, further away and more expensive. Furthermore, children should not be overly involved in sports and other after-school activities. It only leads to women being tied up "running around with kids for days. Kids don't need that," says Metropolitan's Assistant Professor McMillan. People are brainwashed into thinking that children have to do all these things, she insists, but they are spending all day away at school anyhow. So, women ought to make adjustments and find time for themselves. Community College's late career faculty Monet concurs. Children seem to make more demands on young adults today, more so than they did in previous generations, is her opinion. For one, schools tend to demand more parental involvement than they did in the past, and, second, children generally get involved in more activities, all contributing to the pressure on their parents.

Regarding children, Community College's early career faculty member Lilian suggests choosing a partner who is involved in child rearing and avoid having children be overly dependent only on their mother. Mid-career Dr. Schumacher at Metropolitan recommends, "never have children without family in town because you need backup and resources." She tells the story of having to take her smallest child to the hospital in the middle of the night, and the only choice she and her husband had was to wake up the other child, pack her up and take her along. "Because there is no one I can call at three in the morning and say 'can you come over and just stay with her so we can take the other one to the hospital?' We don't have those kinds of networks and resources to call on for backup."

Along similar lines, cultivating both personal and work relationships, and surrounding oneself with enabling people who are loving and supportive of one's goals, is Community College's Ms. Ehrenreich's advice. Get help at home. Talk to your family about the kind of support you may be able to get, and hire someone to clean the house, suggests Metropolitan's Assistant Professor McMillan. "Get help anyway you can get help," echoes her colleague Dr. Schumacher. House cleaning, maintaining the grounds, whatever it takes, hire somebody to do it because . . .

> . . . if you try to run the mundane things of life, you don't have time to be with your kids, or the whole time you're with your kids it's sort of setting them aside so you

can do the dishes. I don't think that is good for them, and when you are at work, at least for me, that is still a burden that I'm carrying into my office. I know when I get home, I have to deal with it if I haven't found help. So, in that sense, get help.

All in all, female faculty in this study supplement their ideas for institutional reform with down-to-earth proposals for how to make it in academe, be successful yet sane, and be able to pursue what women themselves deem important in life. Some of their suggestions are specifically directed at those who prepare to join the professoriate, while others are primarily useful for women who are planning to combine work and children. Many ideas apply to female faculty more generally, regardless of career stage, future plans, or family constellation.

In all, these "tips for an academic life" are not meant to be solutions in a grander scheme, promising to create new conditions in higher education that allow women to better balance their professional and personal lives. They are, instead, pieces of wisdom borne out by experience, and they are immensely useful while we all work and wait for a better world.

Note

1. Interestingly enough, even egalitarian social policies may not necessarily lead to gender equality because of the persistent power of pervasive cultural assumptions and traditions. Finland, for instance, provides paternal leave in cases of birth or adoption of a child. Yet research indicates that Finnish men take less parental leave than their female counterparts (Lammi-Taskula, 2000, pp. 1–24).

Conclusion

"Feminists often say that we have to start with women's own experience if we are to understand how profoundly it influences our perspectives, values, attitudes, and role in society," writes Judith Glazer-Raymo (1999, p. 1). This study started right there. It was the women's experiences with balancing professional and personal lives in the context of higher education that I wanted to unearth, understand, and put on paper—in their own words, as much as possible. Those experiences, I believe, shed light on statistics that stubbornly refuse to change, the numbers that indicate a continuing underrepresentation of women in higher faculty ranks. Little progress has been made in this regard despite narrowing of gender gaps in many societal realms and the drastically increased representation of women in higher education overall. Something continues to plug the pipeline and hold women back, and it was my hunch, supported by a growing body of research, that the difficulties of finding a sustainable balance between professional and personal obligations may be a central reason for the stagnation, one that has not sufficiently been studied. That's what this book set out to investigate.

Studying the sparse literature on the topic of balancing personal and professional lives in academe, it seemed to me that the focus was primarily on women with children, and some of the newest research dealt with questions of babies, and what having babies tends to do to women's careers (Mason, Goulden, & Wolfinger, 2006). I decided to broaden the scope and include women in diverse living arrangements, of different sexual orientations, and with and without partners and/or children. In addition, I sought to include women of middle and advanced age, at mid- and late-career stages, and to find out what issues they face in their quest to balance personal and professional lives in academe.

This study is not longitudinal in nature but compares women who are at different life stages *today*. However, studying the topic across generations provides a unique comparative lens and allows glimpses into the past, an appreciation for progress over time, as well as wake-up calls to face those realities that simply do not get better.

The best fit for this study was a qualitative interview design. It was stories I was after. "[S]tories form the foundation of any teacher's professional life," write faculty developers O'Donovan and Simmons (2006, p. 315), and yet, they say, college and university instructors rarely have opportunities to tell their teaching stories in structured and reflective ways. This research provided such opportunities to female faculty across career spans. Although their stories are not about teaching but about the relationship between their personal and professional lives, the intent very similarly is to give voice to memories and a wealth of experiences women in academe accumulated over time.

And wealth I found. It is clear that exceedingly difficult times often await beginning faculty members when they need to establish themselves professionally, and when those on tenure-track are plagued by nebulous and ever-increasing expectations of what it means to be worthy of institutional commitment. Many are not clear about how to design a life path that allows them to have both a career and a family, if they so desire. Single women have difficulty finding the time to focus on networking and dating, a problem compounded by the fact that many early-career faculty are recent transplants from far-away places. The tenure-clock, for many, coincides with their last child-bearing years, creating the bind of either postponing having children or giving up on them altogether.

Women who decide to become parents anyway pay a high price trying to do it all. While individuals in their lives, be they spouses, partners or colleagues, are often major enablers, institutional support is largely nonexistent. Maternity leave has to be individually negotiated rather than being equally available to all, a finding consistent with existing research (Wolf-Wendel & Ward, 2006). The ramifications of taking leave, or stopping the tenure-clock, furthermore, are unclear, and women are haunted by anxiety that their benefits come with a price tag—also mirroring previous studies (Wolf-Wendel & Ward, 2006; Ward & Wolf-Wendel, 2004; Drago & Colbeck, 2003; Finkel, Olswang & She, 1994). For example, will research expectations go up because these women are perceived to have more time before they come up for tenure? Policies that single out one particular group based on such innate characteristics as gender have a tendency to stigmatize and, despite good intentions, create unintended consequences.

Early-career faculty face other issues; one is the dual-career problem. Since the academic job market is largely a national one, faculty tend to move geographically to take a position, often far away. In many cases, their partners are academics also, confronting a highly selective job market and unable to relocate as easily as the wives of former generations of faculty could. The problem is not entirely new, as has been articulated before, and some institutions are taking steps to address it. Even though more research is needed to adequately gauge progress in that regard, the women in this study seem to experience primarily token efforts to accommodate the career aspirations of significant others. The problem is a vexing one, fraught with ethical and professional dilemmas. I admit not to have ready solutions at hand but do know that more discussion is clearly needed.

And so are efforts to better understand the various challenges faced by an understudied population, immigrant scholars. Partly an outgrowth of a rapidly globalizing world, increasing numbers of faculty posts are held by foreign nationals. Perhaps because they occupy relatively privileged positions as researchers and faculty, not as much attention is being paid to their well-being as, for instance, to that of international students. What international scholars may go through because of cultural barriers, adjustment problems, and emotional, psychological, and social challenges related to their immigrant status and experiences is simply not known. This study suggests that more research is needed to take a closer look at the issues, and that institutions of higher education ought to start paying attention to the needs of this group, which makes highly valuable contributions to the system.

Mid-career faculty on the tenure-track have been able to get out of the shadow cast by the tenure albatross. Yet their lives continue to be extremely busy now that they take on the responsibilities of senior professors. Those with children never get to rest, and largely sacrifice care of self, despite the fact that many benefit from supportive partners who do more at home than "helping out." A sign of the times is the increasing number of faculty women with stay-at-home spouses. Although such arrangements may be just as convenient for women as they used to be for men of past generations, it is my opinion that the model might well be flawed in much the same way that its gender-reversed predecessor was. Some people, women or men, may wish not to enter gainful employment and stay home, if they can afford to do so. Such a choice is theirs to make. Yet if one person in a family *needs* to stay at home in order to make the arrangement work, there is a problem. The world worth striving for, as I see it, includes as one of the choices for both partners in a family to have professional lives and be actively engaged at home, as well. For that to happen in ways that allow women (and men) to maintain a healthy balance in their lives, institutions simply have to change, and we are far from the mark in that respect. Echoing their early-career colleagues, mid-career female faculty report how little institutional support was available when they started their families, and how little continues to be available for them now. The institutions they portray were indifferent to faculty's balancing issues at best, and are probably more adequately described as downright hostile.

Mid-career faculty in this study are working on actively defining their identity and refusing to "play games." They "come out" in more ways than one. One woman reports revealing her homosexual identity and carving out a space for herself that allows her to be who she is without pretense, and a colleague adjusts how she defines boundaries so that she is able to venture into new professional territory as an administrator. This trajectory appears to continue because late-career faculty almost unequivocally seem happy with who they are and where they are in life.

The relative contentment seeping through the comments of the late-career faculty in this study is palpable. Almost all of them say they are happy with the balance they have finally reached in their lives. This finding, of course, needs to be put in perspective given that the participants in this study represent success stories; they are the ones who made it rather than left the system.

Nevertheless, it is heartening to hear how much control they feel they have over how they allocate their time and make choices about what is worth pursuing at work (and what is not), and that they are, finally, in positions to take care of themselves. Some choose to work more, finally able to do so unencumbered, whereas others are happy to have found a level of productivity that allows a life that is relatively sane. One group totally merges personal and professional spheres and effortlessly slides back and forth between the two; another group enjoys finally being able to separate the two without annoying encroachments. Although previous research maintains that in comparison to other work (for example, shift work in a factory) academic work allows for a higher degree of choice as to how flexible and permeable the boundaries between work and life are to be (Colbeck, 2006, p. 35), my study indicates that there are significant differences across generations, and it may only be late-career faculty who truly enjoy a choice.

One of the reasons it was so good to hear late-career women talk about their choices and the healthy state of balance at the present time is that so many of them have gone through so much in the past. Their stories abound with costs and sacrifices unimaginable to many of us in the younger generations. They tell of the subjugation of their careers to family needs, of decades of feeling torn between their personal and professional lives, of unbearable losses and regrets. They were pioneers who did path-breaking work, not just in scholarly terms but also in terms of what they accomplished for generations of women to come. They were shunned by their profession, exploited by the system, but fought for access and, once that was gained, continued to fight for equal, or at the very least decent, treatment.

Despite their successes, however, and their relative bliss currently, challenges continue to exist. For one, the "sandwich generation" finds itself squeezed between two needy populations, their children whom they often still support, and their parents who are reaching advanced ages. Elder care was mentioned as a particular challenge. Furthermore, although some feel they have reached the peak of their careers, others battle feelings of alienation in institutions they fear are changing for the worse and feelings of inferiority because of younger colleagues whom they perceive as better prepared professionally than they ever were. Retirement starts to loom on the horizon, and it looks good to some, whereas others worry how to stay active and engaged and have partners who share the journey with them.

Regardless of career stage, female faculty in this study report not just challenges but enablers as well, ranging from partners, spouses, extended family, and friends to professional colleagues, mentors, other professors, and administrators. To supplement those, the women employ a wide variety of coping strategies, some personal in nature, others involving the way they work, but all of them instructive for others.

Large-scale quantitative research is needed to assess the variations in balancing acts according to institutional makeup. Though the women in this study come from five different institutions, their experiences cannot be generalized as representing the various types of colleges and universities. Lisa Wolf-Wendel and Kelly Ward compared policies at different institutions, but their research focused primarily on maternity policies and other provisions most relevant to women of child-bearing age who are planning to combine families and careers. The balancing issues women in later life stages and/or in different living arrangements face are not addressed (Wolf-Wendel & Ward, 2006).

Across generations, women share positive experiences with individual men in their lives, be they spouses, friends, mentors, or colleagues. At the same time, they work in a system that has been able neither to topple its structure built on male privilege nor shed the remnants of misogynist attitudes and behaviors. They do not doubt that in many ways academic women have come a long way and no longer have to contend with the blatant sexism of previous generations. Both at work and at home, progress is unmistakable. It is disconcerting, however, that much has not changed enough or has simply morphed into a different beast. Women are still forced to make choices between families and careers that men do not have to make; they continue to sacrifice themselves to be able to "do it all," are still disadvantaged in terms of pay, and are still pushed to perform the least rewarded labor. They know all that, and make recommendations for change.

Some of what the participants in this study suggest are well known reiterations of reform proposals made before. They include the provision of child care, for example, and the standardization of university policies and services meant to support life-balancing efforts of faculty. Others are less often talked about.

The exemplar model for tenure is an entirely new idea. It introduces into academic culture the notion that, if we are to take seriously that people's lives do not, cannot, and should not revolve around work entirely, we need to have a tenure policy in sync with that idea. Some would say we should do away with tenure entirely, and might even use "family-friendliness" to support their position. In my opinion, this would be a grave mistake. It is the tenure system that protects academic freedom, and it is the tenure system that gives exemplary scholars such as Drs. Pelletier and Pryzinski in this study the freedom to define how they want to be. That freedom is essential if we want faculty who are creative, productive, and, yes, happy.[1]

Critics of the reform proposals made in this book may argue that to follow the suggestions would be too expensive. I would counter that some reforms would cost nothing and yet go a long way in facilitating better balance. Examples are the exemplar model of tenure or better coordination and advertising of available university services. Other proposals involve costs, such as the provision of decent maternity leave, but they are worthy investments. Just as sabbaticals and research leave invigorate faculty and, ultimately, make them more productive, time to bear and have children or deal with other crucial personal issues will be likely to have similar effects. It will diminish stress and allow faculty to take care of essential things in life, and then come back to productive careers. In a strictly economic sense, hiring and acculturating new faculty is expensive for universities, and it is in their best interest to retain quality people instead of losing them because support is lacking during major life events or crises.

Women in this study do not merely make suggestions for systemic reform, however. They also share strategies on how to survive on a daily basis and, at times, "beat the system." One of these strategies, as useful as it may be at the moment, may well be counterproductive in the long term and, in addition, contradict other aims formulated by the women. I am referring to the women's repeated recommendation not to engage in university service because it is undervalued and will not yield the same recognition for academic work as scholarship and teaching. Although the suggestion is well grounded in reality, to further encourage individualizing behavior such as grant work, research, and publishing at the expense of service strikes me as shortsighted long-term, and as contradicting the expressed needs for collaboration, networks, and community. It is exclusively centered on individuals, their careers, and promotions, whereas service to professional and other communities has a centrally important place in the work of university professors who see themselves not only as creators of knowledge but also as active members of the scholarly community and servants of the greater good.

I fear a "tragedy of the commons" to occur if faculty's only concern with service is how to get out of it. Even though this behavior may well be more typical for men than for women, it is not worth emulating. What needs to happen instead, I submit, is an institutional reevaluation of roles and rewards to align what people are asked to do with how they are rewarded for it. As Jon Wergin argues, such an alignment is a responsibility that does not exclusively fall on the shoulders of university administrators; faculty in such bodies as tenure and promotion committees have a role to play in this as well (Wergin, 2003, p. 19).

According to Wergin, furthermore, faculty tend to be motivated by different things, among them professional autonomy and intellectual community, and these two motivators tend to be in tension. To overcome this tension and build an environment conducive to productive faculty life, he makes several suggestions. One is to create institutions that make it possible for faculty to identify with them because they understand they are part of an academic community that cares about them and respects both their autonomy and their unique contributions to the common good (Wergin, 2003, p. 23). A caring institution, however, can ill afford to ignore the strains put on its faculty when, for one, values, expectations, and rewards are out of step, and for another, women more than men suffer from the consequences of the misalignment.

Some of the challenges experienced by the women in this study may be indicative of problems that go beyond academe. Perhaps, as a culture, we are indeed "in over our heads," as psychologist Robert Kegan suggests (Kegan, 1994). He postulates that adults in general may not be equipped for the cultural demands of modern life given that these have grown ever more challenging over time. Just as most children cannot handle a school curriculum far above their grade level, adults find themselves unable to handle the "curriculum" imposed on them by an increasingly complicated society that offers choices that, if made, place expectations on people that they are not adequately prepared to meet.

Certainly it seems as if the women in this study at times are "in over their heads." Whether men in academe share the feeling has not yet been explored but will soon be studied (Philipsen & Bostic, in preparation). Be that as it may, the question is what to do about the situation. Whereas psychology typically focuses on helping people adapt mentally and learn new ways to cope with situations, I am less convinced that women in academe need to learn new coping skills. As my study illustrates, they have already developed an amazing array of these. Although such publications as *Balancing Work and Family*, published by the American Management Association (Lizotte & Litwak, 1995), may provide many helpful tips on "how to do it," it is based on the assumption that balancing one's life is solely a matter of individual taste and construction. "You will create true balance in your life only by setting your own standards and fashioning your own definition of balance," the publication insists (p. 4). I think not.

Certainly, individual standards are important, yet merely having them does not guarantee successful balance. Standards can only be fulfilled within parameters that are conducive to their fulfillment. The women in this study have all sorts of different standards; they are very different individuals, and yet their balancing acts during their early and middle years are precarious not because of their standards but because of inflexible institutional frameworks still steeped in patriarchal notions of what it means to be a faculty member. So I submit that we need to locate responsibility for a system that does not adequately provide the tools faculty need for a successful balancing of their lives, where it lies: in outmoded structures and old-fashioned mind frames. This continues to be the task to change so that future generations will be able to draw conclusions significantly different from those of Flagship's Professor Seidman, who says:

> I think in terms of doing the balancing, the most important person is me. The second-most person is the person I choose to share my life with, and the other people with whom I share my life. I think people, after you take a look at what you bring and who we are as individuals, it's the people around you that help you do that balancing. It's the people around you that help validate you and tell you it's OK when you constantly don't make the mark. In our profession, we really need to be productive all the time, and be perfect in a sense. Of course, that's not realistic. At the very end, the organization is of the least help in helping you balance.

Note

1. For an extensive analysis of the important connection of happiness and education, see Nel Noddings (2002), *Happiness and Education*, Cambridge, UK; New York: Cambridge University Press.

Appendix A

Balancing Personal and Professional Lives—A Quantitative Assessment

Tim Bostic

Introduction

During my Ph.D. program, I had the opportunity to work with Maike Philipsen on her project researching the issues female faculty face trying to create a healthy balance between their personal and professional lives. The more interviews I transcribed, the more fascinated I became by the stories they shared. At times, I almost wept hearing some of the inequities they faced, and the personal sacrifices they made in order to have a career seemed, at times, almost unbelievable. As I continued transcribing the interview data, I became increasingly curious as to whether other female faculty shared their experiences. In a discussion with Maike about one particularly poignant interview, I asked her if she thought the women's experiences were unique. She was honest enough to say that she was not sure, but she doubted it. At that moment, I knew I wanted to conduct a quantitative survey to try to find out. In early Spring 2007, Maike provided me with the themes from the qualitative data and the statements relevant to them. These themes and statements became the starting point for the survey.

Survey Construction

Unlike most surveys, this one was grounded in real data. Rather than making educated guesses about the issues of balance between life and work that academic women face, I constructed the survey with statements women made in the interviews. At times, I synthesized several statements addressing a similar concern or issue to form one statement. At other times, a particular participant's comment was so salient and concise it stood on its own and did not need to be altered. This process allowed for clear alignment between the findings from the qualitative and quantitative data. The construction of the survey relied on the scale development process posited by Robert F. DeVellis in *Scale Development: Theory and Applications*.[1] The survey used a five-point Likert scale, ranging from "strongly agree" to "strongly disagree." The participants had the option of choosing "not applicable" on any questions that they did not feel applied to them.

After the construction of the initial survey, three expert reviewers provided feedback; appropriate changes were made, and several questions were eliminated because of redundancy or lack of clarity. The survey was piloted before being placed on Survey Monkey. The original survey had seventy-two questions measuring eight different constructs, reduced in its final form to six constructs and forty-seven questions. All versions of the survey have been included in Appendix B. The survey originally attempted to measure eight constructs; however, after performing a factor analysis on the data (see Appendix B), it became clear that four constructs, which seemed distinct at the time of the original construction, actually measured only two separate and distinct ideas. In order to ensure the decision to reduce the constructs was theoretically sound, I consulted with Maike Philipsen on whether she agreed that these were indeed similar and should be placed together.

Constructs Measured

Based on the qualitative data, whether or not academic women are able to establish a healthy balance between their personal and professional responsibilities depends on specific barriers, stressors, and enablers. In the first iteration of the survey, I attempted to measure whether the enablers came from institutional supports or through the support of significant others (spouses, families, colleagues, friends, support groups) in academic women's lives. Stressors included obligations women felt to their families and the academy, work sacrifices due to family obligations, family sacrifices due to work obligations, and personal sacrifices in the struggle to meet both family and work obligations. Also, the survey included questions that explored whether the tenure process acted as a barrier for academic women in their attempt to establish a healthy balance between their personal and professional responsibilities. Finally, several survey questions investigated whether academic women believed that creating a healthy balance proved easier for academic women today than for academic women in the past.

As stated previously, after performing the factor analysis on the survey, the stressors were actually only two constructs rather than the four first envisioned. The factor analysis helped clarify that the obligations women felt were clearly tied to personal sacrifices they made in order to meet their professional and personal responsibilities. Also, although sacrificing either work or home had originally been conceived as two distinct constructs, academic women who completed the survey felt as if they had to sacrifice either work or home in order to accomplish what was necessary in one arena or the other, so the questions measuring this idea were combined into one construct. Thus, the questions on the final survey measured whether institutional supports aid academic women creating a balance, whether the tenure process inhibits establishing a balance, whether the participants believe academic women today have it

Exhibit A.1.   Cronbach's Alpha coefficients for all constructs

Construct	Cronbach's Alpha
Institutional support	.88
Institutional support without college and department	.82
College support	.72
Departmental support	.74
Tenure process inhibits creating a balance between personal and professional responsibilities	.71
Past generations of women had a harder time creating balance compared to the current generation	.64
Obligations to work and home leave me feeling as if I have to sacrifice myself	.86
Significant others in my life help me deal with balance issues	.86
Feel as if either home or work is being sacrifice for the other	.70

easier than their female colleagues in the past, whether the participants believe they have to sacrifice themselves in order to meet their
personal and professional obligations, whether they believe they
must sacrifice either work or home to meet the needs of the other,
and whether significant others help in coping with the personal
and professional pressures these academic women feel. Exhibit A.1
presents the Cronbach's Alpha reliability coefficients for the six
constructs and the three subconstructs. These alphas are in the
"acceptable" range for surveys of this nature.

Recruitment

Due to time constraints, mailing the survey out to women individually or to organizations that may have ties to women academicians
was not possible. Therefore, the survey was posted on Survey
Monkey. A link to the survey was placed on a number of higher

education listservs with a message requesting academic women to complete it. In addition, I requested assistance from the Association of University Women, and Dr. Kelly Anne Ward, the organization's Researcher in Residence, was kind enough to send it along to participants in a study she was conducting. Although this method of recruitment was not the most effective, it was the only method that allowed for a large enough cross section of academic women. In all, 120 academic women filled out the survey. Twelve of them had to be removed from the database for such reasons as incomplete responses given, resulting in a final sample size of 108.

Limitations

Clearly, the biggest limitation is the method of recruitment. First and foremost, it created a situation where self-selection became an issue. Further, it is impossible to calculate the response rate, since it is unknown how many academic women actually saw the recruitment message, opened the survey, and then chose not to fill it out. However, because I was able to create groups of about fifty participants each, I was provided with enough statistical power to perform the descriptive statistical analysis needed to see whether the quantitative findings supported the qualitative findings.

I received three e-mails from potential participants who voiced concerns about the survey. In the first instance, the potential participant felt the survey ignored issues of sexual orientation and the experiences of lesbians in the academy. In the second case, the potential participant believed the survey was defining "family" in a traditional sense, that is, children and a male spouse. In the last case, the potential participant believed that other issues academic women face, such as being a caregiver to an ailing parent, were not addressed. Certainly the survey did not intend to marginalize any group of academic women, nor was it trying to negate less traditional definitions of family, nor was it implying the issues the survey questions were addressing were the only ones of import to academic women. Instead, the aim of administering the survey was to ascertain whether a larger group of academic women had similar experiences, beliefs, and feelings as the women interviewed in the qualitative portion of the study. The survey had an option under the demographic category "family life" (i.e., being partnered with a female) that would have aided me in clarifying how different groups felt about balancing personal and professional responsibilities; unfortunately, not enough respondents fell into those groups for them to be discussed. Fortunately, some of the participants in the interviews had diverse family life constructions, so I hope that academic women from these groups see themselves and their experiences in the stories of those women.

Results

The results section is broken down by the categories early-career women and mid-career women. Unfortunately, not enough women in the late stages of their careers participated in the study; therefore, only results for women in the early and mid stages of their career have been included. In each section, I discuss the findings based on the barriers, stressors, and enablers to creating a balance between personal and professional responsibilities that academic women face. Because some of the responses fell near the midpoint on the scale being used, a frequency exhibit for the constructs and histograms have been provided in Appendix C (Exhibit C.1). The medians and the modes for the constructs, also provided in Exhibit C.1), help paint a clearer picture of where the participants fell on the scale. Since the scale had a "neither agree nor disagree" option, it is easier to see with the histograms that the respondents were not ambivalent about the different constructs.

Early-Career Women

Exhibit A.2 provides the means and standard deviations for each of the constructs for the early career participants. Early-career women agree that the tenure process constitutes a barrier to creating a balance between their personal and professional lives. On this construct, this group of participants have a mean of 4.2. This finding, while not surprising, adds to the growing body of literature that examines the deleterious effects of the tenure process on academic women. The stressors were a little more ambiguous. The participants clearly believed they sacrifice themselves in order to meet their professional obligations (mean of 3.95); they also agree, although moderately, that either work or home is always being sacrificed (mean of 3.45). The implication is that women attempt to sacrifice either home or work in order to meet the demands they face from both spheres of their lives. It may be the need to juggle the responsibilities from both spheres that leads them to agree that they end up sacrificing themselves in order to meet their personal and professional obligations. A sample statement from this construct is "I give up time for things I want to do in order to make sure my work and family are taken care of." Female academics learn to suppress their own needs and wants in order to try to meet the responsibilities they face at home and at work. This fact may help explain why many academic women do not get across the tenure finish line. It seems that institutions must question their practices if the only way female faculty find it is possible to do all that is required of them is to forgo meeting their own needs.

In terms of the enablers, the participants clustered at the middle of the scale when asked whether the institutions at which they work provide support to assist them in balancing their personal and professional responsibilities (mean of 3.03). However, breaking this construct down by departmental support, college support, and institutional support, the research found participants are successively less likely to acknowledge support, depending on the size of

Exhibit A.2.   Means and Standard Deviations for Early-Career Women[a]

Construct	Sample Size	Mean	Std. Deviation
Institutional support	46	3.03	.901
Tenure inhibits balance	46	4.21	.513
Past generations had it harder	46	3.19	.648
Obligations lead to sacrifice of self	46	3.95	.703
Significant others help	46	3.87	.997
Work or home is sacrificed	46	3.45	.625
My department supports me	46	4.25	1.188
My college supports me	46	3.1	1.083
My institution supports me	46	2.51	.923

[a]Five-point Likert scale used ranging from strongly disagree to strongly agree, with 3 being neither agree nor disagree.

the academic unit: the degree of agreement was strongest at the departmental level (mean of 4.25), then decreased at the college level (mean of 3.1), and then decreased substantially at the institutional level (mean of 2.51). This finding illustrates that most of the support systems available to academic women are informal rather than institutionalized. It also suggests that academic women must rely on nonwritten policies in order to find ways to balance their personal and professional responsibilities.

The last questions concerning enablers focused on whether the help of significant others in their lives assists academic women in dealing with the pressure of trying to balance their personal and professional responsibilities. They agreed, on average, that the help of significant others in their lives enables them to achieve a sense of balance (mean of 3.87). Statements in this construct included "my friends who have similar life experiences help me attempt to cope with balancing my personal and professional responsibilities," and "my spouse/significant other allows me to attempt to have a balance between work and home." Therefore, support outside of the academy proves to be the greatest enabler for academic women to achieve a sense of balance. This finding, in conjunction with the finding that academic women do not feel supported by their institutions, helps clarify how the female academics who participated in this survey must look outside of codified, institutional programs to support them. When early-career women move to places where they do not have outside support networks in place, many are left feeling isolated and without any enablers to help them find a healthy balance between their personal and professional lives.

Finally, in response to whether past generations of academic women "had it harder," the mean for this construct was at the middle of the scale (mean of 3.19). An examination of individual questions within this construct reveals, however, that participants are not at all ambivalent: they believe that the institutional support received today is much greater than for past generations, and today spouses take on more responsibility for home and children. The means for these two questions are 3.91 and 3.87, respectively. The divergence of answers among participants on the individual questions led to a regression toward the mid-point of the scale. The early-career participants disagreed that academia is more supportive today than in the past, and that academic women in the past had it easier because they had fewer choices. The means for these two questions are 2.51 and 2.20, respectively. For this subgroup of women, even with many of the strides that female academics have made, they still believe it is difficult for academic women to achieve a balance. Although this group of women feels that they do not receive much institutional support, they do think that in some respects the institutional support female faculty receive today is better than in the past. It should be remembered, however, that the qualitative findings indicate an increase in expectations, so in that respect things have gotten more difficult.

Mid-Career Women

Exhibit A.3 provides the means and standard deviations for each of the constructs for mid-career participants. This group of academic women agrees that the tenure process inhibits balancing personal and professional responsibilities (mean of 3.86). They do not, however, agree as strongly as the early-career women. An independent sample t-test indicates that the difference is significant at the .02 level. Some of this difference may be explained by the completion of the tenure process for the mid-career women; perhaps pressures experienced in the past may no longer seem as severe. Thus, although they are in agreement with the early-career women that the tenure process creates a barrier to achieving a balance, they have made it to the other side and learned how to negotiate the process effectively. It should be remembered that the participants in this group are the "successful" ones who are still in the academy. Regardless of any negative experiences they may have had trying to negotiate the tenure process, they were able to hang on. The

Exhibit A.3.   Means and Standard Deviations for Mid-Career Women[a]

Construct	Sample Size	Mean	Std. Deviation
Institutional support	46	3.03	.901
Tenure inhibits balance	46	4.21	.513
Past generations had it harder	46	3.19	.648
Obligations lead to sacrifice of self	46	3.95	.703
Significant others help	46	3.87	.997
Work or home is sacrificed	46	3.45	.625
My department supports me	46	4.25	1.188
My college supports me	46	3.1	1.083
My institution supports me	46	2.51	.923

[a]Five-point Likert scale used, ranging from strongly disagree to strongly agree, with 3 being neither agree nor disagree.

women who did not make it through the tenure process are not accounted for.

Female faculty, even at mid-career, still feel they must sacrifice themselves in order to meet the obligations they have at home and work, and they believe they must constantly sacrifice either work or home in order to meet their responsibilities (means of 3.96 and 3.87, respectively). Their constant stress may explain why female faculty do not achieve parity with their male colleagues in terms of representation at the associate and full professor ranks. If the only way they can manage to get there is to sacrifice themselves, many may opt to get off the tenure treadmill. From the perspective of the participants in this study, this finding indicates a need for institutions to create support systems for women, so they do not have to make a choice between their work and their home.

Like their early-career colleagues, mid-career women agree that significant others in their lives help them deal with the pressures of trying to find a balance (mean of 3.75). On this construct, there is no statistically significant difference between the two groups. Again, since this group represents the success stories, institutions should try to learn from their resiliency and encourage the creation of appropriate support networks for their female faculty. Institutions committed to creating parity for women among the professoriate would be wise to foster support systems, both formal and informal, that help female faculty deal with the barriers they face in their attempt to create a balance in their lives. Unfortunately, mid-career participants feel even less support from their institutions in terms of balancing their personal and professional responsibilities than their early-career colleagues (mean of 2.69).

Mid-career faculty are split in their views about whether their institutions as a whole help them achieve a balance between their personal and professional responsibilities. Even though the overall mean was 2.99 on a five-point scale, most respondents indicated either agreement or disagreement with this statement. Like the early-career participants, breaking the construct down by department, college, and institution, they indicate that their departments are most supportive (mean of 3.31) and their institutions are least supportive (mean of 2.69). These differences are smaller than those for early-career faculty, however. The histograms for these constructs, provided in Appendix C, help further clarify these findings. Perhaps the early-career women are benefiting on a departmental level from having more female role models who were successful in negotiating the tenure process and making it to the other side. Unlike the early-career women, the possibility exists that the mid-career participants did not have any or as many female role models; thus, they do not feel as supported even on the departmental level as the early-career participants. This finding, in conjunction with the finding that this group of participants believe that they have to sacrifice themselves in order to meet all of their obligations, paints a bleak picture for female faculty, especially at this career stage.

Mid-career participants, like the early-career faculty, agree only slightly that past generations of academic women had it harder than women currently in academia (mean of 3.20). However, they demonstrate stronger agreement that a difference exists in the amount of support women in academia receive today compared to past generations of academic women, and that more institutional supports exist today as well (means of 3.88 and 3.94, respectively). They also agree that women today get more support from husbands and significant others who take on more responsibility for home and children (mean of 3.75). Finally, they agree balancing personal and professional responsibilities was more difficult for female academics in the past (mean of 3.82). However, again, these means are for individual questions and should be explored further in future research. These findings indicate that this group of academic women, relative to earlier generations, believes that things are getting better. Institutions have a long way to go, however, in order to make balancing personal and professional responsibilities easier for academic women.

Conclusion

Clearly, the quantitative data support the findings of the qualitative study. The women who completed the survey feel much the way the women interviewed do. First and foremost, the tenure process, as it stands, intrinsically inhibits creating a healthy balance between personal and professional responsibilities. In addition, regardless of career stage, the participants believe they must sacrifice themselves in order to make both arenas of their lives work. The data indicate that in order to have both professional and personal lives, female academics end up forgoing their own needs. Thus, female faculty believe they either sacrifice work or home in order to meet the demands of the other.

When looking solely at the survey findings, female academics, regardless of career stage, experience similar barriers, stressors, and enablers. Although there are some statistically significant differences between them, none of the differences prove *practically* significant, meaning the results are not large enough to indicate that they are important. The participants in the survey believe that the tenure process creates a barrier to finding a healthy balance between their personal and professional lives. The findings from the interview data help clarify exactly what issues surrounding tenure academic women face. Please note, however, that the qualitative data do not indicate that participants suggested doing away with the tenure process but only a need for reforming it.

Both groups feel they must sacrifice themselves in order to do what is required in their personal and professional spheres. Only through the qualitative findings do we begin to see what a toll these sacrifices take on academic women.

The enablers assisting academic women are insufficient for the types of demands they face. It is discouraging to think that the only available option for academic women is to rely on infor-mal practices within their departments to manage some type of personal/professional balance—discouraging because it forces women to depend on a system that has no clear guidelines. Instead, female academics must hope they end up in a department that supports them because it is clear from both the interview and survey findings that most do not feel supported by their institutions. Further, it is through significant others in their lives that they find a way to deal with the pressures of trying to balance their personal and professional responsibilities. The interview data help clarify not only exactly what these support structures look like, but also, because the support comes from outside of the academy, that women must find them on their own.

One would hope that academic institutions act as leaders in providing more hospitable working environments for women. However, the findings of this survey suggest that this is not the case. As new women enter the academy, it is imperative that they begin demanding formal, institutionalized systems that will allow them to create lives for themselves that are healthily balanced and sustainable.

Note

1. DeVellis, Robert F. (2003). *Scale Development: Theory and Application*. Thousand Oaks, CA: Sage Publications, Inc.

Appendix B

The Survey

Exhibit B.1. First Version of Survey Academic Women: Balancing Personal and Professional Lives

For each statement below, circle the number to the right that best fits your level of agreement with the statement.
If the statement is not applicable to you, please circle n/a.
1 = strongly disagree; 2 = disagree; 3 = mildly disagree; 4 = mildly agree; 5 = agree; 6 = strongly agree

Description/Identification of Survey Item	Strongly Disagree				Strongly Agree		
1. My institution provides support to help me cope with balancing my personal and professional responsibilities.	1	2	3	4	5	6	n/a
2. My department provides a supportive environment which aids my ability to balance the personal and professional.	1	2	3	4	5	6	n/a
3. My college provides a supportive environment which aids my ability to balance the personal and professional.	1	2	3	4	5	6	n/a
4. My institution supports families.	1	2	3	4	5	6	n/a
5. My institution has quality day care available on campus.	1	2	3	4	5	6	n/a
6. My institution has specific policies to help faculty when they have children.	1	2	3	4	5	6	n/a
7. The class schedule at my university makes it difficult for me to spend time with my family.	1	2	3	4	5	6	n/a
8. The administration at my institution does not support me.	1	2	3	4	5	6	n/a
9. The administration of my college does not support me.	1	2	3	4	5	6	n/a

10. The administration of my department does not support me.	1	2	3	4	5	6	n/a
11. My institution has unwritten policies that support my need to balance the personal and the professional.	1	2	3	4	5	6	n/a
12. It is easier to have children after receiving tenure.	1	2	3	4	5	6	n/a
13. The pressure of obtaining tenure makes it difficult to have a personal life.	1	2	3	4	5	6	n/a
14. Tenure rules are male modeled rules and should be changed.	1	2	3	4	5	6	n/a
15. My institution allows pre-tenure women to stop the tenure clock if they have a child.	1	2	3	4	5	6	n/a
16. There are no negative repercussions for women faculty who stop the tenure clock when they have a child.	1	2	3	4	5	6	n/a
17. The pressures of getting tenure cause people to put off making personal decisions.	1	2	3	4	5	6	n/a
18. Needing to get tenure makes it difficult for me to devote time to finding a significant other.	1	2	3	4	5	6	n/a
19. The lack of clarity about what it takes to earn tenure makes it difficult to achieve a personal and professional balance.	1	2	3	4	5	6	n/a

(continued overleaf)

Exhibit B.1. *(continued)*

Description/Identification of Survey Item	Strongly Disagree				Strongly Agree		
	1	2	3	4	5	6	n/a
20. Once I receive(d) tenure it was/will be easier to have a balance between the personal and professional.	1	2	3	4	5	6	n/a
21. Academia supports women balancing the personal and professional more today than for previous generations of academic women.	1	2	3	4	5	6	n/a
22. Academic women in the past perceived themselves differently in terms of their profession than academic women of today.	1	2	3	4	5	6	n/a
23. There is no difference between the way academic women received institutional support for working in the past and today.	1	2	3	4	5	6	n/a
24. Husbands/significant others take on more responsibility for home and children than they did in past generations.	1	2	3	4	5	6	n/a
25. Academic women in the past had it easier because they didn't have a choice between a professional and personal life.	1	2	3	4	5	6	n/a
26. Balancing the personal and professional was more difficult for female academics in the past.	1	2	3	4	5	6	n/a
27. This generation of academic women has more institutional resources than past generations.	1	2	3	4	5	6	n/a

	1	2	3	4	5	6	n/a
28. Older academic women feel sorry for what younger academic women have to go through.	1	2	3	4	5	6	n/a
29. Younger academic women feel sorry for what older academic women had to go through.	1	2	3	4	5	6	n/a
30. Having responsibilities outside of work makes my work time more effective.	1	2	3	4	5	6	n/a
31. I have to compartmentalize the different areas of my life in order not to be overwhelmed.	1	2	3	4	5	6	n/a
32. Having a child/children made/makes balancing the personal and professional impossible.	1	2	3	4	5	6	n/a
33. When I'm at work, I feel like I should be at home.	1	2	3	4	5	6	n/a
34. When I'm at home, I feel like I should be at work.	1	2	3	4	5	6	n/a
35. In attempting to create a balance, I always feel like something is being sacrificed.	1	2	3	4	5	6	n/a
36. I feel like I am robbing one part of my life in order to maintain other parts.	1	2	3	4	5	6	n/a
37. I always feel like either my students or my children are getting short changed.	1	2	3	4	5	6	n/a

(continued overleaf)

Exhibit B.1. *(continued)*

Description/Identification of Survey Item	Strongly Disagree					Strongly Agree	
38. Support groups outside of the academy help me achieve a balance between my personal and professional lives.	1	2	3	4	5	6	n/a
39. My extended family helps me cope with balancing the personal and professional.	1	2	3	4	5	6	n/a
40. My friends who have similar life experiences help me cope with balancing the personal and professional.	1	2	3	4	5	6	n/a
41. My spouse/significant other allows me to have a balance between work and home.	1	2	3	4	5	6	n/a
42. My spouse/significant other is very interested in my professional life.	1	2	3	4	5	6	n/a
43. My spouse/significant other's job creates a barrier to achieving a balance between my personal and professional lives.	1	2	3	4	5	6	n/a
44. Having a spouse/significant other in the academy makes it easier for me to strike a balance between my work and home.	1	2	3	4	5	6	n/a
45. My personal life allows me to create time for my professional responsibilities.	1	2	3	4	5	6	n/a

46. My spouse/significant other's support makes it easier for me to achieve a balance between my work and home life.	1	2	3	4	5	6	n/a
47. I do not allow myself to sacrifice everything else in my life for work.	1	2	3	4	5	6	n/a
48. I have changed how I do my job because I have a child/children.	1	2	3	4	5	6	n/a
49. My institution bears the cost of juggling my family and work responsibilities.	1	2	3	4	5	6	n/a
50. My job is my second priority; my family is my first priority.	1	2	3	4	5	6	n/a
51. I make a personal choice to create a balance between my personal and professional life since it is not provided by my institution.	1	2	3	4	5	6	n/a
52. I feel pressured to have a husband/significant other who takes on most of the household responsibilities in order to meet professional obligations.	1	2	3	4	5	6	n/a
53. The energy I have left for my family after meeting my professional obligations is not the best.	1	2	3	4	5	6	n/a
54. As a working mother, I don't have time to create support networks for my child(ren).	1	2	3	4	5	6	n/a

(continued overleaf)

Exhibit B.1. (*continued*)

Description/Identification of Survey Item	Strongly Disagree					Strongly Agree	
55. It is/was a good idea to wait to have children until I have/had my career established.	1	2	3	4	5	6	n/a
56. As an academic woman, I often felt that I couldn't or shouldn't have children.	1	2	3	4	5	6	n/a
57. An academic job requires women to move away from family support networks.	1	2	3	4	5	6	n/a
58. Demands from students make it difficult for me to achieve a balance between work and home.	1	2	3	4	5	6	n/a
59. I believe my only option was not to have children or get married in order to have a successful academic career.	1	2	3	4	5	6	n/a
60. Doing work I enjoy allowed me to be comfortable giving up having a family life.	1	2	3	4	5	6	n/a
61. My child(ren) bears the cost of my need to juggle family and work responsibilities.	1	2	3	4	5	6	n/a
62. My job hinders my ability to create a personal life.	1	2	3	4	5	6	n/a
63. I do not allow others to tell me what is or is not enough in terms of my work.	1	2	3	4	5	6	n/a

	1	2	3	4	5	6	n/a
64. I have learned to live with a certain amount of guilt about not being able to do everything.	1	2	3	4	5	6	n/a
65. I give up time for things I want to do in order to make sure my work and family are taken care of.	1	2	3	4	5	6	n/a
66. I do not have a personal life due to work obligations.	1	2	3	4	5	6	n/a
67. It is up to me to negotiate the balance between work and home.	1	2	3	4	5	6	n/a
68. It is not difficult balancing my personal and professional lives.	1	2	3	4	5	6	n/a
69. My personal and professional responsibilities impinge on my ability to do what I want to do.	1	2	3	4	5	6	n/a
70. If I try to create a balance between my personal and professional lives, I feel like I don't succeed.	1	2	3	4	5	6	n/a
71. As an academic woman, I feel that I have to prove myself to my institution and my male colleagues.	1	2	3	4	5	6	n/a
72. I feel that I am under pressure to be a success both personally and professionally.	1	2	3	4	5	6	n/a

Demographic Information

Please select all options from the choices below that apply to you.

Institution Type

> Community college: □; Small, private liberal arts college: □; Comprehensive public university □; HBCU □; Selective public research institution □; Private research institution □.

Career Stage

> Pre-tenure □; Post-tenure (mid-career) □; Post-tenure (5 or less years from retirement) □; Non-tenured track □; Adjunct □.

Discipline

> Social-Sciences □; Humanities □; Hard-Sciences □; Arts □;
>
> Professional (law/education/medicine/social work/engineering, nursing, etc.) □.

Family Life

> Partnered/Married to male □; Partnered/married to female □;
>
> Married with child (children) at home □; Divorced with grown child(ren) □;
>
> Married with grown child (children) no longer at home □; Single without children □;
>
> Single with child(ren) □; Divorced without child(ren) □; Divorced with children at home □;
>
> Spouse/Significant other works full-time outside of academia □; Spouse/Significant other works full-time inside of academia □; Spouse/significant other is stay-at-home partner □.

Age

> Under 30 □; 31–40 □; 41–50 □; 51–66 □; 67–70 □; over 70 □.

Exhibit B.2. Second Version of the Survey After Expert Review Academic Women: Balancing Personal and Professional Lives

For each statement below, circle the number to the right that best fits your level of agreement with the statement. If the statement is not applicable to you, please circle n/a.

1 = strongly disagree; 2 = disagree; 3 = mildly disagree; 4 = mildly agree; 5 = agree; 6 = strongly agree

Description/Identification of Survey Item	Strongly Disagree				Strongly Agree	
1. My institution provides support to help me cope with balancing my personal and professional responsibilities.	1	2	3	4	5	n/a
2. My department provides a supportive environment which aids my ability to balance the personal and professional.	1	2	3	4	5	n/a
3. My college provides a supportive environment which aids my ability to balance the personal and professional.	1	2	3	4	5	n/a
4. My institution supports families.	1	2	3	4	5	n/a
5. My institution has quality day care available on campus.	1	2	3	4	5	n/a
6. My institution has specific policies to help faculty when they have children.	1	2	3	4	5	n/a
7. The class schedule at my university makes it difficult for me to spend time with my family.	1	2	3	4	5	n/a
8. The administration at my institution does not support me.	1	2	3	4	5	n/a

(continued overleaf)

Exhibit B.2. *(continued)*

Description/Identification of Survey Item	Strongly Disagree				Strongly Agree	
9. The administration of my college does not support me.	1	2	3	4	5	n/a
10. The administration of my department does not support me.	1	2	3	4	5	n/a
11. My institution has unwritten policies that support my need to balance the personal and the professional.	1	2	3	4	5	n/a
12. It is easier to have children after receiving tenure.	1	2	3	4	5	n/a
13. The pressure of obtaining tenure makes it difficult to have a personal life.	1	2	3	4	5	n/a
14. Tenure rules should be changed.	1	2	3	4	5	n/a
15. My institution allows pre-tenure women to stop the tenure clock if they have a child.	1	2	3	4	5	n/a
16. There are no negative repercussions for women faculty who stop the tenure clock when they have a child.	1	2	3	4	5	n/a
17. The pressures of getting tenure cause people to put off making personal decisions.	1	2	3	4	5	n/a
18. Needing to get tenure makes it difficult for me to devote time to finding a significant other.	1	2	3	4	5	n/a
19. The lack of clarity about what it takes to earn tenure makes it difficult to achieve a personal and professional balance.	1	2	3	4	5	n/a

20. Once I receive(d) tenure it was/will be easier to have a balance between the personal and professional.	1	2	3	4	5	n/a
21. Academia supports women balancing the personal and professional more today than for previous generations of academic women.	1	2	3	4	5	n/a
22. There is no difference between the way academic women received institutional support for working in the past and today.	1	2	3	4	5	n/a
23. Husbands/significant others take on more responsibility for home and children than they did in past generations.	1	2	3	4	5	n/a
24. Academic women in the past had it easier because they didn't have a choice between a professional and personal life.	1	2	3	4	5	n/a
25. Balancing the personal and professional was more difficult for female academics in the past.	1	2	3	4	5	n/a
26. This generation of academic women has more institutional resources than past generations.	1	2	3	4	5	n/a
27. Having responsibilities outside of work makes my work time more effective.	1	2	3	4	5	n/a
28. I have to compartmentalize the different areas of my life in order to not be overwhelmed.	1	2	3	4	5	n/a

(continued overleaf)

Exhibit B.2. *(continued)*

Description/Identification of Survey Item	Strongly Disagree				Strongly Agree	
	1	2	3	4	5	n/a
29. Having a child/children made/makes balancing the personal and professional impossible.	1	2	3	4	5	n/a
30. When I'm at work, I feel like I should be at home.	1	2	3	4	5	n/a
31. In attempting to create a balance, I always feel like something is being sacrificed.	1	2	3	4	5	n/a
32. I feel like I am robbing one part of my life in order to maintain other parts.	1	2	3	4	5	n/a
33. I always feel like either my students or my children are getting short changed.	1	2	3	4	5	n/a
34. Support groups outside of the academy help me achieve a balance between my personal and professional lives.	1	2	3	4	5	n/a
35. My extended family helps me cope with balancing the personal and professional.	1	2	3	4	5	n/a
36. My friends who have similar life experiences help me cope with balancing the personal and professional.	1	2	3	4	5	n/a
37. My spouse/significant other allows me to have a balance between work and home.	1	2	3	4	5	n/a
38. My spouse/significant other is very interested in my professional life.	1	2	3	4	5	n/a

39. My spouse/significant other's job creates a barrier to achieving a balance between my personal and professional lives.	1	2	3	4	5	n/a
40. Having a spouse/significant other in the academy makes it easier for me to strike a balance between my work and home.	1	2	3	4	5	n/a
41. My personal life allows me to create time for my professional responsibilities.	1	2	3	4	5	n/a
42. My spouse/significant other's support makes it easier for me to achieve a balance between my work and home life.	1	2	3	4	5	n/a
43. I do not allow myself to sacrifice everything else in my life for work.	1	2	3	4	5	n/a
44. I have changed how I do my job because I have a child/children.	1	2	3	4	5	n/a
45. My institution bears the cost of juggling my family and work responsibilities.	1	2	3	4	5	n/a
46. I make a personal choice to create a balance between my personal and professional life since it is not provided by my institution.	1	2	3	4	5	n/a
47. I feel pressured to have a husband/significant other who takes on most of the household responsibilities in order to meet professional obligations.	1	2	3	4	5	n/a

(continued overleaf)

Exhibit B.2. (*continued*)

Description/Identification of Survey Item	Strongly Disagree				Strongly Agree	
48. The energy I have left for my family after meeting my professional obligations is not the best.	1	2	3	4	5	n/a
49. As a working mother, I don't have time to create support networks for my child(ren).	1	2	3	4	5	n/a
50. It is/was a good idea to wait to have children until I have/had my career established.	1	2	3	4	5	n/a
51. As an academic woman, I often felt that I couldn't or shouldn't have children.	1	2	3	4	5	n/a
52. An academic job requires women to move away from family support networks.	1	2	3	4	5	n/a
53. Demands from students make it difficult for me to achieve a balance between work and home.	1	2	3	4	5	n/a
54. I believe my only option was not to have children or get married in order to have a successful academic career.	1	2	3	4	5	n/a
55. Doing work I enjoy allowed me to be comfortable giving up having a family life.	1	2	3	4	5	n/a
56. My child(ren) bears the cost of my need to juggle family and work responsibilities.	1	2	3	4	5	n/a

	1	2	3	4	5	
57. My job hinders my ability to create a personal life.	1	2	3	4	5	n/a
58. I do not allow others to tell me what is or is not enough in terms of my work.	1	2	3	4	5	n/a
59. I have learned to live with a certain amount of guilt about not being able to do everything.	1	2	3	4	5	n/a
60. I give up time for things I want to do in order to make sure my work and family are taken care of.	1	2	3	4	5	n/a
61. I do not have a personal life due to work obligations.	1	2	3	4	5	n/a
62. It is up to me to negotiate the balance between work and home.	1	2	3	4	5	n/a
63. It is not difficult balancing my personal and professional lives.	1	2	3	4	5	n/a
64. My personal and professional responsibilities impinge on my ability to do what I want to do.	1	2	3	4	5	n/a
65. If I try to create a balance between my personal and professional lives, I feel like I don't succeed.	1	2	3	4	5	n/a
66. As an academic woman, I feel that I have to prove myself to my institution and my male colleagues.	1	2	3	4	5	n/a
67. I feel that I am under pressure to be a success both personally and professionally.	1	2	3	4	5	n/a

Demographic Information

Please select all options from the choices below that apply to you.

Institution Type

Community college: □; Small, private liberal arts college: □; Comprehensive public university □; HBCU □; Selective public research institution □; Private research institution □.

Career Stage

Pre-tenure □; Post-tenure (mid-career) □; Post-tenure (5 or less years from retirement) □; Non-tenured track □; Adjunct □.

Discipline

Social-Sciences □; Humanities □; Hard-Sciences □; Arts □; Professional (law/education/medicine/social work/engineering, nursing, etc.) □.

Family Life

Partnered/Married to male □; Partnered/married to female □;

Married with child (children) at home □;

Married with grown child (children) no longer at home □; Single without children □;

Single with child(ren) □; Divorced without child(ren) □;

Divorced with children at home □; Divorced with grown child(ren) □;

Spouse/Significant other works full-time outside of academia □; Spouse/Significant other works full-time inside of academia □; Spouse/significant other is stay-at-home partner □.

Age

Under 30 □; 31–40 □; 41–50 □; 51–66 □; 67–70 □; over 70 □.

Exhibit B.3. Final Version of Survey Academic Women: Balancing Personal and Professional Lives

For each statement below, circle the number to the right that best fits your level of agreement with the statement. If the statement is not applicable to you, please circle n/a.

1 = strongly disagree; 2 = disagree; 3 = mildly disagree; 4 = mildly agree; 5 = agree; 6 = strongly agree

Description/Identification of Survey Item	Strongly Disagree				Strongly Agree	
1. My institution provides support to help me cope with balancing my personal and professional responsibilities.	1	2	3	4	5	n/a
2. My department provides a supportive environment which aids my ability to balance the personal and professional.	1	2	3	4	5	n/a
3. My college provides a supportive environment which aids my ability to balance the personal and professional.	1	2	3	4	5	n/a
4. My institution supports families.	1	2	3	4	5	n/a
5. The class schedule at my university makes it difficult for me to spend time with my family.	1	2	3	4	5	n/a
6. The administration at my institution does not support me.	1	2	3	4	5	n/a
7. The administration of my college does not support me.	1	2	3	4	5	n/a
8. The administration of my department does not support me.	1	2	3	4	5	n/a
9. My institution has unwritten policies that support my need to balance the personal and the professional.	1	2	3	4	5	n/a

(continued overleaf)

Exhibit B.3. *(continued)*

Description/Identification of Survey Item	Strongly Disagree			Strongly Agree		
10. The pressures of getting tenure cause people to put off making personal decisions.	1	2	3	4	5	n/a
11. Needing to get tenure makes it difficult for me to devote time to finding a significant other.	1	2	3	4	5	n/a
12. The lack of clarity about what it takes to earn tenure makes it difficult to achieve a personal and professional balance.	1	2	3	4	5	n/a
13. Once I receive(d) tenure it was/will be easier to have a balance between the personal and professional.	1	2	3	4	5	n/a
14. Academia supports women balancing the personal and professional more today than for previous generations of academic women.	1	2	3	4	5	n/a
15. There is no difference between the way academic women received institutional support for working in the past and today.	1	2	3	4	5	n/a
16. Husbands/significant others take on more responsibility for home and children than they did in past generations.	1	2	3	4	5	n/a
17. Academic women in the past had it easier because they didn't have a choice between a professional and personal life.	1	2	3	4	5	n/a
18. Balancing the personal and professional was more difficult for female academics in the past.	1	2	3	4	5	n/a

19. This generation of academic women has more institutional resources than past generations.	1	2	3	4	5	n/a
20. When I'm at work, I feel like I should be at home.	1	2	3	4	5	n/a
21. In attempting to create a balance, I always feel like something is being sacrificed.	1	2	3	4	5	n/a
22. I feel like I am robbing one part of my life in order to maintain other parts.	1	2	3	4	5	n/a
23. I always feel like either my students or my children are getting short changed.	1	2	3	4	5	n/a
24. Support groups outside of the academy help me achieve a balance between my personal and professional lives.	1	2	3	4	5	n/a
25. My extended family helps me cope with balancing the personal and professional.	1	2	3	4	5	n/a
26. My friends who have similar life experiences help me cope with balancing the personal and professional.	1	2	3	4	5	n/a
27. My spouse/significant other allows me to have a balance between work and home.	1	2	3	4	5	n/a

(continued overleaf)

Exhibit B.3. *(continued)*

Description/Identification of Survey Item	Strongly Disagree				Strongly Agree	
28. My spouse/significant other is very interested in my professional life.	1	2	3	4	5	n/a
29. My spouse/significant other's job creates a barrier to achieving a balance between my personal and professional lives.	1	2	3	4	5	n/a
30. Having a spouse/significant other in the academy makes it easier for me to strike a balance between my work and home.	1	2	3	4	5	n/a
31. My personal life allows me to create time for my professional responsibilities.	1	2	3	4	5	n/a
32. My spouse/significant other's support makes it easier for me to achieve a balance between my work and home life.	1	2	3	4	5	n/a
33. I have changed how I do my job because I have a child/children.	1	2	3	4	5	n/a
34. As a working mother, I don't have time to create support networks for my child(ren).	1	2	3	4	5	n/a
35. It is/was a good idea to wait to have children until I have/had my career established.	1	2	3	4	5	n/a
36. As an academic woman, I often felt that I couldn't or shouldn't have children.	1	2	3	4	5	n/a
37. An academic job requires women to move away from family support networks.	1	2	3	4	5	n/a

	1	2	3	4	5	n/a
38. Demands from students make it difficult for me to achieve a balance between work and home.	1	2	3	4	5	n/a
39. I believe my only option was not to have children or get married in order to have a successful academic career.	1	2	3	4	5	n/a
40. Doing work I enjoy allowed me to be comfortable giving up having a family life.	1	2	3	4	5	n/a
41. My child(ren) bears the cost of my need to juggle family and work responsibilities.	1	2	3	4	5	n/a
42. I have learned to live with a certain amount of guilt about not be able to do everything.	1	2	3	4	5	n/a
43. I do not have a personal life due to work obligations.	1	2	3	4	5	n/a
44. It is not difficult balancing my personal and professional lives.	1	2	3	4	5	n/a
45. My personal and professional responsibilities impinge on my ability to do what I want to do.	1	2	3	4	5	n/a
46. If I try to create a balance between my personal and professional lives, I feel like I don't succeed.	1	2	3	4	5	n/a
47. I feel that I am under pressure to be a success both personally and professionally.	1	2	3	4	5	n/a

Demographic Information

Please select all options from the choices below that apply to you.

Institution Type

Community college: □; Small, private liberal arts college: □; Comprehensive public university □; HBCU □; Selective public research institution □; Private research institution □.

Career Stage

Pre-tenure □; Post-tenure (mid-career) □; Post-tenure (5 or fewer years from retirement) □; Non-tenured track □; Adjunct □.

Discipline

Social-Sciences □; Humanities □; Hard-Sciences □; Arts □; Professional (law/education/medicine/social work/engineering, nursing, etc.) □.

Family Life

Partnered/Married to male □; Partnered/married to female □;

Married with child (children) at home □;

Married with grown child (children) no longer at home □; Single without children □;

Single with child(ren) □; Divorced without child(ren) □; Divorced with children at home □;

Divorced with grown child(ren) □;

Spouse/Significant other works full-time outside of academia □;

Spouse/Significant other works full-time inside of academia □;

Spouse/significant other is stay-at-home partner □.

Age

Under 30 □; 31–40 □; 41–50 □; 51–66 □; 67–70 □; over 70 □.

Exhibit B.4. Factor Analysis: Rotated Component Matrix

	Obligations Lead to Sacrifice of Self	Work or Home Is Sacrificed	Institutional Support	Significant Others Help	Past Generations Had It Harder	Tenure Inhibits Balance
Q1 IS	-.583		.574			
Q2 IS			.703			
Q3 IS	-.498		.612			
Q4 IS	-.371		.618			
Q7 IS			.459			
Q8 IS			.775			
Q9 IS			.805			
Q10 IS			.745			
Q11 IS			.600			
Q12 TI						.386
Q15 TI						.610
Q16 TI						.584
Q17 TI						.448
Q18 TI						.671
Q19 TI						.599
Q20 TI						.751

(continued overleaf)

Exhibit B.4. (continued)

	Obligations Lead to Sacrifice of Self	Work or Home Is Sacrificed	Institutional Support	Significant Others Help	Past Generations Had It Harder	Tenure Inhibits Balance
Q21 PHARD					.517	
Q22 PHARD					.410	
Q23 PHARD				.476	.486	
Q24 PHARD					.664	
Q25 PHARD					.739	
Q26 PHARD					.690	
Q30 OBLVTRN	.650					
Q31 OBLVTRN	.840					
Q32 OBLVTRN	.874					
Q33 OBLVTRN	.542	.501				
Q34 SOSUPPORT				.355		
Q35 SOSUPPORT				.365	.447	
Q36 SOSUPPORT				.360		
Q37 SOSUPPORT				.825		
Q38 SOSUPPORT				.852		
Q39 SOSUPPORT				.656		
Q40 SOSUPPORT		.429		.588		

	Component 1	Component 2	Component 3	Component 4	Component 5
Q41 SOSUPPORT			.326	.484	
Q42 SOSUPPORT				.731	
Q44 SACW4FAM		.598		.479	
Q49 SACFRWORK		.696			
Q50 SACFRWORK		.633			
Q51 SACFRWORK		.715		-.334	
Q54 SACFRWORK		.514			.368
Q55 SACFRWORK		.385		.310	
Q56 SACFRWORK		.736			
Q59 SACSELF4BTH	.439				
Q61 SACSELF4BTH	.476			-.308	-.440
Q63 SACSELF4BTH	.756				
Q64 SACSELF4BTH	.655		-.324		
Q65 SACSELF4BTH	.573		-.393		
Q67 SACSELF4BTH	.515				

Extraction method: principal component analysis. Rotation method: Varimax with Kaiser normalization.
While some of the questions are cross loading, the similarity among the questions would seem to account for it.

Appendix C

Frequencies and Histograms

Exhibit C.1. Means and Standard Deviations for Early-Career Women

	Valid	Mean	Median	Mode	Std. Deviation	Percentiles		
						25	50	75
Institutional support	46	3.0300	3.0000	2.56(a)	.90110	2.5278	3.0000	3.8056
Tenure inhibits balance	46	4.2100	4.0000	4.00	.51357	3.3750	4.0000	4.1875
Past had it harder	46	3.1900	3.1429	3.14	.64830	3.0000	3.1429	3.5714
Obligations lead to sacrifice of self	46	3.9500	3.9000	3.90	.70323	3.5000	3.9000	4.2000
Significant others help	46	3.8700	3.8333	4.67	.99707	3.3333	3.8333	4.5000
Work or home is sacrifice	46	3.4500	3.5000	3.70(a)	.62540	3.1000	3.5000	3.9000
Departmental support	46	4.2500	4.0000	5.00	1.18862	2.5000	4.0000	4.5000
College support	46	3.1000	3.0000	2.50	1.08339	2.5000	3.0000	4.0000
Institution support 2	46	2.5100	2.6667	2.33(a)	.92265	2.3333	2.6667	3.3333

aMultiple modes exist. The smallest value is shown.

Exhibit C.2.   Institutional Support

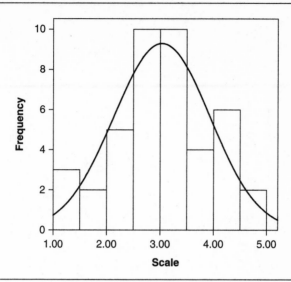

Exhibit C.3.   Tenure Inhibits Balance

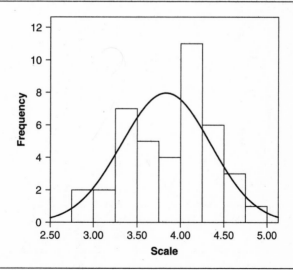

Exhibit C.4.   Past Had It Harder

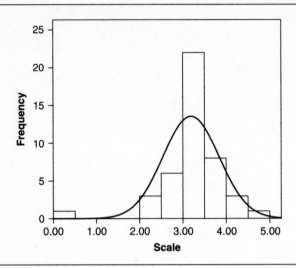

Exhibit C.5.   Obligations Lead to Sacrifice of Self

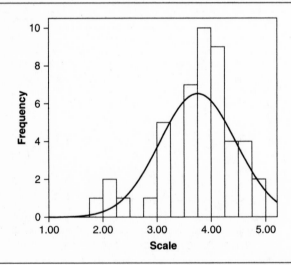

Exhibit C.6.   Departmental Support

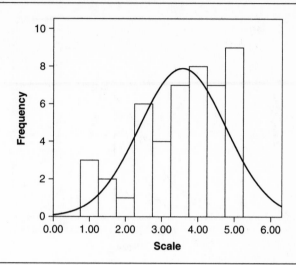

Exhibit C.7.   Significant Others Help

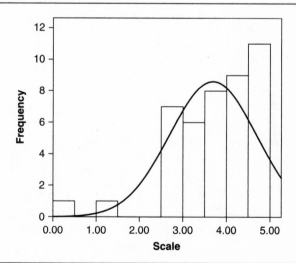

Exhibit C.8.   Work or Home Is Sacrificed

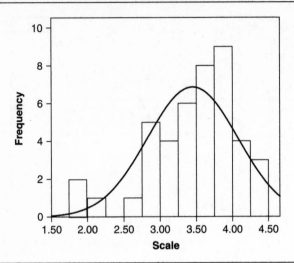

Exhibit C.9.   College Support

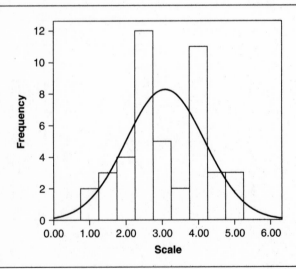

Exhibit C.10.   Institutional Support 2

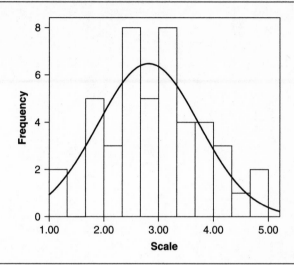

Exhibit C.11. Means and Standard Deviations for Mid-Career Women

	Sample Size	Mean	Std. Error of Mean	Median	Mode	Std. Deviation	Percentiles		
							25	50	75
Institutional support	44	2.8100	.14478	2.9400	2.44	.84420	2.4444	2.9444	3.5833
Tenure inhibits balance	44	3.8600	.13744	3.6250	3.88	.77746	2.9375	3.6250	3.8750
Past had it harder	44	3.2000	.07840	3.1429	3.00[a]	.45038	3.0000	3.1429	3.4286
Obligations lead to sacrifice of self	44	3.9600	.14837	3.5000	3.10[a]	.83930	3.1000	3.5000	4.1750
Significant others help	44	3.7500	.13376	3.8333	3.33[a]	.76840	3.3333	3.8333	4.3333
Sacrifice work or home	44	3.8700	.13892	3.7000	3.90	.77349	3.0000	3.7000	3.9000
Departmental support	44	3.3100	.18113	3.5000	4.00	1.07160	2.5000	3.5000	4.0000
College support	44	3.0200	.17507	3.0000	2.50[a]	1.03571	2.5000	3.0000	4.0000
Institutional support 2	44	2.6900	.16757	2.6667	2.00[a]	.99137	2.0000	2.6667	3.3333

[a]Multiple modes exist. The smallest value is shown.

Exhibit C.12.   Institutional Support

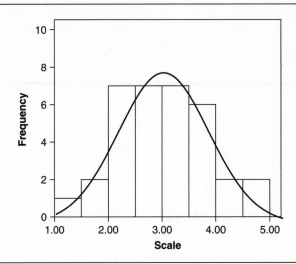

Exhibit C.13.   Tenure Inhibits Balance

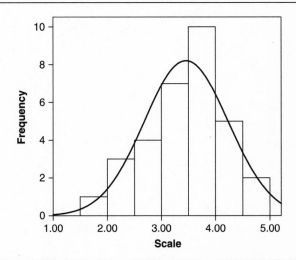

Exhibit C.14.   Past Had It Harder

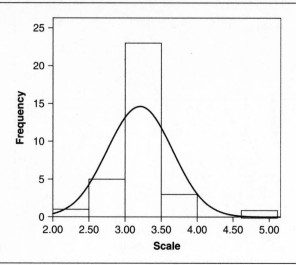

Exhibit C.15.   Obligations Lead to Sacrifice of Self

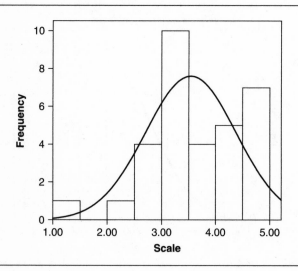

Exhibit C.16.   Significant Others Help with Pressure

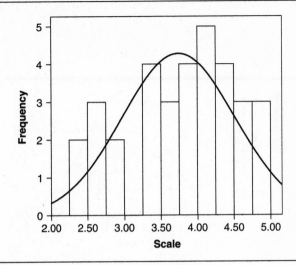

Exhibit C.17.   Worker or Home Is Sacrificed

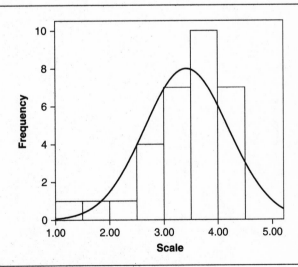

Exhibit C.18. Departmental Support

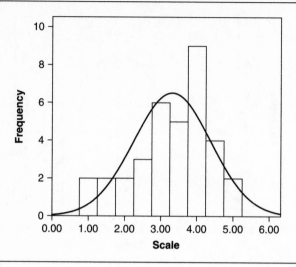

Exhibit C.19. College Support

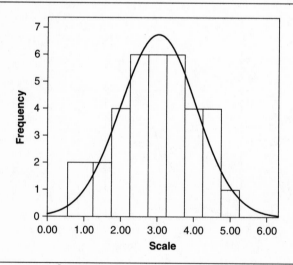

Exhibit C.20.   Institutional Support 2

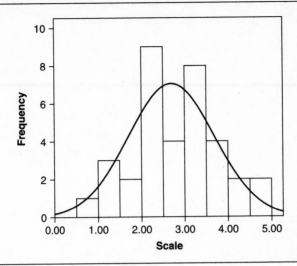

References

Austin, A. (January/February 2002). Preparing the next generation of faculty: Graduate school as socialization to the academic career. *Journal of Higher Education, 73* (1), 94–122.

Austin, A. (2006). Foreword. In S. J. Bracken, J. K. Allen, & D. R. Dean (Eds.), *The balancing act: Gendered perspectives in faculty roles and work lives* (pp. ix–xiv). Sterling, VA: Stylus.

Baker, S. M. (1999). Success for women in academia: "Choices, experiences, and challenges." *Annals of the New York Academy of Sciences, 869,* 210–218.

Bee, H. L. & Bjorklund, B. R. (2004). *The journey of adulthood.* 5th ed. Upper Saddle River, NJ: Pearson/Prentice Hall.

Bracken, S. J, Allen, J. K., & Dean, D. R. (2006). Introduction: The past, present, and future. In S. J. Bracken, J. K. Allen, & D. R. Dean (Eds.), *The balancing act: Gendered perspectives in faculty roles and work lives* (pp. 1–8). Sterling, VA: Stylus.

Brantner, C. (2005). Adoption angles and maternity leave suggestions. In R. Hile Bassett (Ed.), *Parenting and professing: Balancing family work with an academic career* (pp. 192–203). Nashville, TN: Vanderbilt University Press.

Caplan, P. (1993). *Lifting a ton of feathers: A woman's guide to surviving in the academic world.* Toronto, Canada: University of Toronto Press.

Chronicle of Higher Education Almanac (2007–2008). Number of full-time faculty members by sex, rank, and racial and ethnic group, Fall 2005. 54 (1), 24.

http://chronicle.com/weekly/almanac/2007/nation/0102402.htm (accessed November 7, 2007).

Colbeck, C. (2006). How female and male faculty with families manage work and personal roles. In S. J. Bracken, J. K. Allen, & D. R. Dean (Eds.), *The balancing act: Gendered perspectives in faculty roles and work lives* (pp. 31–72). Sterling, VA: Stylus.

Colbeck, C. & Drago, R. (November/December 2005). Accept, avoid, resist: How faculty members respond to bias against caregiving . . . and how departments can help. *Change: The magazine of higher learning, 37* (6), 10–17.

Department of Education, Institute of Education Sciences, National Center for Education Statistics. *Digest of Education Statistics 2005.* http://nces.ed.gov/programs/digest/d05/tables/dt05_252.asp (accessed May 1, 2007).

Drago, R. & Colbeck, C. (2003). *Final report from the mapping project: Exploring the terrain of U.S. colleges and universities for faculty and families.* University Park: Pennsylvania State University.

Fine, M. (1991). *Framing dropouts: Notes on the politics of an urban public high school.* Albany: State University of New York Press.

Finkel, S. K., Olswang, S., & She, N. (1994). Childbirth, tenure, and promotion for women faculty. *Review of Higher Education, 17* (3), 259–270.

Folbre, N. (2005). Eliminating economic penalties on caregivers. In J. Heyman & C. Beem (Eds.), *Unfinished work: Building equality and democracy in an era of working families* (pp. 348–370). New York/London: The New Press.

Glazer-Raymo, J. (1999). *Shattering the myths: Women in academe.* Baltimore, MD/London: Johns Hopkins University Press.

Gornick, J. C. & Meyers, M. K. (2005). Supporting a dual-earner/dual-career society. In J. Heyman & C. Beem (Eds.), *Unfinished work: Building equality and democracy in an era of working families* (pp. 371–408). New York/London: The New Press.

Holden Rønnig, A. (2000). Gender, culture, and power-sharing in academia. In M. L. Kearney (Ed.), *Women, power, and the academy* (pp. 99–109). New York: Berghahn Books.

Jaggar, A. M. (1983). *Feminist politics and human nature*. Totowa, N.J.: Rowman & Allanheld.

Jones, K. B. (2005). Boomerangst. In R. Hile Bassett (Ed.), *Parenting & professing: Balancing family work within an academic career* (pp. 173–181). Nashville, TN: Vanderbilt University Press.

Kamerman, S. B. (2005). Europe advanced while the United States lagged. In J. Heyman & C. Beem (eds.), *Unfinished work: Building equality and democracy in an era of working families* (pp. 309–347). New York/London: The New Press.

Kegan, R. (1994). *In over our heads: The mental demands of modern life.* Cambridge, MA: Harvard University Press.

Kelly-Gadol, J. (1987). The social relation of the sexes: Methodological implications of women's history. In S. Harding (Ed.) *Feminism & methodology* (pp. 15–28). Bloomington and Indianapolis: Indiana University Press, Open University Press.

Lammi-Taskula, J. (2000). Combining work and fatherhood in Finland. In C.D.H. Hervey (Ed.), *Walking a tightrope: Meeting the challenges of work and family* (pp. 1–24). Aldershot, UK: Ashgate.

Lesko, N. (Ed). (2000). *Masculinities at school.* Thousand Oaks: Sage.

Letherby, G., Marchbank, J., Ramsay, K., & Shiel, J. (2005). Mothers and "others" providing care within and outside the academy. In R. Hile Bassett (Ed.), *Parenting & professing: Balancing family work within an academic career.* (pp. 204–216). Nashville, TN: Vanderbilt University Press.

Liu, M. & Mallon, W. (2004). Tenure in transition: Trends in basic science faculty appointment policies at U.S. medical schools. *Academic Medicine, 79* (3), 205–213.

Lizotte, L. & Litwak, B. A. (1995). *Balancing work and family*. American Management Association, The WorkSmart Series. New York: amacom.

Madden, M. (2002). The transformative leadership of women in higher education administration. In J. Digeorgio-Lutz (Ed.), *Women in higher education: Empowering change*. Westport, CT: Praeger.

Marcus, J. (2007). Helping academics have families and tenure too. *Change, 39* (92), 27–32.

Mason, M. A., Goulden, M., & Wolfinger, N. (2006). Babies matter. In S. J. Bracken, J. K. Allen, & D. R. Dean (Eds.), *The balancing act: Gendered perspectives in faculty roles and work lives* (pp. 9–29). Sterling, VA: Stylus.

Miller, K. L. & Miller, S. M. (2002). A model for evaluating gender equity in academe. In J. DiGeorgio-Lutz (Ed.), *Women in higher education: Empowering change* (pp. 103–114). Westport, CT: Greenwood Publishing Group.

National Center for Education Statistics (NCES). (2005). Digest of Education Statistics 2005: Table 227. Full-time instructional faculty in degree-granting institutions, by race/ethnicity, residency status, sex, and academic rank, Fall 2003. http://nces.ed.gov/programs/digest/d05/tables/dt05_227.asp (accessed May 4, 2007).

National Family Caregivers Association. (1997). *A profile of caregivers*, member survey. Quoted in Folbre, N. (2005). Eliminating economic penalties on caregivers. In J. Heyman & C. Beem (Eds.), *Unfinished work: Building equality and democracy in an era of working families* (pp. 348–370). New York/London: The New Press.

Noddings, N. (2002). *Happiness and education*. Cambridge, UK: New York: Cambridge University Press.

O'Donovan, K.F. & Simmons, S. (2006). Making meaning of a life in teaching: A memoir-writing project for seasoned faculty. In D. R. Robertson & L. B. Nilson (Eds.), *To improve the academy: Resources for faculty, instructional, and organizational development, 25* (pp. 315–326). Bolton, Mass.: Anker.

Ogbu, J. (1987). Variability in minority school performance: A problem in search of an explanation. *Anthropology and Educational Quarterly, 18*, 312–335.

Olsen, D. & Sorcinelli, M. D. (1992, Summer). The pretenure years: A longitudinal perspective. In M.D. Sorcinelli & A. Austin (Eds.), *Developing new and junior faculty*. New directions for teaching and learning, no. 50, 15–25. San Francisco: Jossey-Bass.

Philipsen, M. & Bostic, T. (in preparation). *Across the life span of male faculty: Stages, challenges, and coping strategies* (working title). San Francisco: Jossey-Bass.

Raymond, J. (2007, June 18). A guide for caregivers. *Newsweek*, 62–64.

Rice, R. E., Sorcinelli, M. D., & Austin, A. (2000). *Heeding new voices: Academic careers for a new generation*. Washington, D.C.: American Association for Higher Education.

Rimer, S. (1999, November 27). Study details sacrifices in caring for elderly kin. *The New York Times*, p. 9; quoted in Folbre, N. (2005). Eliminating economic penalties on caregivers. In J. Heyman C. & Beem (Eds.), *Unfinished work: Building equality and democracy in an era of working families* (pp. 348–370). New York/London: The New Press.

Rosser, S. (2002). Institutional barriers for women scientists and engineers: What four years of survey data of National Science Foundation POWRE awardees reveal. In DiGeorgio-Lutz, J. (Ed.), *Women in higher education: Empowering change* (pp. 146–159). Westport, CT: Greenwood Publishing Group.

Seidman, I. (2006). *Interviewing as qualitative research* (3rd ed.). New York: Teachers College Press.

Simeone, A. (1987). *Academic women: Working towards equality*. South Hadley, MA: Bergin & Garvey.

Spalter-Roth, R. & Erskine, W. (November/December 2005). Beyond the fear factor: Work/family policies in academia-resources or rewards? *Change: The Magazine of Higher Learning, 37* (6), 18–25.

Stanley, T. L. (2005). The one with the baby: Single-mothering in academia. In R. Hile Bassett (Ed.), *Parenting & professing: Balancing family work within an academic career* (pp. 88–88). Nashville, TN: Vanderbilt University Press.

Trower, C. (2005, Fall). Gen X meets theory X: What new scholars want. *The Department Chair, 16* (2), 16–18.

Trubek, A. (2004). When a spousal hire becomes a single mom. *The Chronicle of Higher Education/Chronicle Careers.* http://chronicle.com/jobs/2004/02/2004022 001c.htm (accessed May 16, 2007).

Tyack, D. (1974). *The one best system: The history of American urban education.* Cambridge, MA: Harvard University Press.

Unesco (2000). *Women, power and the academy: From rhetoric to reality,* M. L. Kearney (Ed.). New York: Berghahn Books.

University of Michigan Faculty Handbook. (Fall 2006). *Section 6.d. Extensions of the probationary period for childrearing, dependent care, or medical leave.* Ann Arbor Campus. http://www.provost.umich.edu/faculty/handbook/6/6.D.html#6.D.3 (accessed June 26, 2007).

USA Today (2005). U.S. stands apart from other nations on maternity leave. http://www.usatoday.com/news/health/2005-07-26-maternity-leave_x.htm (accessed September 28, 2005).

U.S. Department of Labor (2007). The Family and Medical Leave Act of 1993: Public Law 103-3, Enacted February 5, 1993. http://www.dol.gov/esa/regs/ statutes/whd/fmla.htm (accessed May 11, 2007).

Vygotsky, L. (1987). *Thought and language* (A. Kozulin, Ed.). Cambridge, MA: MIT Press, 236–237; cited in Seidman, I. (2006). *Interviewing as Qualitative Research* (3rd ed.). New York: Teachers College Press, p. 7.

Ward, K. & Wolf-Wendel, L. (November-December 2004). Fear factor: How safe is it to make time for family? *Academe, 90* (6), 28–31.

Warner, J. (2005). *Perfect madness: Motherhood in the age of anxiety.* New York: Riverhead Books.

Wergin, J. F. (2003). *Departments that work: Building and sustaining cultures of excellence in academic programs.* Bolton, MA: Anker.

West, M. S. & Curtis, J. W. (2006). *AAUP Faculty Gender Equity Indicators 2006* (pp. 10–11). Washington, DC: American Association of University Professors.

Williams, J. (2000). *Unbending gender: Why family and work conflict and what to do about it.* New York: Oxford University Press.

Wilson, R. (December 5, 2003). How babies alter careers for academics. *The Chronicle of Higher Education, L(15)*, A1–A8.

Wolf-Wendel, L. & Ward, K. (2006). Faculty work and family life: Policy perspectives from different institutional types. In S. J. Bracken, J. K. Allen, & D. R. Dean (Eds.), *The balancing act: Gendered perspectives in faculty roles and work lives* (pp. 51–72). Sterling, VA: Stylus.

Index